A HISTORY OF SEAMANSHIP

A HISTORY
OF
SEAMANSHIP

DOUGLAS PHILLIPS-BIRT

DOUBLEDAY & COMPANY, INC.
GARDEN CITY, NEW YORK 1971

DEDICATION
To Maurice Michael
who suggested the subject
and collected the illustrations

First published in 1971

Library of Congress Catalog Card Number 70–157617
Copyright © 1971 by
Douglas Phillips-Birt and Maurice Michael
All Rights Reserved

Printed in Great Britain

Contents

ACKNOWLEDGEMENTS

The thanks of the author and publishers are due to the following for permission to reproduce items in their possession.

Antikvarisk Topografiske Arkivet, Stockholm.
Arkeologiska Museet, Göteborg.
Associated Press, London.
Messrs Beken and Sons, Cowes.
The Directors of the British Museum.
British Steel Corporation.
Henry Browne and Sons Ltd.
Centraal Museum der Gemeente Utrecht.
Decca Navigator Co. Ltd.
Direzione Antichità, Belle Arti e Storia del Commune di Genova.
Egypt Exploration Society, London.
The Director of the Maritime Museum, Haifa.
David Goddard Esq. of the ISCA, Exeter.
Gotlands Fornsal, Visby.
Lehnert and Landrock, Cairo.
Hr Walter Lüdens.

The Master and Fellows of Magdalen College, Cambridge.
John Mannering Esq.
The Director of the National Maritime Museum, Greenwich.
Nationalmuseet, Copenhagen.
Die Österreichische Nationalbibliothek, Vienna.
Soprintendenza alle Antichita di Ostia.
Real Bibliotheca el Escorial, Madrid.
Mr Morris Rosenfeld, New York.
Editions J.-L. Roth and Cie, Paris.
San Francisco Maritime Museum.
The Directors and Secretary of the Science Museum, London.
Shell International Marine.
The Times.
Transworld Feature Syndicate Inc.
Mark Wickham Esq.

Preface

To write a comprehensive history of seamanship, as defined in the early paragraphs below, within the scope of a book the length of this, even when assisted by so many illustrations, is clearly impossible. The subject is both vast and necessarily detailed. Seamanship began at some unknown period in the Stone Age, and, advancing in complication with man's experience, has at the moment reached ships and submarines propelled by nuclear power and navigated by the aid of man-made satellites. Also, the operations of seamanship are intensely practical and often their adequate explanation requires most detailed treatment. A book the size of this could be written on each of the six sections into which the subject is divided here, and still there would be numerous omissions.

The author is aware of how much in the practice of seamanship is missing from the following pages. Ruthless selection has had to be made, with, in places, something like impressionistic treatment, significant details being chosen for examination because of light they may shed on so much that cannot be considered.

It has been said that Gibbon could not have written *The Decline and Fall* today because his vision would have been stunned by the mass of material available. For the full history of seamanship an author today would find more material than all that was handled by Gibbon (he used, I believe, purely printed sources). The author need hardly say that the sources of this book are also purely secondary. As one eminent historian said lately: 'My sources are all in my library.' Otherwise this book could not have been written. Had we paused down the path of history, we would have written a treatise on various moments (and many moments the author has longed to linger on), but it could not have been this book.

1
The Earliest Days

When the *Titanic* glanced off an iceberg in 1912 and sank quickly, it was appalling not merely that foolish publicists should have called the ship 'unsinkable', but that highly qualified seamen had sunk her on a calm, cold Atlantic night when there was no adequate excuse for doing so. It was a spectacular failure of latter-day seamanship.

The wreck of the tanker *Torrey Canyon* is another example of the fragility of the art of seamanship, which now has had computers and automation added to it.

The sea is all unloving; but men have always been drawn to it, not by sentiment, but because there lies produce and profit. This is the story of seamanship, part of the story of man.

Seamanship may be defined as the alliance of art and science by means of which a ship is conducted from one part of the earth's shorelines to another. To achieve this it is necessary firstly to control the ship, secondly to find the way. The two combined make the ancient art of seamanship.

Since the earliest times finding the way has been complicated by the trackless character of the ocean, the lack of marks to guide except when land is in sight, the difficulties of identification when it is, and the uncertainties about outlying dangers set to wreck the ship. The business of finding the way safely is navigation in the narrow sense and is the task of the navigator.

In the broader sense navigation must include the seamanship by means of which the ship is handled, a skill determined by the characteristics of the ship. 'Bound is boatless man.' But if the art of finding the way is to be practised, man must have ships that may be handled with some safety at sea. Handling the ship is the task of the seaman. Seamen in the fullest sense can both find the way and handle the ship.

According to the evidence man made baskets before he made pots. Thus, though his first craft was probably a raft, the boat of skin over a wicker frame, i.e. the coracle, was his first actual boat. Models of Babylonian river craft

9

This book is a study of this combined activity down the ages – the art of the sea captain. There has never been more of them than today.

The limitations of the ship have always made the difficulties of seafaring parallel with the complications of finding the way. Throughout the history of seafaring the design of ships and the natures of navigational instruments and methods have been changing and reacting on each other. The story of seamanship is composed of two

The raft of pots – one of man's early craft

strands: that of finding the way and that of creating ships with the ability to travel along that way with reasonable efficiency, two problems, both of which have been slowly solved during the centuries.

The discovery of a means of steering a ship with some degree of certainty, to which various solutions, more or less imperfect, were found in the course of time, was a mechanical problem whose apparent complexity appeared originally to be no less than that of discovering how a sense of direction might be maintained when out of sight of land. And having steered for many days, a method of discovering precisely where the ship might be was no less necessary than that of possessing a ship with enough sailing ability to reach land before its limited stores of food and water were exhausted.

While it is a common error to over-emphasize the inadequacies of past techniques, and equally to underestimate the abilities of man's trained senses, some of which have been dulled by the conditions of modern civilization, we still must remember how long seafaring lacked what now seem the bare essentials of competent seamanship.

For example, the busy medieval seas had long become a thing of the past; the tremendous saga of Elizabethan England and the Spain of Philip II was over; round the coast of Europe shipping was busied in the trade of a new era, yet the coasts of England were still largely uncharted; indeed, until 1693, only seven years from the eighteenth century, no adequate survey of the British coastline had ever been made. Such work as had been done, was done by the Dutch, and inaccurate, for the surveyors were engaged in hostilities off the coast they were surveying.

By A.D. 1700 man had been practising seamanship in some form for perhaps

12,000 years; for in the Palaeolithic we believe there was water transport on the rivers and lakes. But of the first seamen we shall never gain direct knowledge. '. . . These were floats not boats.' So Professor Lionel Casson says in his book *The Ancient Mariners*, and he passes quickly on to ships with more far-reaching potentialities, but perhaps we may pause and wonder a little about the child-seamen of the human race. Wondering and guessing makes up much, but not all, of what is known about these unrecorded times.

Unrecorded, yet leaving a curious legacy. For today the earliest kinds of marine craft invented some time in the Mesolithic, or Middle Stone Age, are still in use in some parts of the world, still serving man in the early years of the Nuclear Age. The craft may be classified as (i) inflated skins; (ii) bundles of branches; (iii) raft; (iv) reed boat; (v) dugout; (vi) skin boat; (vii) bark boat. From these, and in comparatively recent times – perhaps before 4000 B.C. in the Middle East and by 2500 B.C. in northern Europe – the boat of wood planks developed.

We shall never know the details of how on lakes, the upper reaches of rivers, swamps and floods, or in creeks opening out to the yet unreached sea, man long boatless, eventually became some kind of seaman with craft, however inadequate, to carry him over appreciable stretches of salt water. Early man would often have found himself afloat against his will owing to a sudden flood, which for coastal

American Indians using fire to hollow out a canoe

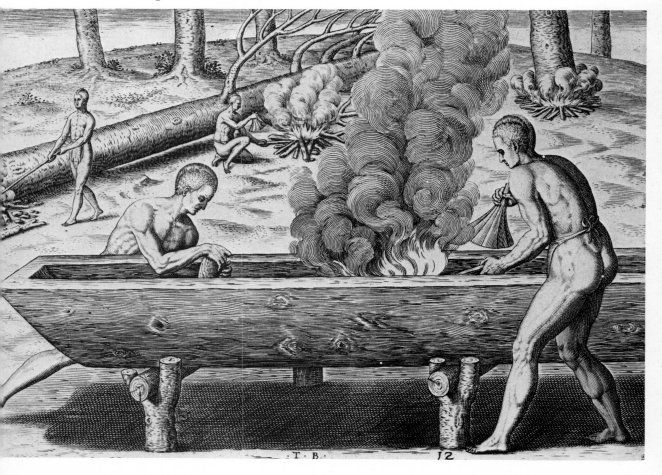

Solomon Islands sailing canoe. Note the mast step

dwellers might have been a wind-driven spring tide, in the season of what became known as 'live water'; and man would have found himself more adroit than the animals in saving himself by means of drifting tree trunks. We have to reach back to the Palaeolithic and Neolithic before 10,000 B.C. in the roundest numbers, to find the first seamen. By the sides of many estuaries whose geography differed from that of today – by the Nile and Red Sea when what is now the eastern desert was rich with vegetation, a thousand years before the Old Kingdom was even young; by the Tigris, Euphrates and Indus before the Bronze Age civilization had appeared; perhaps before the English Channel had broken through and today's bottom of the North Sea was the soggy western plain of the European and Asian land mass, men were learning how to bear themselves up on water in what were boats rather than floats.

Floats included drifting branches or logs and inflated animal skins. The latter are still used today in Tibet. Western seamanship has just made a return to an extensive use of the same principle in inflatable dinghies, lifeboats and rafts, the air contained now within a plastic material, the craft driven by outboard motors with twentieth-century citizens in anxious control (outboards being temperamental) instead of the paddling hands of even more apprehensive savages. Logs or branches lashed together to form a raft were once feats of technology representing immense strides towards seagoing craft. Pots were among the early artefacts of man, to the advantage of the archaeologists who discovered how to use these items of durable kitchenware as a means of identifying sequences of cultures. Man having become a potter at some time in the Neolithic, which may be placed about the middle of the third millennium B.C. in the East, and the middle of the second in the North, rafts with the added floatation power of pots would then have become possible. The sophistication of the dugout would have been evolved while man shared the world on precarious tenure with the overwhelming forests and the mainly hostile animals; and then in what has sometimes been called the 'Skin Age' – skins for clothing, for the roofs of dwellings, or to hang as a curtain before the draughty entrance to a cave – appeared the boat of skin; not just skin inflated, but skin laid over intelligently shaped frames of basketwork.

Basketry appears to have been older than pottery, and to have been practised in the Palaeolithic, when stone axe, scraper and knife, assisted by fire which was not easily produced or controlled, were the only means of hollowing the dugout from the tree-trunk – though any rottenness in the tree itself would help. It might appear that the covering of the familiar basket with the familiar skin would be an easier means of making a boat than digging out a tree. All we may claim is that both types of craft were among the earliest boats as opposed to floats. In other areas rich in reeds, that refinement of the raft represented by the reasonably well-shaped but perishable boat of sausage-like bundles of papyrus lashed together into an initially not inelegant ship shape, became the usual type. Much later, when a new breed of shipwright was practising the subtler art of making boats from many pieces of timber fastened together, with the innate conservatism of his kind he clung to the shape of the reed-bundle boat, reproducing it in wood.

At some early age of seamanship the paddle was evolved, a neat extension of and improvement on the hands for digging into the water and securing some forward thrust. For unknown ages the paddle was the one means of propulsion, and this simple device must be placed alongside the sail as one of the most important developments of primitive seamanship. The oar, involving the principle of the fulcrum and the use of a rowlock or thole-pin or a strop of leather fixed in a rigid gunwale, was a device lying yet far in the future. The early seamen paddled and, we are now able to believe, paddled far.

Because of the persistence of early boat types into the twentieth century, we may understand more than might be expected of these creations of long ago. But the minds and skills of the seamen who handled them are hidden more deeply. Men

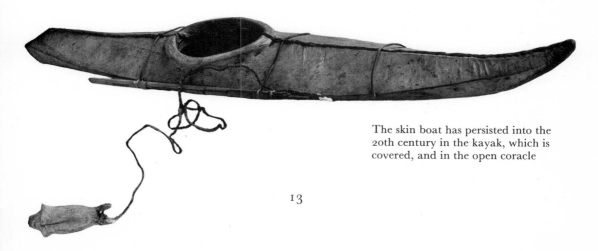

The skin boat has persisted into the 20th century in the kayak, which is covered, and in the open coracle

13

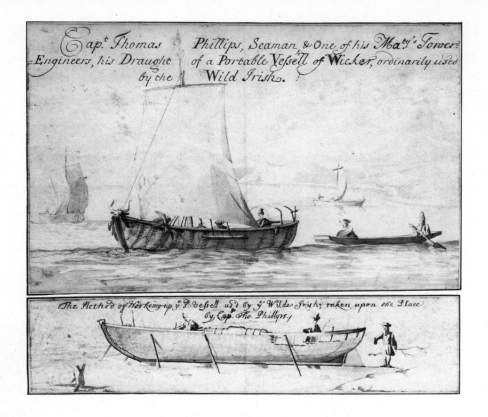

Cap.ᵗ Thomas Phillips, Seaman, & One of his Ma.ᵗʸ Tower-Engineers, his Draught of a Portable Vessell of Wicker, ordinarily used by the Wild Irish.

The Method of Workeing up y.ᵉ s. vessell us'd by y.ᵉ Wilde Irish; taken upon the Place by Cap.ᵗ Tho. Phillips.

contrived to evolve the first arts of seamanship, the handling of their dangerous craft when wind brought waves, and when inshore currents swirled them from their course. They had to learn how to react to all the multitudinous effects of wind on the water through which they sought to drive their boats; and as today yachtsmen find fascination in the same study and practice, so, too, are they often mystified by the problems of wind and water which are at the root of seamanship. But in some respects it was the ancient and not the modern seamen who had crucial advantages.

Always to be remembered is the fact that what modern man has gained in philosophical ability has been won at the cost of atrophying some useful and once instinctive powers – accurate observation, memory that did not require records, sense of direction and locality that had no need of instruments or maps, smell (often so invaluable to the seaman), kinship with natural phenomena – all now mislaid in the Broadways of industrial civilization. A philosopher once remarked that the human mind is a poor thing to use for reasoning about the nature of reality, since it originally evolved in order to help the swinging monkey find nuts. The first seamen had passed beyond swinging for nuts. But, hunters and fishermen, they were harshly pressed to find the equivalent; and the equivalent, too, of the monkey's fur and home up among the leaves, for the more complicated 'civilized' ways of keeping alive had not yet been revealed to them. The earlier instincts were intact. Early seamanship, and even much that was achieved later during historical times, will never be understood unless this is remembered.

In our own day we have the examples of the unlettered men who, a generation ago, were often placed in charge of steam-trawlers that remained at sea for weeks on end, and yet they never thought to consult the charts provided by the owners which remained in their first folds year after year. These men when making a landfall in thick weather, could identify it though they may have faced it last a decade or more before. So, too, skippers of fishing-smacks found their way to a precise spot on the fishing-grounds and back to port again without chart or accurate compass. Of such is the essence of ancient seafaring, beyond the comprehension of the sophisticated. Research in recent years has shown that birds conduct their migrations by means of celestial navigation, using the direction of the sun and stars for course, their altitude for position. There is evidence that fish do likewise, making the necessary allowance for the refraction of light. Man, driven by necessity, might distantly have approached these achievements.

We may believe that the men of the long Palaeolithic, the Old Stone Age, reaching back at least half a million years from today, kept to the rivers and lakes. By some time not later than 10,000 B.C., and perhaps much earlier, those of the

Modern
reproductions
of the earliest
type of skin
boat. These are
Welsh coracles
in canvas

North had dugouts and skin boats. Among the earliest drawings of boats are the few dozen rock carvings discovered near the Stone Age coastal settlements of northern Norway, and many more dating from the Northern Bronze Age have been found in southern Scandinavia. Many of these are of the utmost simplicity, like outline drawings by children, and it used to be argued that they did not represent boats at all, but possibly sledges. Today it is no longer doubted they are boats; and in this gallery of drawings spread over the rocks of the Scandinavian coast, amplified by other archaeological hints, we are able to watch what might be a flickering ciné

Irish curragh with a small running sail set

picture, tantalizing in its dark moments and bad focus, showing the activities of seamen who were among the earliest and the first of all on the Atlantic. The testimony of the Northern rocks has indicated that it was not only in the Mediterranean and further east that seamen first crossed wide stretches of sea; it suggests, too, that it was perhaps in the North that man first learned habitually to handle ships in severe ocean conditions.

A. W. Brøgger, Professor of Archaeology at the University of Oslo, has written: 'Myriads of such islands lie to seaward, west of all the skerries in Norway, and they were all reached by men, as far back as there were men in Norway at all. . . . The earliest traces go a long way back; it must be ten thousand years at least since the hunting tribes of Finmark, of the Helgeland-Fosna coast and of Østfold journeyed along the coast and out upon the deep sea which furnished a great part of their livelihood.'

The fact now accepted is that these Stone Age seamen used skin boats, boats of hide covering a wooden framework, of which the representatives today are found in the Irish curragh and the Welsh coracle. So long as it was believed that only the dugout was known to ancient seamen, the limitations of this type precluded any deep-sea operations. The hollowed-out tree-trunk is ill-shaped, fragile and heavy. Ancient dugouts in literal thousands have been found in various parts of the world; it has to be accepted as the commonest type of early boat in all places that provided suitable trees, which in ancient times included many localities that no longer do so. But the lack of buoyancy and stability in the type must have kept them off all but relatively calm water. Dugouts are still hollowed from tree-trunks and in daily use. One of them is now on exhibition at the International Maritime Museum for Sailing Craft at Exeter. It was found drifting off the East African coast, the record perhaps of an unwatched tragedy of the latter half of the twentieth century, repeating un-numbered others which have been occurring since men first dared broader waters in such craft. The casual, wandering curves of the simple dugout, with still so much of the tree from which it was hewn and hollowed in its narrow form, makes a touching commentary on unsophisticated man's efforts to become a seaman.

The first Northern seamen to go offshore in their skin boats were fishermen, and it is reasonable to believe that seamanship was developed alongside hunting as one of the two means of sustaining life in the period which preceded agriculture and settlement. On one Stone Age site near Stavanger have been found numerous bones of deep-water fish (cod, pollock and ling), and of Greenland seals and porpoises; also fish-hooks of a size required for deep-water fishing with sinkers of various weights graduated in the manner still accepted today and ranging up to the heaviest needed for fishing depths of up to 90 fathoms. To use these fishermen would have had to go some 20–30 miles offshore.

We see then the spectacle of Stone Age seafarers in the North working on the edge of the Continental Shelf in seas where even in summer changes from calm to high wind might be sudden; where a wind of only Force 4 blowing off the Atlantic could raise ugly seas out of the great ocean reach to windward; where fog might suddenly drench a clear day, and from which the seamen lacked any means of making a fast return to shore. For the speed the Stone Age seamen, bending to their paddles, could achieve in wicker-framed craft, loaded perhaps with a good catch, would be minimal, much slower than the waves with their curling crests which chased them. The handling of those rudderless boats in seas from the stern and

Curraghs, with the wooden framework covered in canvas, are used today. This example was made in Tralee

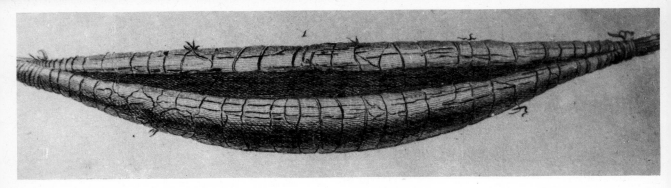

quarter must have been one of the first operations of deep-water seamanship.

Also in the Exeter Museum are examples of coracles and an Irish curragh, the latter newly constructed, at Castle Gregory near Tralee, with canvas replacing the hide of the ancients. The performance of Irish seamen with the curragh in the former and present centuries vividly illustrate the activities of Stone and Bronze Age seamen. The modern curragh's interlaced framework of elm laths is very strong and flexible, and the 'skin' is composed of tarred calico in two layers separated by a kind of brown paper. As late as the 1930s such boats were used as a means of communication between Aran Island, County Donegal, and the mainland, a stretch of water in Galway Bay open to the long ocean seas of the Atlantic. In a curragh 9 feet in length and 4 feet in beam, not only people and goods are transported but sheep and cows; and these light, wonderfully buoyant craft, capable of setting a small sail forward, scurry over the valleys and hills of the Atlantic-born rollers that come in upon Ireland's west coast. We may see here in the sea traffic to the offshore isles of Galway and County Mayo in say A.D. 1900 the pattern of that between the north-western coast of Norway and the outer skerries in 2900 B.C. and earlier.

Dugouts have reached nearly 50 feet in length – one such was found at Brigg in Lincolnshire in 1866 – and various means were devised of improving their innate lack of seaworthiness. But after controversy spread over many years, the dugout of Antiquity is relegated to the lakes and rivers, and the earliest seagoing boats, at least in the North, are accepted to have been skin boats, which were ultimately replaced in a transitionary process which can only be conjectured, by the earliest boats made of wooden planks. And in this later art the Mediterranean and the East are assumed to have been in advance of the North and West.

The men who used the dugouts were boatmen of lake, river and estuary; and in some places they evolved a kind of craft better suited to the exercise of rudimentary seamanship. Raising the inadequate freeboard of the hollowed log by sewing to its upper part a roughly hewn plank on either side was one possible course of advance, beset with the difficulty of splitting planks from the tree-trunk with stone, or even bronze axes. Internal timbers of branches might be added to hold the hollowed log, which had a tendency to split, and the added planks together. The use of two and even three hollowed logs lashed side by side enabled the inadequate breadth of the single dugout to be compensated. While the dugouts in one form or another have served boatmen through all ages down to the present time, the type has remained inherently fragile, lacking in buoyancy and excessively heavy.

Tied to craft derived from the dugout, however modified, boatmen could never

18

have become seamen. But how the boat, built in some way of planks sewn together and caulked with moss or resin, was evolved from more primitive forms is at the moment unknown. It happened in different ways in different places, and we reasonably believe today that two of the historically most important genres of wood-planked seagoing craft came about, by unknown stages, from the skin boat in the North and the reed-bundle boat in the South, the resulting wooden boats in either case retaining the shapes characteristic of the primitive craft from which they had been derived. It has also been suggested that one form of planked boat evolved from the dugout by the addition of further planks to increase freeboard and more logs to increase beam, until the logs themselves became no more than the solid keels of the new creations. We do not know. But it now appears likely that the original seagoing boats of Scandinavia and, perhaps of further south, though for this there is less evidence, were evolved from the primitive skin boat. This transition from skin to wood was made in the Neolithic period. In the Bronze Age was evolved the kind of craft exemplified by the Hjortspring boat and possibly others more seaworthy. The numerous Bronze Age rock carvings of southern Scandinavia are a record of seafaring that was perhaps extensive. Meanwhile, the more backward boatmen continued to paddle their boats of skin, log and reed down the winding streams of history.

Trobriand Island canoe

Opposite page
A reed-bundle boat from Cape Diemen. See also pages 34 and 35

Pre-dynastic Egyptian rock painting
of papyrus boats

The scene now shifts from the rocky west coast of Norway above the Arctic Circle that faces the storm-swept seas of latitude 70 degrees north, and moves south to the semi-tropical waters in only 25 degrees of northern latitude of the Red Sea and Persian Gulf. Once again it is the ships drawn on rocks that claim our attention as the earliest evidences of seafaring.

It appears that during recorded history there have been no permanent inhabitants of the eastern desert of Egypt, between the Nile and the northern Red Sea coast, but that in prehistoric periods this baked and barren region was fertile, like that of the Arabian coast opposite, and supported a population where now 'the only people met were a weary camel man and his son passing Nilewards' as James Hornell has said. On the sandstone rocks of Egypt's present eastern desert are found numerous rock drawings of boats.

There is little doubt that in lands lacking big timber but rich in the reeds of hot swamp and marsh, the earliest boats were made of papyrus-reed bundles. Essentially such craft are rafts, the tapered reed bundles tightly bound together with twine taking the place of logs. Illustrations that may be dated around 6,000 years ago show the ends of the craft rising in a noble sweep, which in practice the reed boat soon loses once it is afloat; and inside the outer bundles there might be others to give as much dryness and buoyancy as possible to the soggy outer reeds. Such craft in modern times have reached a length of 35 feet and carried a load of up to 3 tons.

20

It is possible that the ancient papyrus boats had a tent-like shelter nearly amidships. They had a short life and were paddled and steered with an oar. They did not have the ability to face stormy seas of the skin boats in which, at the same period, the first Northern seamen may have been putting out into the Atlantic. For a time, in the dawn of seamanship, the seamen of the North may have been superior to those in the Middle East.

But the cradle of more advanced seafaring and voyaging, and the earliest practice of navigation in the sophisticated sense, lay in the coast lands around the head of the Persian Gulf, in the Nile Valley and the eastern Mediterranean. Here as in the North, and possibly no earlier than in the North, the boat of wood appeared, its development handicapped by the lack of long timber. Typical of human conservatism, the boats made from short lengths of acacia, or sunt timber, were given the shape of the papyrus-bundle boats. Made of numerous short lengths of plank dowelled together, with no continuous strakes of planking, and at first built without ribs, some rigidity was given to the hull by numerous beams across its topsides, which passed through the planking and were pegged.

The sail appeared. James Hornell has suggested that by the third millennium B.C. there were on the Persian Gulf 'a people similar to the Omanites today – expert shipwrights, ocean carriers trading in their own *baghlas* or *bums* to ports in India, Iraq, Iran, Arabia and East Africa, fishing along the coast in innumerable small

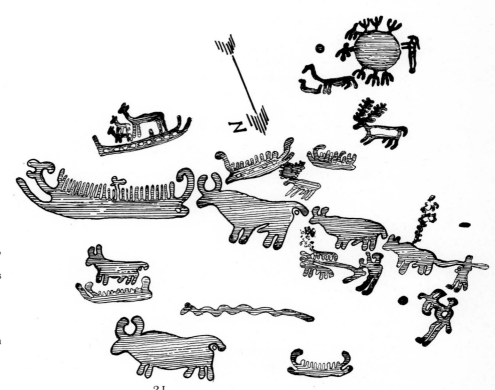

Rock drawing of skin boat, Norway, Stone Age. The two vertical strokes are assumed to represent bulkheads
Petroglyph of boats, bifid at both ends. Bronze Age, Sweden

21

craft and cultivating in their valleys the date, the vine, the mango, the apricot and the orange'.

Clearly, the art of seamanship had advanced far, but of the course of its development little is known. Compared with the men of the North, who were still in the Stone Age, the Early Bronze Age dwellers in the Fertile Crescent had many advantages. The storms they knew could be no less violent than those of the North, but they were less frequent. Their winds were more predictable, and they did not have to face the seas regularly raised by the great fetch of the Atlantic out to windward. The effects of tidal scour and sandbanks did not worry them in the Mediterranean. The lack of tides enabled them to concentrate on the winds, and they moved by day over seas whose colour and visibility were brilliant and whose night skies were their glory. The indented Northern coastline with its countless bays and inlets, and the dust upon the sea of the Aegean islands, gave the seamen the boon of numerous safe, natural harbours. Calms, so rare in the North, were prevalent enough during the Mediterranean summer to give prominence to the oar even after sail had been devised, and eventually it was this that led to the most advanced development of the rowing technique ever reached, in the many-oared, multi-banked Classical galleys. But it was the sail that gave the seaman his widest-ranging powers and was the key to the future influence of seamanship.

Clearly the invention of sail is the most crucial event in the story of seamanship, paralleled only by the development of mechanical power afloat possibly 6,000 years

Rock drawings at Leirfall, Norway, depicting footprints and ships. Bronze Age. An element of the mystical appears in the Bronze Age rock carvings

Opposite page
Model Twelfth Dynasty, *circa* 1900 B.C. Notice that the crew is shown rowing, not paddling

later. Whatever may have been the achievements of the Northern seamen during the later Stone and Bronze Ages, the wider oceans must have been for ever closed to man unless something better than propulsion by oar or paddle could be devised. We might note, incidentally, that sail itself, even after millennia of development, had inadequacies that produced the seamen's major problems, and surmounting these has been down the ages the sublimest test of his skill. Wind propulsion by sail, setting such rigorous limits upon the direction in which a ship could move, and enforcing, by the nature of the winds, a very low average speed between ports, is a far from satisfactory way of achieving motion over great tracts of ocean. But for so long it was the only way; it was a case of this or nothing; and herein lies much of the story of seamanship.

There is reason to suppose that the origins of rudimentary sail are to be sought further east than the Mediterranean, the Red Sea or the Persian Gulf where sail made its appearance at some date before 3500 B.C. Perhaps the first sail known was a large leaf from a palm tree, erected aloft; a design on a pre-dynastic Egyptian vase of *circa* 5000 B.C. suggests this practice. Out of the palm sail could have evolved the sail of matted leaves, or coconut leaflets, known during much later eras, and the venue of such devices may have been the Indian Ocean. A similar picture of an Egyptian pot shows a square sail with yard and boom. The date of this, once considered to be *circa* 6000 B.C., is now considered to be more like 4000–3000 B.C. No rigging is illustrated.

There is yet little evidence of the sail being used in northern Europe before the Christian era, and direct evidence that it was not used in prominent types of

23

Northern boats even later. The Saxon migrations, for example, were made in sail-less boats of up to 80 feet in length. Mention should be made, however, of features on certain Scandinavian rock carvings which have been interpreted as sails, and may be suspected to have been leafy branches poised aloft in a manner similar to that practised in the Mediterranean and further east. Too little is known about the evolution of sail in the North. On the one hand is the fact that the *idea* of sail is almost a matter of common sense in a seaman – at least of sail in the limited role of something to assist being blown along faster by a following wind – something that would have become evident to the sailorman who stood up on his raft and found himself moving downwind faster than when he was sitting. On the other hand, we find in the North the development of boat-building techniques that were advanced far beyond mere common sense, revealing the skills of long experience, yet used for vessels which structurally were unable to set sails.

Yet Julius Caesar found that the Veneti of Brittany had craft with sails of hide. The Scandinavians for all the brilliance of their seamanship, were still backward in the development of sail when in southern Europe, with its several thousand years of experience, Rome was being supplied with corn from Egypt by the sophisticated merchant sailing-ships of the Empire. And not for another thousand years after this were the seamen of northern Europe, despite Viking achievements in seamanship,

The earliest known seagoing ship, modelled from an Egyptian bas-relief of 3000 B.C. Note that there are three steering oars and that the mast is bipod

to produce sailing merchantmen the equal of those regularly using the Mediterranean when the Christian era opened.

Thereafter the North moved ahead of the South, to produce in the medieval period the three-masted sailing-ship which opened the way for the age of discovery. But we should notice that, until the early centuries A.D., seamanship as practised to the west of Gibraltar was largely a matter of navigation under oars; while to the east seamen were gaining centuries of confidence in harnessing the wind.

With sail came the necessity for a positive means of steering ships. Initially this was achieved by the unsatisfactory device of a steering oar, essentially the same, though perhaps longer, than the propulsion paddles, and not pivoted or hung but simply held in the hand. Steering was effected by sweeping the oar towards or away from the ship's side. The more desirable steering action would be to rotate the oar without any transverse motion. The problem of how the oar might be fixed to the hull yet have the freedom to rotate on its axis, and thus become a true side rudder as opposed to a mere steering oar, was mechanically not easy to solve. The fact that Egyptian ships had two and sometimes three or even five side rudders on either quarter would suggest a certain inadequacy in the equipment; while bowling along before a stiff breeze steering would evidently need sympathetic team-work between the two or more helmsmen, controlled by the master, who might have seemed to be

25

Model of an early Egyptian
sailing-boat found in a grave in
the Valley of the Kings. The
steering method is already
more advanced . The many
lifts for the boom are to ease
the stress in the fragile
sail-cloth

in the position of conducting an orchestra rather than guiding a ship. But in the last days of sailing-ships, when in heavy weather there would be steering tackles on the wheel with men heaving on the falls, a similar corporate effort was necessary to keep control.

Steering oars might have been lashed to a crossbeam or placed between Sampson's-posts. In a more developed form, the side rudder would pass through a wooden block with a hole in it, secured to the topsides of the hull, and have a line to enable it to be swung upwards when not in use. A greater area of blade and increased

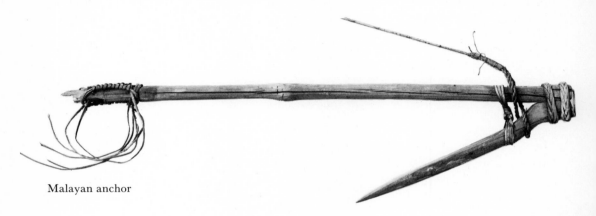

Malayan anchor

depth gave more power to the rudder, in time enabling control to be assured with one rudder only on each quarter. And this became the classical Mediterranean form of ship's steering. A short tiller, set horizontally at right angles to the oar's axis, or sometimes vertically downwards, was the means by which the helmsman rotated the oar.

In the galleys the steering oars were hung from the after end of the parados, or outrigger, and a variant of this arrangement persisted in Mediterranean sailing-ships until the stern rudder was adopted. In the great Roman corn-ships, such as that in which St Paul was wrecked, the twin quarter rudders of Mediterranean shipping reached their ultimate state of development. The ship's topsides at the quarters were carried out beyond the hull proper to form an open-ended projection which carried the rudders, into which they might be housed when they were raised on board by the tackles. It appears that both rudders might be used simultaneously – certainly in the long, narrow galleys. At other times one of them might be lifted, the helmsman using the rudder to leeward.

It is a measure of the backwardness of Northern seafaring that the fixed steering oar, or stern rudder, does not appear to have been used until the Early Iron Age. In the Norse ship found at Nydam, and dating in the third or fourth century A.D., the inadequate fastenings of the steering oar would have precluded sailing the ship. By the time of the Viking expansion the single side rudder of the North, counterpart to the twin side rudders of the South, had reached its fully developed form. This is described below in detail. It is worth noting at this point, however, the contrasting systems of steering evolved in the North and Mediterranean. The single steering oar on the starboard side was a fragile device compared with the large, heavy twin quarter rudders of the South lodged in their massive quarter galleries.

Anchoring, like steering, is a fundamental operation of seamanship, and the anchor, more than any other part of a vessel's equipment, has gathered symbolical undertones. The stone with a rope round it, or preferably with a hole through it to take the cable, is the obvious and earliest anchor. Marine archaeology has recovered a stone anchor with holes to take a wooden stock, a notable advance in the technique of anchoring. More simple, and sometimes used today, is the bag filled with shingle having a cable secured to one of the top corners and a tripping line to the bottom. Having lowered the bag carefully, it is easily hoisted empty, having been relieved of its stones by hauling on the tripping line.

The simple stone anchor might be encased in timber. Anchors were hewn from stone in the familiar double hook form, with a hole in the top of the shank to allow a wooden stock to be fitted. The stock is of crucial importance to the basic type of anchor, assisting the flukes to dig and get a hold. Anchors had been made of lead, of wood weighted with lead, even of solid silver in days when silver was worthless, before iron established itself as the best material. The Viking anchor found with the Gokstad ship was a little more than 3 feet 6 inches from the crown to the middle of the stock, where a ring was forged to take the cable. There was also a ring at the crown for a tripping line. And the stock was significantly massive, just short of

A further improvement in the steering method

Canoe of the New Hebrides

9 feet in length, giving the anchor great stability when on the bottom. This suggests the later Norse seaman's concern for reliability in anchoring, and will serve to remind us, should the impressions of their superb ocean voyages become too dominant, that much of their time was spent close to the shore, where their chief purposes, usually nefarious, lay. Spending much of their time in the immediate offing of the coast, when the sun became low the ship would be run in close to a beach and an anchor dropped astern while a warp was taken ashore and made fast. Over the gangplank rigged from the bow to the beach would go the cook with his pots, while busy hands on board rigged the tent over its ridge-pole and verge-boards to cover the midships.

This, however, was in a later period of seamanship, when the pagans from the fjords were spreading over the waters of Europe, far up the rivers and out into the Atlantic to America. This period of the Viking expansion used to be regarded as the first great age of north European seamanship. But now we have to consider the extent of the much earlier Bronze Age seafaring, about which some modern ideas are exciting. They owe much to Professor Brøgger, who set out his ideas to an archaeological congress in Oslo in 1936. Essentially his idea is that the voyages made by Greek and Phoenician seamen out into the Atlantic in the fifth to sixth centuries B.C. were in fact the later achievements of a long preceding and hitherto unrecognized period of bold seamanship during the earlier Bronze Age.

'In my student days', he said, 'it was considered a completely revolutionary thought . . . that there had been a direct connection between England and Sweden in the Stone Age. For there were no steamship lines across the North Sea during the Stone Age.' The truth is quite simply that it is *we* who have had our conception of distance destroyed. For the men of the Stone and Bronze Ages distance was no object. They knew no frontiers, needed no passports or identity papers or tickets. The earth was free, the world lay open, and they wandered across it as though a thousand miles was nothing but a joyous adventure. . . . Decisive for a true understanding of pre-history is the archaeological evidence for *the Bronze Age as the great millennium of seafaring.*'

The Bronze Age in the Scandinavian North opened in about 1900 B.C., at which time it was already 1,000 years old in the eastern Mediterranean. It was at the beginning of this period that the Phoenicians had begun to settle on their strip of the Syrian coast, and had learned their first shipbuilding from the Egyptians. By the beginning of the first millennium B.C. they were sailing along all the Mediterranean coasts. But were the seamen of northern Europe also making extensive voyages, and even reaching the Mediterranean? In 1951 Professor Brøgger was repeating the substance of his 1936 ideas: 'Nevertheless, to judge from the source material, it seems clear that the Bronze Age was an age of seafaring, the first we know . . . tribes of Western Europe and the Mediterranean created in the Bronze Age the first great seafaring period, in which they not merely sailed along the main coasts, but put out to sea and sailed the ocean. It is probable that this applies especially to the later Bronze Age.'

Of the achievements of Mediterranean seamen we have little doubt, though their exact scope remains uncertain. But what about the Northern peoples? Brøgger's ideas have lit many imaginations. Thus, in *The Testimony of the Spade* Geoffrey Bibby writes: 'We see the younger sons of Northern European husbandmen going to sea, and returning with the tales of tropical shores and dark-skinned beauties, and memories of nights spent drinking the resin-flavoured wine in the harbour dives of Tartessus or of Corinth. . . .'

Were the Northern seamen during the first millennium B.C. ranging so far over the oceans? There are little firm data to guide us. As far as the Scandinavian seamen are concerned, we believe they had no sail until about A.D. 600, when we find the first archaeological evidence of a wooden clinker-built boat with the capability of sailing; it was excavated at Kvalsund in 1920. Until the latter half of the first millennium the Scandinavian seamen may not even have used oars, but paddled, as had their Stone Age ancestors in their skin boats. There is the evidence of the Hjortspring boat, found in the Danish island of Als. It dates from the Late Bronze Age of Scandinavia and is the earliest surviving example of a Northern wood-planked boat, which we have already seen to have been in existence for possibly 2,000 years by this time.

31

The Hjortspring boat has no keel. A broad bottom plank extends forward of the hull proper into a beak, which is matched by a similar extension of the two thickened gunwale planks – a configuration clearly seen in the Bronze Age rock carvings. What we should now call a stem and stern-post are fixed vertically to the bottom plank near either extremity, and these support the ends of the gunwale planks. A few wide, thin planks between gunwale and bottom form the hull, which has slender ribs, at the upper ends of which are struts crossing the hull at gunwale level. The length of the craft is 43 feet, the beam 6 feet. She was paddled and could carry no sail.

The tremendous seagoing of the Bronze Age could not have occurred in such light and fragile craft as the Hjortspring boat, or in the craft shown in the Bronze Age rock carvings if, as appears to be so, they were like her. Professor Brøgger at moments appears to question the ancient scene he has envisaged. Of the rock carvings he asks 'whether these ships were ocean-going. At first sight it appears a fairly hopeless enterprise to row a good-sized craft over such waters as the Skagerrak and the North Sea. But it would be a mistake to draw the conclusion that these ships did not cross the sea. . . . it has been shown, from indirect evidence, that even in the early Stone Age they must have crossed even the great *waters*, where they had to be several days at sea.'

The Scandinavian seamen's lack of sail and oar might seem an insuperable obstacle to deep-water voyages other than accidental ones, driven by storm and followed by miraculous survival, which may be the explanation of a number of the prodigious ancient voyages, including those in the Pacific. Then again, our lights on the means of ancient seafaring are so scattered and focus momentarily so small an area, that much remains unseen. We are confronted with such apparent facts that while the Scandinavian seamen did not use sail until several hundred years of the Christian era had passed, we know, as will be shown, that the seamen of Britanny were using it shortly before this era, perhaps long before, possibly making coasting voyages at slow speeds covering long periods 'when a thousand miles was nothing but a joyous adventure'. These may have carried seamen far. But in our present state of knowledge we can only feel that the 'younger sons of Northern European husbandmen' would have had a rough time reaching the 'dark-skinned beauties, and . . . the resin-flavoured wine in the harbour dives of Tartessus or of Corinth' and would have earned them had they succeeded in getting there.

It is from Egypt that may be gleamed something of the details of ancient seamanship. The sail had long been known, but it must be visualized as something loosely woven and relatively fragile, resembling that of the dhow today with its slack seams that open to release the wind pressure. We find methods of rigging and sail-handling totally different from anything that has become familiar since. This was due partly to the fact that the block and tackle had not yet been invented; seamen were without that method of deriving mechanical advantage which is at the heart of all advanced rigging systems and which alone made it possible to handle ships of large size with considerable areas of canvas.

Sail was hoisted on the bipod, or sheerleg, mast, which like the shape of the hull, was inherited from the reed boat. The latter was unable to stand the compression of a single mast stepped on the centre-line, where the hull was weakest. The sides of

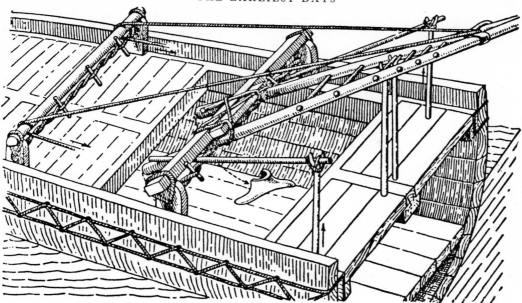

Reconstruction of the mast arrangement of one of the
ships of Fifth Dynasty King Sahure (*circa* 2480 B.C.).
The pivoted sheer mast is raised out of its position over
the after part of the vessel by falls leading forward.
(After Borchardt, *Das Grabdenkmal des Königs Sahu-re*)

the hull alone could take the stress, and this led to the double mast with half the load
being carried in each leg. The origin of the bipod mast is unknown: it is suspected to
have been an Egyptian invention and it served them for centuries.

Many features of the Egyptian rig during the third millennium B.C. have puzzled
students today, but an explanation produced lately by the American nautical
archaeologist Richard LeBaron Bowen may reveal the most ancient sailing practices
of which we have detailed knowledge. The single square sail was tall and narrow. To
set it the bipod mast was first raised by ropes led from the masthead forward, and
the pivoted mast was hauled beyond the vertical until it raked forward over the bow.
The yard and narrow sail was now hoisted with a halyard, which in the absence of a
sheave, or pulley, must have simply passed through a hole in the top of the mast
where the two legs of the bipod were united. Friction and the weight of the yard and
sail would have made it impossible to set the sail up hard. It is here that the numerous
'backstays' – as many as six to eighteen separate lines led from the mast just below
the hoisted yard – came into use. So many stays as this could only seem otiose if they
were assumed to be merely supports for the mast. It would appear that they were the
subsitute for the missing blocks and tackles. With a number of men hauling on each
of these lines a considerable force could be produced, pulling the top of the mast aft
until it was upright and thereby stretching the bagging sail taut. The sail had a boom
along its foot, but differently arranged from the boom in later sailing-craft. It was

33

The reed boat, now in the ISCA Museum, Exeter,
under sail on Lake Titicaca. The sail is a lug with
kinship to the Nile *naggar* lug

fixed across the hull, and presumably could neither be swung nor lifted; and against it the sail would be stretched. The many lines would then be belayed. While the sail was still billowing, prior to the mast being pivoted back to the vertical, it was controlled by ropes secured to the leeches.

If we accept this method of rigging, the sail with its fixed boom could not be

The same boat in the Museum

The Eskimo kayak as depicted in the 16th century

35

trimmed round by the braces on the yard without twisting, and we must accept that it could be used only in fair winds. Ideas that the Egyptian seamen of the Old Kingdom were able to sail to windward are unacceptable. And it has to be noted too that the hull, as well as the rig, was unsuitable for windward sailing owing to its spoon shape and lack of lateral resistance.

Some experiments made with a hull having the shallow draught of the Egyptian vessel and a square sail of similar proportions have been revealing. With the wind brought 50 degrees round from the stern towards the quarter, the leeway became prohibitive. Furthermore, the sail had a boom which was allowed to rotate, which we assume was not so in boats from the Old Kingdom, in which any trimming of the yard made a twist in the sail destroying its efficiency. It is a reasonable estimate that the ancient Egyptians never sailed with the wind more than 30 degrees from dead

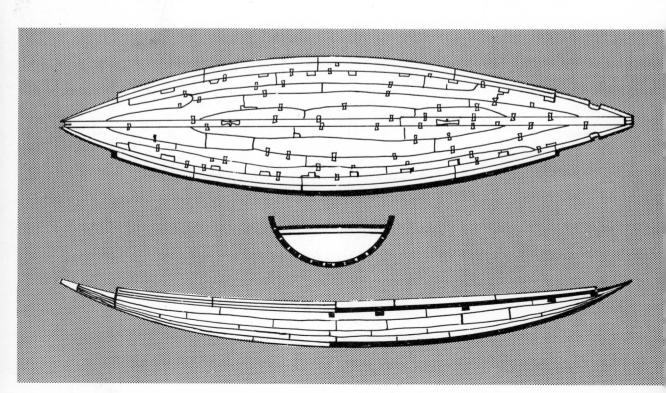

astern. The (inadequate) steering oars also precluded bringing the wind closer to the beam.

It was in vessels so rigged that voyages north to Syria were made, into the eye of the prevailing wind. For the passage up the Syrian coast, which runs nearly northward, rowing or paddling would have been necessary. Such voyages were made in the reign of King Sahure (*circa* 2480 B.C.) and though we think oars had by this time been invented, his ships were apparently paddled. For the return voyage, the bipod mast would have been hauled up, the tall sail hoisted and stretched, and with the coast on the left hand the vessel would have run home before the northerly. We cannot discover how far from the coast they went, or whether they clung to it and

Egyptian ship of about 7th century B.C. Note the bipod mast and greatly improved steering bar

Opposite page, top
Egyptian bas-relief of the Middle Kingdom depicting a ship being built of short planks

Bottom
Twelfth Dynasty boat recovered at Dahshur. The planks lie edge to edge and are joined directly by flat dowels and dovetail-shaped tenons sunk in the surface. The deck beams go through the planking. (After Reisner and de Morgan)

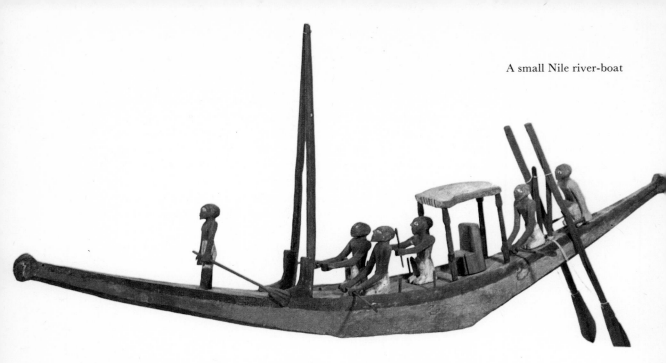

had to turn almost due west, taking again to the oars or paddles, along the north shore of the Sinai Peninsula leading to the treacherous Nile Delta. But to use the wind with any effectiveness they had to follow almost directly along its path, either rowing out to sea on leaving the Syrian coast, until they judged the Nile to lie due south, in the eye of the summer midday sun, or following the coast. It is probable that the latter course was followed. From the time of the Pharaoh Snefru, *circa* 2650 B.C., such voyages up the Syrian coast as far north as Byblos, near today's Beirut, were common. They may have begun very much earlier. That there was former communication between Egypt and Byblos is undoubted, but to what extent it was by land is unknown. It is considered, too, that trade under sail in the Red Sea was more common than was once believed. Here was a sea difficult to navigate and lacking in shelter, and what appears to be the earliest surviving account of a shipwreck occurred in these waters. It has been published in A. Erman's *The Literature of the Ancient Egyptians*. The ship concerned, 180 feet in length with a beam of 60 feet has the proportions we might expect but is unexpectedly large, and according to the narrator 'we had a crew of 120, the pick of Egypt. . . . A storm broke while we were still at sea; we flew before the wind. The ship went down; of all in it only I survived.'

There were links, too, at the period between Minoan Crete and Egypt. The rhumb-line course between Crete and the Nile exceeds 400 miles, and under average summer conditions would have entailed a voyage out of sight of land for between five and six days. It is at least possible that the goods of Egyptian and Minoan origin that have been discovered so far from their place of origin travelled partially by land. Possibly the Sea Kings of Crete may have been more advanced sailors than the Egyptians. Professor Lionel Casson has observed that 'the sailors of Crete travelled to far more distant places; the direct voyage to Egypt could have held no terrors to them.' But this is one more aspect of the unknown extent of Bronze Age seafaring.

In the reign of Queen Hatshepsut a fleet of five Egyptian ships was sent to fetch from the land of Punt a load of fashionable freight, which, apart from various exotic commodities for the comfort of the gods, included apes, monkeys, dogs, skins of the Southern panther and natives with their children. The date was *circa* 1600 B.C. The land of Punt lay somewhere beyond the Red Sea, possibly on the northern coast of the present Somali Republic; perhaps much further south, round that easternmost tip of Africa, Cape Guardafui, and south beyond the River Juba. It is indicative of the state of seafaring that the voyage was extensively recorded, and in a series of reliefs we may study the ships of this period in detail. They show interestingly close similarities to those of more than a thousand years earlier, together with appreciable differences in rig revealing a superior mastery of the sailing art.

The old, tall square sail with presumably its boom fixed to the deck has been replaced by one as wide as the former one was tall, and with a boom that could be trimmed to the wind, well above the deck. But first it should be noted that the hull appears not to have changed much. There is the same truss to brace the hull against hogging, and the artist still presents the hull with long overhangs reaching nobly

Egyptian seagoing ship in the reign
of Sahure, 25th century B.C.

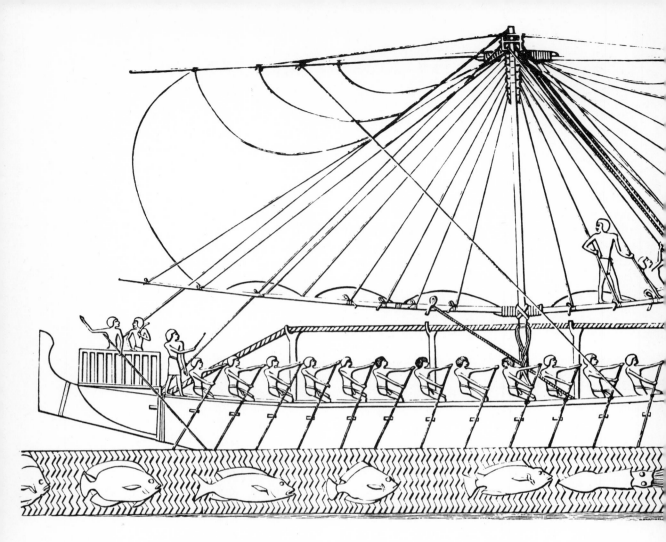

beyond the waterline length. The fully laden ships were obviously deep in the water
and without the luxury of outreaching ends stretching far beyond the buoyant hull.
With their fifteen oarsmen per side, the overall length of the ships was about 70 feet
and the beam 17–18 feet. The fully laden draught may have been perhaps 3 feet
6 inches.

The mast is no longer a bipod, but stands as a single spar on the centre-line of the
hull. That bipod masts were still used is not to be doubted; but the best in naval
architecture, which these ships of the Queen are assumed to be, had in this respect
reached beyond the racial memory of the reed boat. The mast is supported by two
forestays, a backstay and by the halyard, which was belayed aft when the sail was
hoisted, forming another backstay. The halyard was formed by a doubled rope
looped round the middle of the yard. Near the masthead was a rectangular framework, and the two lengths of the halyard led each round one side of the mast and
rested on the bottom rung of the frame. There was no sheave or purchase, and the
yard had to be hoisted against the friction of the rope on the frame. There were no

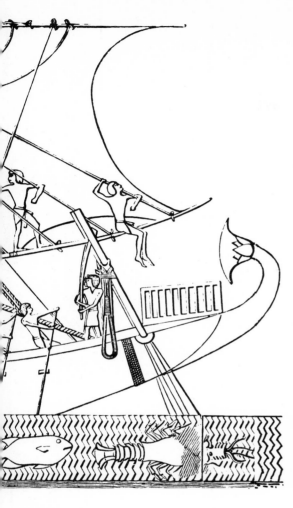

Egyptian ship of the Punt Expedition. About 1600 B.C. From Der-el-Bahari. Note the rigging and the man in the bows with the sounding-rod

Below
Sixth Dynasty Egyptian ships from a relief at Deir el-Gebrawi in Middle Egypt. Note that the left ship has a tripod mast, and the sails are wider than high. But other Sixth Dynasty ships still have tall square sails. (After Davies, *Rock Tombs of Deir el-Gebrawi*)

shrouds, or lateral support for the mast, which may be revealing of the seamanship at the time.

The running rigging includes what must appear to be a great excess of lifts for the yard and boom. The number of individual lines involved is alarming. Eight lifts on either side of the mast support the boom; the same number support the yard. With the yard aloft, all but one lift on either side were slack and hung in bights,

The papyriform
hull of an Egyptian
ship *circa* 1800 B.C.
with yard and
boom and
numerous lifts

gracious for the artist and prettily illustrated in the Egyptian low reliefs. With the sail hoisted the boom lifts were taut; when sail was lowered these became slack while the yard lifts tightened to carry the yard's weight. All this array of lines would appear to indicate intense concern about the sail-cloth. It could carry little load.

The yard was controlled by braces, the boom by sheets, and their positioning provides a clue to the sail-handling practices of the time. The braces led from the yards at about the mid-point between the outer end and the mast, while the sheets were even closer to the mast. The artist, in order to reveal details of the rig shows the yard and boom braced round fore and aft, which does not mean that the vessels could have sailed with the wind abeam. The lack of shrouds on the mast left the latter unsupported against a beam wind, and even with a step in which the mast might be buried deeply this would have been a dangerous arrangement. The sail itself, so shallow and wide, was a bad shape for close-winded sailing, and the short luff presented to the wind and the lack of bowlines would have absolutely prohibited

Opposite page
Dionysios at sea. Perhaps the first representation of the
traditional link between drink and the sea

Stern of a Greek war galley

sailing with the wind anywhere ahead of the beam. The control of the ship, with its single steering oars, is an improvement on the three steering paddles of the past; but we may reasonably assume that these Egyptians, the most sophisticated seamen of their day, did not sail with the wind more than some 40 degrees forward of dead astern.

The voyage to Punt could have been no light achievement. Initially it was

facilitated by the canal which then existed between the Nile and Red Sea. Then lay some 1,500 miles of the Red Sea's length, with the seasonal wind from the NNW. blowing on the stern and allowing sail to be carried. There was also the current running down the Red Sea to help. Wherever on the North-east African coast Punt may have been, once beyond the Red Sea they would have had the chance of making use of the alternating south-west and north-east monsoon. If the voyage started early enough in the year, it might have been possible to catch the last of the north-east monsoon to take them down the coast, and return when the south-west monsoon had set in.

But still there would be hours of rowing, when the great yard was lowered and lay in the ship with the sail bundled along it between the two lines of oarsmen

Egyptian warship, 12th century B.C.,
in reign of Rameses III

Phoenician-Assyrian bireme
of the 8th century B.C.

Scratched on the handle of an amphora excavated at Thasos, a sailing-vessel with a lateen sail of the triangular type that became so characteristic of the Mediterranean

Opposite page
Bows of Greek war galley

bending to their short oars and making quick strokes in time with the notes of a flute played by their rowing-master. And despite the thirty oarsmen, the fluting and the ready whip, progress then would have been slow.

A voyage made by a twentieth-century seaman in a Red Sea dhow may throw some light on the ancient seamanship in that area. Alan Villiers, who sailed a replica of the *Mayflower* across the Atlantic in 1957, made a passage in 1938 from Ma'alla to Gizan in a 55-foot Arab *sambuk*. With her settee lateen sail and deep, teak-planked hull, the Arab ship, though primitive to twentieth-century eyes, would have had better sailing qualities than the Egyptian vessels in the time of the dynasties, though the later ship lacked the oars and oarsmen of the ancient. And in certain other respects she may have been less favoured.

Villiers wrote of her: 'Without any kind of windlass (and no anchor save two rusty small grapnels), with no boat other than a small dugout canoe which could support five excellent balancers in a mill-pond, with no instruments of any kind save one ancient and very inefficient compass, without even a leadline to sound (sometimes the Nkhoda used part of a fishing line weighted with a stone) . . . without charts, without log, without even a pump . . . still that little ship wandered pleasantly enough along, delivering her cargoes in good condition at the tiny outposts of one of the worst seas in the world, full of reefs and sets and maritime dangers which still, upon occasion, prove the undoing of great steamers. She had been doing that for years. There was not even a flag on board, and no clock; no one had heard of a barometer.'

Elsewhere Villiers writes: 'She is exceedingly ill-found. There is not a decent piece of line on board, nor a piece of good canvas. The main halyards are plaited straw.' The lack of instruments the Egyptians would have shared with the dhow, except we may expect her to have had a proper leadline, and if not some form of chart there would have been sailing directions. The Egyptian, however, would not probably have been ill-found. The dhow was a poor man's vessel working in a petty trade on the outskirts of the civilized world; the Egyptian operated in the centre of civilization, belonged to some of its richest members and represented one of the greatest technological achievements of the day.

The dhow sailed only by day, anchoring every night; we do not know if this was the Egyptians' practice. Navigation was purely visual except for occasional soundings made with the fishing-line; and Villiers noticed that whenever the captain did this there transpired to be only a small depth. The skipper knew his waters well. On hazy days he would send one of the crew aloft to pick out landmarks. Then in the last light of the day he would con the ship into an anchorage, getting under way again probably before dawn. Sailing north along the Arabian coast off Yemen Villiers recalls 'the reefs, which for all their sinister thickness and their jagged teeth

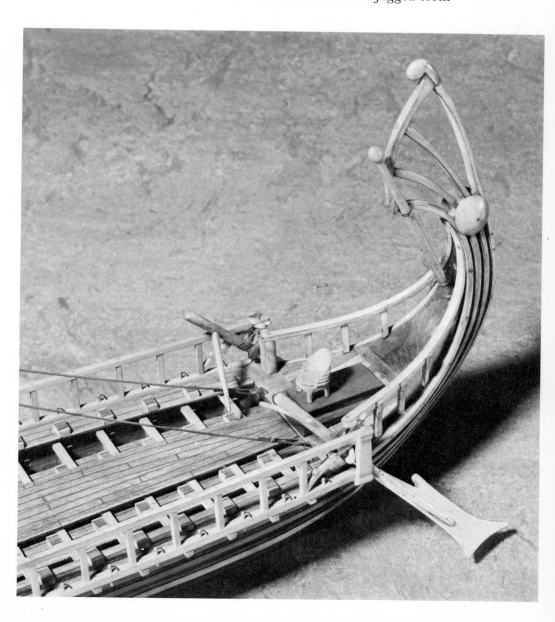

Phoenician merchant ship,
8th century B.C.

gave surprisingly little evidence of themselves; we sailed for days between scattered lines of flat sand cays and the low shore of the mainland.' They passed steamers 'For all their size and their obvious power and contempt of the elements, they seemed in the distance always dead things . . . like clockwork things let loose on a big pond: for it seemed to us being alive in a ship that lived that the great powered things could not belong to our world. . . . The mate sometimes pointed and said: "Barbor" with great contempt.'

And thus a survival of the kind of seamanship that was very ancient greeted the thing it had become in the course of several thousand years.

By the end of the second millennium B.C. the ships of which we know most, the Egyptian, showed further advances compared with those of Queen Hatshepsut. An important change in rigging had occurred. No longer was sail lowered by letting go of the halyard, but the practice of brailing the sail up to the yard, which remained aloft, was adopted; and for a thousand years hence this was to be the practice of the Phoenicians, who learned their seafaring initially from the Egyptians. This never became the seafaring practice of the North, where the use of brails was confined to inland waters. The Egyptian brails hung from the yard, and their use meant doing away with the boom. That gone, the very broad sail could no longer be sheeted and trimmed within the beam of the ship and had to be made more nearly square. By this time, too, the structure of the Egyptian ship had been improved, making it

50

possible to eliminate the hogging truss which hitherto had been an essential feature of Egyptian seagoing vessels, and this had an indirect effect upon seamanship. The inevitable tendency of the earlier hulls built of short lengths of plank and with considerable length of hull overhanging the water at the bow and stern, had been to hog, or droop at the ends. This has always been a problem. The builders of the North, whose ships were smaller than those of the Egyptians, initially solved it by using long planks and a sectional shape of hull with a steep rise to the floor, or bottom, and finally by fitting a sturdy, moderately deep keel. The truss was a large cable fastened round bow and stern and led over a series of queen-posts with crutch tops spaced along the length of the hull on the centre-line. The cable was made taut by an

Sidonian merchant ship
of 3rd century A.D.

Masts and sails of the Roman merchantman of 2nd
century A.D. Largest type of ship of her time

application of the tourniquet principle, or Spanish windlass, applied at either end of
the truss. Such ships were fragile and fraught with peril for the mariner.

The age of the many-oared galleys, yet to come, was to put upon the sea ships
that were inevitably weak; and even the heavy merchantmen of the yet unrisen
Imperial Rome were structurally such that a severe seaway endangered them. The
much later Vikings' mastery of the limited range of materials available for ship construction produced a ship that combined flexibility with strength and these long-
ships from the fjords were triumphs of shipbuilding and led to the supremacy of the
North over the South, which for so long had been the leader in this field.

But the seamen of the Mediterranean at the beginning of the first millennium

B.C. had much superior seagoing vehicles to those of the Bronze Age North. The ships of the Pharaohs Snefru and Sahure with their tall, narrow sails and fixed booms had become those of Queen Hatshepsut, with shallow, broad sails and swinging booms, while by the reign of Rameses III the truss had been eliminated and the system of brailing the sail up to the yard been invented.

During these first millennia of seamanship we have to suppose that only one navigational instrument was available – the leadline, together with its counterpart for shallow waters, the sounding-rod. There are pictures of men standing forward and using the latter in the second millennium B.C., as there are in medieval illustrations 2,000 years later. Once boats had grown into ships having appreciable draught the depth of water below the keel was of vital importance, amplified by the relatively delicate structure of ships which made all but the most carefully arranged groundings a peril. The greater subtlety of arming the lead, and so bringing up a sample of the bottom, which on the evidence of seamen's lore might be identified as belonging to a certain locality, raised the leadline to the status of an important navigational aid.

Knowledge of the seaman's practical methods have not only become lost in the flowing stream of history, but when they were contemporary practices they were still known only to the few whose way of life was on the sea, and even among these the tricks of the trade were most carefully guarded secrets. The freemasonry of the sea is a modern conception. Sailors plied a dangerous trade not in the cause of international learning or to extend the human horizon, but for profit. The secretiveness of the Phoenicians was famous.

Essential to the seaman's trade was a rich store of remembered landmarks. The speed of the ship and distance travelled could only be guessed, but at least under

Graffiti of the *navis bucius* (Katergon) from Hagia Sophia

Model of a two-masted bireme
with sails set

better conditions the experienced seaman would be able to make a remarkably close estimate of speed under oars or in various wind strengths under sail. The later Norse seamen used a 'turn' as a measure of distance run, this being derived from the practice when under oars of having the oarsmen change sides every two hours. A 'turn' was the distance run between the changes, and measurements have indicated that this was about 6 miles. The galleys averaged about 3 knots. A day's sail was a Mediterranean unit of distance, but there is vagueness as to what the distance was assumed to be; it was something between 100 and 130 miles.

But the first knowledge of such matters that we have been able to discover belongs to a later period of seafaring than these earliest days. At some point seamen learned to use the height of the fixed stars to get an idea of latitude. In the Red Sea from north to south there is a change in latitude of some 18 degrees, making this amount of difference in the altitude of the Pole Star. 'We do not follow any of the restless stars which move in the sky, for they deceive poor sailors. We follow no stars but one, that does not dip into the waves, the never-setting Axis, brightest star in the twin Bears. This it is that guides the ships.' The words, from the poet Lucan, are dated as late as

Model of Judean merchant ship *circa* 14th century B.C.
Note the fencing to hold in the cargo; the amphora, the
usual cargo container in the Mediterranean for such
materials as wine, oil, grain; the bipod mast

Opposite page
Judean merchant ship *circa* 3rd century A.D. Note the
form of the lug rig. The deadeyes for setting up the
shrouds, and the ratlines, may be questioned in a
Mediterranean ship of this date

Steering oar, which was actually a true side rudder, and
hull of the Gokstad ship

A.D. 63–5, yet are the first direct evidence of the seaman's use of star altitudes to discover position as opposed merely to giving direction. Whatever it was that the Egyptian astronomers knew about the stars for time telling, we cannot find out what was taught to their sailors. Dr Jules Sottas has written: 'There was, in fact, now a Semitic race whose sailors voyaged regularly to the very ends of the Mediterranean and even passed through the Ocean Gate. These Phoenicians who could navigate by the stars – though they kept their knowledge and practice to themselves – had the monopoly of long-distance navigation: they imported goods into ancient Egypt, into decadent Crete and into Greece, now at the dawn of her destiny.' What today we know of navigation by the stars began at this period.

2
Antiquity

In all parts of the world men paddled their craft before they learned to row them, and there is little doubt that in the East the sail preceded the oar. But the reverse was true of the North. The oar, in terms of mechanical advantage, is a more efficient device; but the principle of the fulcrum and the practical means of arranging one afloat, though it was well enough known ashore, was something lying well along the devious path of ancient seamanship. The paddle, the oar, the sail are three crucial stages in the development of the seaman's art.

In the North, from the evidence of rock carvings, it is known that boats were being rowed in the Early Iron Age, or say 300 B.C. in Scandinavia. But the evidence is scanty. Oars may have been used there earlier. It would have been difficult to arrange oars in a reed boat; but they were in use in Egypt in wooden boats by 3000 B.C. It was a decisive step in the progress of seamanship, and the ship propelled mainly by oars, evolving into the later forms of multi-banked galley and subsequently reverting to the single bank, served seamen for perhaps more than 5,000 years, large galleys being still in use in the Baltic during the nineteenth century.

But oar propulsion suffers from the limitation set by human muscle as a means of producing power. This was to become a capital problem of ancient seamanship productive of remarkably ingenious solutions. A man was such an inefficient means of providing power. His weight in relation to his strength, the brief periods during which full strength might be developed, his requirements in food and (in a hot climate) drink while doing so, entailed entirely filling the ship with the means of propulsion in order to achieve even a modest speed. Professor A. V. Hill of the Biophysics Research Unit, University College, London, considers that the equivalent of half an accepted horsepower (1 h.p. being equivalent to 550 foot-pounds per second) can be delivered by a well-trained man during a period of twenty minutes. The inefficiency of rowing as a means of propulsion is clear. A 10-stone man will have a power-to-weight ratio, expressed in pounds weight per horsepower, of 280. The ratio is about 34 in the diesel engines now used in the larger ships; a Rolls-Royce Merlin petrol engine weighs only 2 pounds per horsepower.

Seamen would appear to have been rowing galleys for some 3,000 years before the mechanically ingenious idea of packing more power into a given length of ship by means of superimposed banks of oars was evolved. With the bireme and later the trireme appeared two of the best-known devices of ancient seamanship.

Immense erudition has been devoted to the arrangement of oars in the bireme, trireme, and thence on to whatever it may have been that quadreremes, quinqueremes were, and further multiremes ranging through ships with eleven, fifteen, twenty, thirty and forty 'banks'; a word which in the higher numbers has clearly

Ship found at Nydam of the 4th century. The vessel pre-dates Norse sail, is narrow, without a keel, and the side rudder is in a yet crude state of development

changed in meaning from that of indicating levels of oars in some manner super-imposed. A school of thought once insisted that oars were always carried in a single horizontal line. Most people now believe that the bireme had two rows of oars at different levels; that the trireme was developed from this by adding a third bank above the other two and having the tholes on an outrigger. Beyond this doubt is still widespread, and while some authorities will accept superimposition up to the quinquereme others stop at the trireme. What is certain is that between *circa* 700 B.C. and the Christian era a new kind of seamanship came into being, limited in range, in terms of seagoing, but of immense complexity compared with any former seagoing operations based upon oar propulsion.

A typical Roman corn-ship on a sarcophagus at Sidon

Long and fierce arguments have ranged over the question of possible oar arrangements, all suffering from the handicap that no seagoing replica has ever been built of even a bireme or trireme; so that while modern seamen have had experience of handling a variety of old ships at sea, from the Viking to medieval and Renaissance vessels, for the multireme all is theory, with some of the contestants in the arguments lacking, one suspects, experience of handling oars under any conditions. So it has been argued that rowers cannot keep time if they are using oars of different lengths, the example of the differing periods of pendulums being cited. Having cleared up the fact that an oar is not a free-swinging pendulum – as the galley slave knew too well – there arises the question of what *is* an oar? Is it a lever of the first or second order? It is now widely considered to be the latter. It may further be said that two oarsmen may keep time with oars of different lengths provided the oars are pivoted so that proportionately the same length of each is inboard and outboard. For each stroke the shorter oar will travel through a greater angle, but will move the ship a similar distance and with the same time of stroke as the longer oar. But the practical mechanics of the multi-bank galley is inevitably complex and offers a great variety of solutions. And when we consider how many galleys were built and the great period of time involved, and set this against the small amount of information there is

64

about them, we can only guess that there was a great variety of arrangements adopted by different builders at different times.

With the galley, seamen became what they had never been before. Man may be a fighting creature, but he had not previously been a fighting seaman using vessels and methods of seamanship devised purely for battle. The fighting seaman's weapon was the ram. Until the appearance of the gun the ram was the one formidable destroyer of ships, and it is this object of destroying ships that defines the fighting seamen. The ram, devised in the earlier half of the first millennium B.C. remained a respected weapon in the most advanced navies of the world until late in the nineteenth century A.D.

We may picture a Greek trireme as a narrow vessel some 130 feet in length with a beam of about 18 feet and 170 oarsmen arranged thus:

Upper bank (thranites)	31 oars per side
Middle bank (zygites)	27 oars per side
Lower bank (thalamites)	27 oars per side

American whaling-boat showing the steering oar still in practical use in the 20th century. The sail is a lug.

The oars were relatively short considering the size of the ship: 14 feet in the upper bank; 10 feet 6 inches in the middle bank; and a mere 7 feet 6 inches in the lower bank. In later centuries, when there was a reversion to single-banked galleys, oars became considerably longer and the rowing-boats in modern navies may have oars as long as 18 feet, while in the racing eight of today they may be 12 feet 6 inches.

Below the lower deck of the Greek galley, which was about a foot above the water, was the hold, where some stone or sand ballast was stowed, and through hatches in this deck buckets were lowered for bailing, which was a continuous operation when at sea as the narrow and flexible ships worked under the stresses of the 170 oars. The spectacle of a slim trireme cutting through a glistening sheet of Mediterranean water, the crowded, disciplined oars simultaneously lifting and dipping to the time of the metronomic notes played on the ship's flute, must have been a study in motion inspiring above all others. And thus indeed it did inspire the sculptor of the Winged Victory of Samothrace, who carved the marble pedestal in the form of a galley's prow.

But the beauty was less than skin deep, and the vision of smooth motion falters when the reality is examined more closely. The author has calculated, using the conventional methods of naval architecture, and accepting Professor Hill's estimate above, that the maximum speed of a trireme would have been little more than 8 knots, this achieved only spasmodically and briefly.

Apart from the oarsmen, the crew would be composed of some twenty seamen and ten marines, a helmsman and navigator, and the captain. The helmsman's literal title in Greek was 'steering oar holder,' though the actual manipulation of the oar was not his function. In these intensely specialized ships various of the crew concentrated upon particular duties essential to effective operation. Thus there was an 'oar-binder' probably in charge of the straps securing the oars; an 'oil-anointer' who may have been generally in charge of all leather-work; the flutist; a carpenter; a boatswain; a number of seamen forward and aft. During the numerous generations of the galley's use by Phoenician, Greek and Roman, the organization on board as well as the ships themselves must have varied widely. In the centuries immediately before Christ remarkable developments in oar arrangements were being made. From the relative simplicity of one man per oar, the oars arranged as we now believe in up to three superimposed banks, there appeared the quadriremes, quinqueremes and other multi-banks, in which more than one man worked on each oar – the practice that was to persist into the latest days of the galleys, but in classical times to be applied to biremes and triremes. Oars became longer, and various permutations of oar levels and arrangements of men were tried, details of which can today only be guessed. We can imagine those distant scenes and the densely crowded ships with their massive crews going on board in carefully organized rotation to each level of the rowing-benches until, with everyone in place, there was, as Cicero pointed out, not space for one man more.

The galleys were capable of sailing, and used sail when possible for passage-making, but lowered sail and even left it and all gear ashore before action. But

Looking down into a Greek galley

This carving of ships under sail in Ostia harbour from
a 3rd century A.D. sarcophagus shows that sprits were
known and used then

whatever the limited capabilities under sail of the beamier and deeper freight-
carrying ships of the times, those of the galleys were even more limited by the narrow-
ness and lack of stability of their hulls which were designed for rowing. The sails were
square and brailed up to the yards, and braces enabled the yards to be trimmed fore
and aft; but this does not indicate that the craft sailed with the wind on the beam or
from ahead. The yards had to be trimmed within the beam of the hull when the
galleys were packed tightly in the small harbours. It is surprising, in view of the fact
that these were not primarily sailing-craft, that it was on the galley, later in its history,
that the fore-and-aft rig first appears, giving an ability to sail closer to the wind than
is possible with the square rig. But this rig, the hard-worked tool of coastwise seamen
in later ages, is considered in the next chapter.

The classical galley, for all the dominating place it has in history, was a fragile
and specialized instrument of seamanship, devoted purely to speed and manœuvrability. Their passage-making was coastal, and they were tied to the land not only by
the needs of the crew, but by the necessity for the ships to be often run ashore for
repairs and to dry out the hull, the weight caused by soakage lowering the speed that
was crucial to them. Their immense crews and light draught deprived them of carrying power, and they were lacking in any ability to face stormy seas.

Many centuries later the merchant galleass evolved from it, and even in the
North vessels of this type continued to be used for various purposes. But essentially
the oared sailing-ship, in whatever form, as opposed to the sailing-ship with possibly
some oars, was the creature of Mediterranean conditions of seamanship. It persisted

there at the expense of the development of the sailing-ship, which advanced to superiority on the Atlantic coasts, where the oared ship lost importance. In so far as the latter could be made into a sea- and ocean-going vessel, this was achieved by the Vikings and their immediate successors, who were shortly to evolve from this kind of galley the northern seagoing sailing-ship. The southern galley in its various forms and throughout its immense span of life was an instrument of seamanship capable of nothing but specialized development and it was ever confined to the edges of the oceans. We find here an anomaly: the sailing-ship, vessel of subservient movement, is able to win the freedom of the oceans, while the galley, vessel of free movement, remains tied to the coasts.

It was not in such craft that the Phoenicians made the voyages that give them today the premier place among ancient seamen. Some of the highlights of Phoenician history are unproved, but we may be sure that following the Minoans, who may have depleted Crete of shipbuilding timber, and the Egyptians, from whom the Phoenicians learned both shipbuilding and seamanship, it was the ships of this secret people which became most numerous in the Mediterranean. We may still sense the beat of the rowdy Viking's heart, and even think we understand – we, so different – a little about his love of a ship. In this we may be grossly mistaken, but we cannot make a similar mistake about the Phoenicians. They remain impenetrable, as they appear to have been to their contemporaries. Yet in the story of seamanship it is the way of the Phoenician that later ages have followed. Canny, unimperial, intent on profit, they are the prototype of the seamen of the ages and the tradesmen of the sea.

It has even been suggested that they reached America, an idea that should not be accepted as other than not impossible. It is usually believed that they came to Britain in search of tin, the latter a potent encouragement of seagoing in the Bronze Age. It has been suggested that having reached Britain they pressed on with the south-westerlies until the Norwegian coast came over the bow, and that they later sailed their Mediterranean craft in the Baltic, whose clear waters and small tides may have recalled to the dark-skinned seamen their home at the end of the slow sea miles astern. These ideas may remind us of the beliefs entertained by Professor Brøgger of the wide-ranging Norse seamanship during the Bronze Age, discussed in the first chapter.

The fact that men have rowed across the Atlantic in small boats during recent years makes it clear that Phoenicians in their trading vessels *could* have reached America, though it may have been by chance rather than choice. In June in the latitude of Gibraltar winds of over Force 8 Beaufort may occur no more often than on 2–3 per cent of the days over the breadth of the Atlantic, and calms are usual on about one-third of the days. In a slightly lower latitude are the north-east trade winds and the ocean current setting to the westward. The Atlantic passage could have been made in this month of ancient seafaring, but when the time involved is considered and the weaknesses of the ships, it becomes impossible to believe that such voyages were other than freaks. That the Phoenicians reached the Azores is a belief hardly less firm than that of their trading with Britain. The former would be an easier passage than the one to the north, with light though variable winds. It should be emphasized, however, that neither in Britain nor the Azores is there any proof of

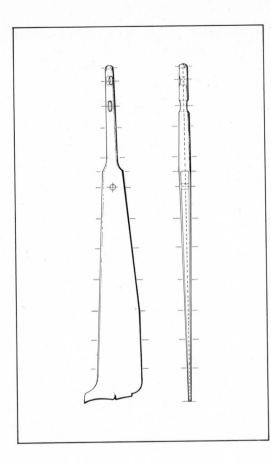

Vorså side rudder, probably 9th century A.D. found in the Kattegat in 1958 and now in Bangsbo Museum

Opposite page
The Hjortspring boat. Found on the Danish island of Als and dated *circa* 200 B.C., 43 feet 6 inches in length, this craft has features that are clearly suggested in the rock drawings (see pages 21 and 22) and though built of wood the design of the hull indicates an inheritance from the skin boat

Phoenician visits; and when the design and construction of their ships are considered, the feats of seamanship that would be represented by these oceanic voyages will be appreciated. That they reached beyond Britain to the Baltic requires a still greater stretch of belief.

Later, when we examine the corn-ships of Imperial Rome, which were to remain the largest ships for some 1,000 years, and note their deficiency in oceangoing qualities, it will serve to reflect upon the ability of the much earlier and smaller Phoenician trading vessels. The fact that they were smaller might be to their advantage. But the Phoenicians' ships could have been no superior in general design and construction, and must have had similar weaknesses in sails and rigging.

The Phoenicians walked out of what is still legend into Mediterranean history, and what details we may gather of the ships which enabled them to reach over the Mediterranean come from the ships of the Egyptians. In the second millennium B.C., including the latter half, they appear to have been using the typically Egyptian broad and shallow square sail with yard and boom both in two pieces fished together, the latter supported by numerous lifts, the sail furled by brailing up to the yard. Perhaps there was still the hogging truss supporting the hull.

While we know so little in detail about the Phoenician trading-ships, it cannot be doubted that they soon advanced far beyond the Egyptian in their design and construction. The Egyptian seagoing ships were over much influenced by the Nile craft from which they were descended, while the Phoenicians had no river-boats to misguide them. And they also had what Ptolemaic Egypt lacked, a supply of the finest shipbuilding timber in the Lebanon forests. Behind the Phoenician seamen were the skilful Phoenician lumbermen. Greek and Phoenician together developed the sailing cargo-ship which ultimately resembled the Roman corn-ships, a type of trading vessel of which details have been preserved and which are able to suggest some of the features of earlier Phoenician and Greek vessels.

One of the most debated questions of the Phoenician achievement is whether, as Herodotus recorded with frank scepticism, they sailed round Africa in the time of the Pharaoh Necho (610–594 B.C.). The tale as Herodotus picked it up, was that a fleet manned by Phoenicians set out from the Red Sea and sailed south down the Indian Ocean. They put ashore each autumn at some point on the African coast to sow a crop they could harvest before again putting to sea. After three years they reached what is today Gibraltar and sailed the length of the comparatively familiar Mediterranean back to home waters.

This is one more Phoenician exploit that may have occurred but cannot be proved. It is not impossible. Starting in the autumn they would have had the northeast monsoon and the current in the Red Sea to row against, but after rounding Cape Guardafui wind and current would have favoured them, as would the current in the Mozambique Channel and round the Cape. It has been estimated that a year after starting they could have harvested a crop, planted in June after rounding the Cape.

With twelve hours per day at sea, the daily rate of progress necessary to complete the rounding of the Cape and reach some way north before planting the crop in June, is not excessive – say between 2 and 3 knots, allowing for delays and accidents. Then during the next year they would find favourable currents and north-easterly winds up the west coast of Africa to the southern tip of the continent's westerly bulge. The year would end with hard rowing against the current and the north-east trade wind

Ship on a sculptured stone *circa* 8th century, found in Gotland. The many bridles along the foot of the sail are to distribute the load over the loosely woven cloth. The criss-cross lines represent doublings, perhaps in leather, to strengthen it.

as far as somewhere off the coast of today's Morocco, when again they would land and sow and reap; after which a further long spell against prevailing wind and current would bring them to Cape Spartel and the return to the Mediterranean.

So brief a summary barely suggests the measure of the achievement represented by such a voyage. The risks inseparable from so long a coasting passage in totally unknown waters, the torrid climate over part of the distance, the likelihood of illness, and the need, except during the periods spent ashore growing food, of pressing on day after day into the unknown, call for qualities of endurance and fortitude that raise it to the level of the magnificent; while the problem of preserving the fabric of the ships during three active sailing seasons must have verged on the insuperable. The voyage might have been made; it is more likely to have been attempted and achieved only to the limited extent of sailing as far south as some distance beyond the equator; perhaps to the Mozambique Channel. For the Phoenicians reported having the sun on their right hand at midday, which they would have found here when working along the coast to the south-west. This is the most convincing piece of evidence in the story.

The methods by which they navigated was one of the best-kept secrets of this evasive people, for herein lay their profit. Strength and direction of wind was the primary concern of the navigator. He named the winds after the country from whose direction they blew, but his crucial skill, the result of long experience, was to recognize the places towards which they would carry him in his ships whose power of sailing was so limited. The wind-rose of the ancients was their mariners' compass, the points being eight in number, placed by eight recognized winds thus: Tramontana (north); Greco (north-east); Levante (east); Syroco (south-east); Mezzodi (south); Garbio (south-west); Pomente (west); Maestro (north-west).

Winds varied with seasonable regularity in the areas important to the ancient seamen and this enabled them to use their wind-rose with some confidence. (Originally and until a late date in the history of seafaring, the mariner's compass, later associated with a magnetic needle, was quite distinct from the wind-rose.) Setting sail from Tyre or Sidon on a voyage down the Red Sea, the ancient seamen would find a fair wind from approximately the north-west, but when the time came later in the season to return home, they were conveniently provided with a wind from the opposite direction – a home-blowing wind, to carry them back up the Red Sea to the coastline of their Syrian home.

Mariners would recognize not only the difference between the mild wind that blew from the direction of the sunset, or the dry wind from the east or the cold wind from the north, but also the more subtle intermediate winds, one bringing a trace of damp, another squalls and rain.

To establish a compass by means of a wind division of the horizon's circle does not bring with it the ability to maintain a course when out of sight of any guiding mark; except in so far as a steady wind may provide a sense of direction. The stars are a means of orientation that no doubt was very old when we first read of it in

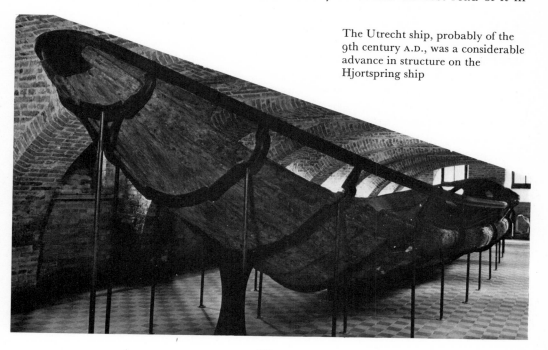

The Utrecht ship, probably of the 9th century A.D., was a considerable advance in structure on the Hjortspring ship

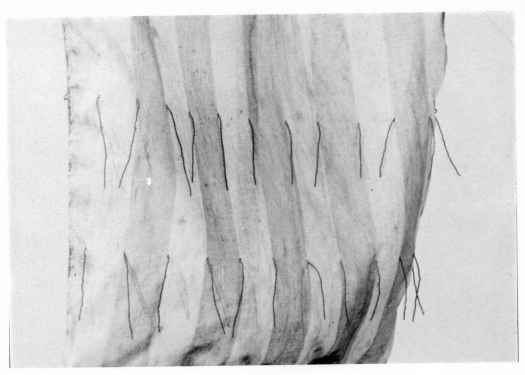

Reef-points on the sail of a model of a Viking ship in
the National Science Museum, London. This feature
may not be correct. It is uncertain whether the Vikings
used reef-points.

Homer. The Phoenicians were the most skilful people of their day in using the stars
as a guide. They knew a better way of distinguishing north than by means of the
Great Bear group of stars. This was by using the Little Bear, which had the advantage
of appearing brighter and earlier in the night. Furthermore, the Little Bear was at
that time more nearly circumpolar than the Pole Star, also used by the Phoenicians;
circumstances differing from those of today when the precessional movement has
brought the Pole Star almost coincidental with the Pole, while the Bear constella-
tions are further away from it. 'By her [the Little Bear's] guidance the men of Sidon
steer the straightest course', said the Greek poet Aratus in 275 B.C. when the practice
was already old.

To use the stars to guide was a less sophisticated process than that referred to in
the first chapter, involving their value for determining position, which was to lead
in the later ages of instruments to the highest subtleties of celestial navigation. When
the Phoenicians sailed down the Red Sea and further south, the Great Bear, which
Homer said 'wheels round and round where it is and never takes a bath in the ocean',
would take a bath, and instead the seamen would observe the brilliant light of
Canopus, which could not be seen from their own coast. Star altitude, like all else
in ancient navigation, was bereft of accurate measurements, which were totally

Opposite page
Remains of a Viking trading vessel *circa* 800 A.D.
Particularly notice the tabernacle for the mast showing
that the vessel could sail.

A small Mediterranean ship *circa* 14th century A.D.,
about 32 feet in length overall, showing some features
typical of Mediterranean craft at this period – the lateen
rig, twin rudders, shrouds set up by tackles and without
ratlines: instead there is a ladder abaft the mast

unfamiliar to the world of the seafarer. The stars, like the winds, were guides to be snatched at and welcomed for a little help; to judge position by the aid of stars was the rudimentary process of noting their height when observed from, say, the helm, using the ship's mast and rigging, or a man at a certain distance as a crude scale of altitude.

The Italy of Imperial Rome was overpopulated and undeveloped while Egypt was the land of corn. It was this fact, as much as her charm, that gave power and influence to the last Cleopatra of the Ptolemies in a Roman-dominated Mediterranean. In a world where sea trade was still so largely involved with luxuries – as it had been in the past – with silks and spices, incense for the gods and gold and ivory, the most important trade in the Mediterranean was carried by the corn-ships from Alexandria into the mouth of the Tiber to Ostia, the port of Rome.

The Macedonian Greek port of Alexandria, raised by Alexander to surpass Tyre – which he had recently destroyed – had a splendid double harbour behind which were the broad and gracious streets of a polyglot town where most of the languages of the Imperial world might be heard. Familiar to every Alexandrian was the colossal lighthouse of gleaming white marble on the island of Pharos, about three-quarters of a mile offshore and linked to the mainland by a magnificent causeway. This lighthouse, with the light burning on its 600-foot summit, was not only regarded as one of the wonders of the world; in view of the importance of Roman-Egyptian trade it was the most crucial sea-mark in the Mediterranean, guiding ships into the flat and featureless Nile Delta, with its shallows and dangerous reefs, and up to the haven lying between Pharos and the mainland known as the 'Harbour of Good Homecoming', or in less emotional style merely as the 'Great Harbour'.

Here the grain-ships, which carried the crop of the Nile Valley to Rome during the season of seagoing (extending, it should be remembered, only from April to October) arrived and left in a steady procession. Another cargo taken on board would be Egypt's other source of wealth, gold from the Nubian mountains. These were the finest sailing vessels the world had yet seen, and probably the largest. Lucian wrote of one 180 feet in length: 'What a tremendous vessel it was . . . the crew was like an army.'

But the more usual size was about 100 feet with a beam of some 30 feet and able to carry perhaps 280 tons of cargo. Various representations of such vessels have survived – reliefs at Porto and Ostia on the Tiber, a tombstone at Pompeii, sarcophagae on the Syrian coast at Sidon and Tarsus. These, together with Lucian's description, have allowed detailed drawings and models to be made of this important class of vessel in the early Christian Mediterranean, which was hardly improved upon for 1,000 years.

The merchantman, beamy and deep, was purely a sailing vessel, quite unlike others in that galley-strewn sea. This emphasizes the sluggishness of marine trade during the summer months of navigation with their long periods of calm. But like all sailing vessels before her day, and for centuries after until they became too large, a few sweeps would be carried on board for manœuvring in port and constricted waters and for swinging the ship in near calms. The largest vessels of their time, they offered some comforts for a few of those on board. There may have been a raised

awning-covered balcony aft, beneath the curve of the great swan's neck, the characteristic stern decoration of merchantmen, which carried no figureheads. There would
have been a deckhouse further forward on a lower level, close to which the helmsman
stood at the double steering oars. Ahead would be the hatches, and in chocks near
amidships the ship's boat, which so nearly came to grief at an early stage in St Paul's
voyage, and in the bow the two anchors.

As the largest sailing-ship yet to have been evolved the rig should be studied
carefully. Some 800 years later we find the most advanced rig of northern Europe in
the Viking ships, and this, apart from being simpler in construction, showed how in
important respects methods of seamanship differed in these two parts of the world.

On the central mast of the Roman merchantman was a square sail, with sometimes a triangular topsail above it. Here is the first-known evidence of the superimposed sail which does not seem to have been in use in the North even 1,000 years
later; yet it was in the North that this early step towards the full-rigged ship resulted
in up to six superimposed working sails being set with light weather canvas above.
In the extreme bow was another spar which might be regarded as a heavily steeved
bowsprit or a heavily raked foremast. It carried the sail known as the *artemon*, an
essential feature in the concept of the rig, for it gave a limited power of sailing with
the wind on and a little forward of the beam. The Vikings were later to achieve this
by quite a different means. In some of the largest ships it appears that there was also
a mizzen-mast carrying a third square sail.

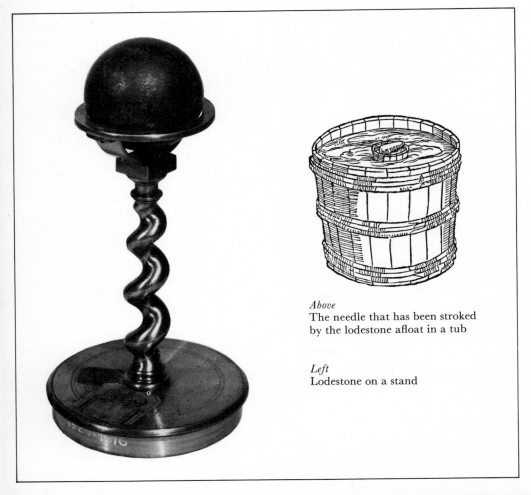

Above
The needle that has been stroked
by the lodestone afloat in a tub

Left
Lodestone on a stand

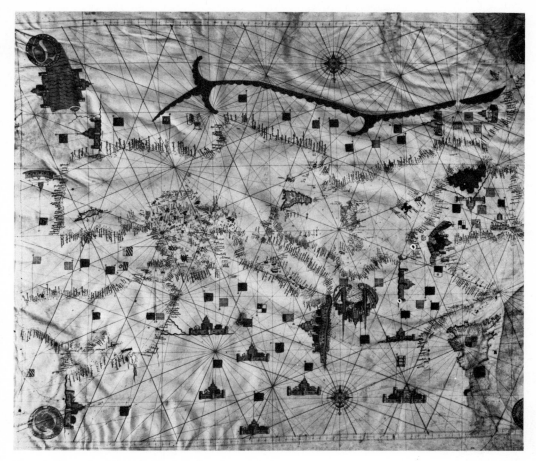

Part of a Portulan of 1456 showing the criss-cross of
rhumb-lines from the various roses

There were the braces and sheets for trimming the yards and the foot of the sails,
a heavy forestay and backstay, and shrouds, four per side, all set up by deadeyes.
The blocks for the halyards and braces probably did not have sheaves, and therefore
were essentially deadeyes. These elements of the rig were to become common in all
square-rigged ships until they disappeared. Indeed, the twentieth-century seaman
able to handle this rig would have found much familiar in the Roman merchantmen.
But he would have had to learn many forgotten tricks in connection with the
handling of the vessel and in the manipulation of the twin side rudders.

The sails were brailed up to their yards. The brails were lines running from the
foot of the sail through rings sewn to the seams up to the yard, and thence down
again. This formed the hauling part. There were perhaps nine brails in the width of
the mainsail, and when hauled on these lifted the foot of the sail in pleats to any
required level or right home to the yard itself, where the furling would be completed
by the crew up on the yard, presumably on foot-ropes. The *artemon* had a similar

79

brailing system, with perhaps five brails. Either sail might thus be partially brailed, or brailed on one side and not the other, producing numerous permutations of sail balance, and in using these adroitly lay the skill in coaxing these unquestionably unwieldy and not very easily controlled vessels along.

There were no reef-points, the brails serving their purpose. The only method of achieving a degree of progress in adverse winds lay in the *artemon*. The Viking ships of centuries later, so much less sophisticated in many respects, had achieved some weatherliness in a single-masted, square-rigged ship by means of bowlines and bearing-out poles. One cannot avoid the impression, however, that Roman seamen did use bearing-out spars to spread the square sails when the yards were hauled round to take an adverse wind.

In ordinary weather the two-piece yard would remain aloft. But in severe conditions the difficult operation of lowering it would have to be undertaken, and as we shall see this was probably done when the storm overtook St Paul's ship. The yard, of two spars fished together, was hoisted on a halyard passing through a heavy block secured near the masthead, and there were lifts above the yard, their hauling parts leading to the deck. In these vessels we see a high development of the sailing vessel. The rig of the ships in northern Europe 1,000 years later, though different in important ways, cannot in the main be described as superior in concept, though possibly the ships were easier to handle in the tidal and stormy waters of the North.

It was in such a ship as this that St Paul was wrecked in about A.D. 61 when on passage from Caesarea to Rome. We have to be grateful that since the voyage and shipwreck showed the Apostle in a favourable light, it was most carefully recounted in Acts 27, which has thus become the most interesting and accurate picture to have reached us of the seamanship involved in handling one of the most important classes of ancient merchant ships.

St Paul embarked at Adramyttium, an important Greek city seaport in Mysia, on the coast a little south of the present Dardanelles. The ship, a small coasting vessel touched at Sidon. Putting to sea from there, foul winds – the prevalent westerly – forced her to take shelter under the lee of Cyprus to the eastward of the island. They then sailed along the south coast of what is now Turkey to Myra, then one of the important harbours of the grain trade route; and here was picked up 'a ship of Alexandria sailing for Italy'.

Portulan of about 1529

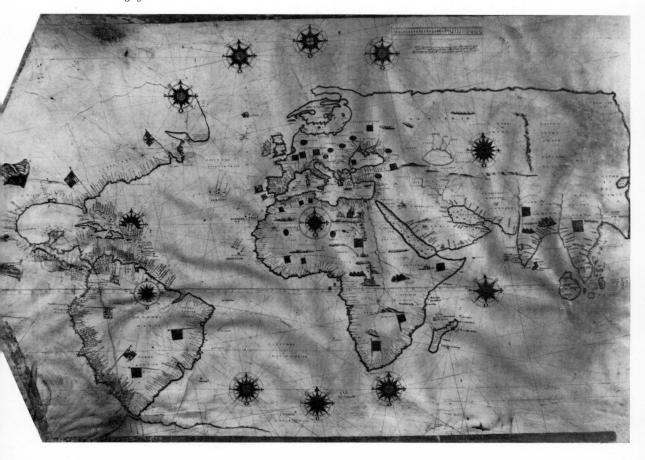

Rudder of a Japanese junk. Note the tunnel in which it could be raised or lowered, a feature common to junk's rudders

On board when the ship sailed were 276 people, and for some days the wind was light and progress slow – typical of the conditions in the Mediterranean summer, when for long, slow hours the grain-ships would be lying like great sea birds asleep in blue circles of calm. What winds there were came mainly from ahead, prohibiting the direct course to Italy; and having coasted slowly to the south-west corner of Asia Minor off Cape Crio, these forced the ship down to Crete, where she with difficulty worked along the coast and made Fair Havens, at the extreme south of the island. They had sailed late in the season, and the Apostle advised them to winter here – speaking from the experience of three former shipwrecks.

It would appear that St Paul's ship may already have completed one round trip carrying grain during the season that was now quickly passing, and the slowness of this second passage was making it dangerously late in the year to keep at sea. But Fair Havens was not considered a suitable port, 'not commodious to winter in'. It was, in fact, sheltered only against the north and north-west winds. So in light airs from the south-west they put to sea, keeping close along the south coast of the island, bound for the port of Phoenix, some 40 miles further west, which was a well-protected

82

harbour suitable for the winter which was fast setting in. 'And when the south wind blew softly . . . they weighed anchor and sailed along Crete. . . .' This anxiety to make a well-sheltered port as soon as possible and then to lie snugly there throughout the long winter months vividly portrays the limitations on seagoing in even the best found of vessels about 1,000 years ago.

During this short passage the head wind freshened, rising to gale strength and veering through north-east to east. Thereafter the ship was barely under command and was swept away from the south shore of Crete. They ran under the lee of Cauda, or Gaudos Island, which lies about 40 miles and a little south of west from Fair Havens. Here they were able 'with difficulty, to secure the boat; and when they had hoisted it up, they used helps, undergirding the ship'.

This passage must have a familiar ring to many yachtsmen who, like this Roman corn-ship's master, have towed the dinghy astern in the expectation of a short, smooth passage, only to find, too late, that it has been filling as the sea increased and at the worst has to be cut adrift, at the best got on board and secured with great

Stern lifting rudder of a Chinese
fish-carrying boat

difficulty. But the yachtsman will never have undergirded his craft. This was the practice of passing ropes under the hull to steady the planking and frames and keep them together.

Then, 'fearing lest they should be cast upon the Syrtes they lowered the gear and so were driven. And as we laboured exceedingly with the storm, the next day they began to throw the freight overboard; and the third day they cast out with their own hands the tackling of the ship.'

They had now been driven under that easterly wind of Euraquilo far to the westward, and the Greater Syrtes on the African shore, on to which they feared they might be swept, has been described as the Goodwin Sands of the Mediterranean. The Authorized and Revised versions of the Acts describe the subsequent operations of seamanship in slightly different terms, and where the latter speaks of lowering the gear, the former says that they 'strake sail'. We may assume that they lowered the mainsail but kept the *artemon* set for a time. But they lightened ship by heaving some of the grain overboard, and on the third day cast out 'the tackling'. This is sometimes taken as meaning that much of the furnishing of the vessel was put over the side; sometimes that they discarded the heavy yard of the mainsail and the masthead blocks; possibly the mainsail, too.

'And when neither sun nor stars shone upon us for many days, and no small tempest lay on us, all hope that we should be saved was taken away.'

They were without food, and, having no compass, could in the circumstances know only vaguely from the continuing wind that they were being driven far to the west, though how far, and with how much north or south in their furious course could hardly be guessed after so many days of uncertainty. At about this time, when they had been at sea for almost a fortnight, St Paul, who initially had been against ever leaving Fair Havens and attempting to make Phoenix, appears to have been in an 'I told you so' mood, and he told them so, but added the comfort that 'there shall be no loss of life among you, but only of the ship'. This, it will be recalled, an angel had told him.

It was during the fourteenth night, when all they knew was that they 'were driven to and from in the Sea of Adria,' which is today's Adriatic and the waters south of it, that the seamen smelled land. Perhaps they detected a difference in the run of the violent waves in which they were tossing, indicating shoal water, so that the lead was immediately cast. A depth of 20 fathoms was quickly followed by one of 15 fathoms, and, fearing that it might be rocks down to leeward, four anchors were dropped from the stern. At this point some of the sailors panicked and lowered the boat, but before they could embark, its lines were cut and it drifted away. The ship was further lightened by throwing overboard more of the wheat.

Daylight revealed a shore where there was a beach, unrecognized by anyone, on which it might be possible to run up the ship. And while the steering oars were put into position the anchors were slipped and the *artemon* hoisted. The process of running the ship upon the beach does not seem to have gone smoothly. The helmsman headed for the beach under the *artemon*, but the ship appears to have struck earlier than expected: 'the foreship struck and remained unmoveable, but the stern began to break up by the violence of the waves.' But all the ship's company, by

84

Contrasting Chinese and Occidental
rudders, the former in a south China
trading vessel

85

swimming or clinging to planks 'or other things from the ship' reached the shore safely. And it was realized that they were on the island of Malta, 'and the barbarians showed us no common kindness.'

The weakness of the apparently splendid Roman corn-ships, which disappeared after a few centuries and were not to be exceeded in size for 1,000 years, should be emphasized. Drawings and models fail to convey the difficult seamanship involved when handling them in even the relatively placid Mediterranean sailing season.

Chinese compass

The not ungracious rig was the root of most troubles. To drive a ship that may have been of 400 tons, the source of power was divided into a rig having only two principal sails, and of these the mainsail was very much the larger. The area of the mainsail may have been appreciably more than 2,500 square feet, perhaps as much as 2,700 square feet. A nineteenth-century brig of comparable size carried a greater sail area, but the total was divided between eight square sails on two masts, plus the spanker on the mainmast and three triangular headsails, or jibs. The largest sail in the ship, the mainsail, would have been half the size of the corn-ship's.

The brig was a fast and heavily sparred vessel. If the comparison be made instead with a similar size of three-masted barque, the sails would have been spread over three masts and a dozen square sails apart from the fore-and-aft canvas. In addition to the task of handling so large a sail as the corn-ship's mainsail, there was the greater danger of the concentrated stresses with which the sail loaded the mast and the few members of the standing rigging. Supporting the masts in the barque might have been a total of twelve shrouds to take the load at any moment on the weather side; the Roman ship had four shrouds and a backstay. Loosely woven sails and twisted ropes accentuated the weakness of the rig. The materials were not good enough for the stresses which fell upon them. This applied equally to the construction of the hull. The thrust at the heel of the mast, the tension at the chain-plates, had the effect of forcing the hull apart; a tendency that has to be countered in all ships when pressed under sail, but that was particularly dangerous in the relatively fragile corn-ship with its immensely loaded mainmast. For these reasons, as much as the aerodynamic inadequacy of the rig, the ships could not be sailed close to the wind. Carrying the wind on the beam the rig loadings are much increased, and the high stresses involved in beating to windward would have been altogether too much.

Ceylon outrigger.
Note the version
of the spritsail

These weaknesses occurred in ships which carried only a small area of sail in relation to their considerable bulk, and which inevitably were slow in the only wind strengths they were able to withstand. It was beyond the vessels to cross oceans, and they were evidently inferior to the smaller and earlier Phoenician merchantmen about which so little is known. But our greater knowledge of the corn-ships, though their size may have made them less seaworthy than their predecessors, serves to reveal the weaknesses in all ancient sailing craft, whose challenge to the oceans thus appears the more impressive.

Five hundred years after the corn-ships, the Viking galleys were proving themselves, when in the hand of fine seamen, able to achieve ocean voyages and to make the coastal seas their home in a way quite beyond their larger and more elaborately rigged predecessors.

Professor Holland Rose in his *The Mediterranean in the Ancient World* has emphasized his belief that the importance to the Roman Empire of its maritime supremacy in the Mediterranean has never been sufficiently appreciated by historians. It was control of this sea that held the Empire together. We might modify one line of Lord Byron on the Mediterranean to make it particularly applicable to the *Pax Romana*:

'Thy shores *one* Empire, changed in all save thee.'

Before returning to the seamen of the North, we should note one aspect of the Roman attitude to the sea which may throw some light upon seamanship everywhere. Professor Holland Rose has emphasized the Romans' dislike and fear of

A steering oar extended to give the helmsman visibility

Outrigged craft had no place in the northern and
Mediterranean traditions of seafaring

even the Mediterranean, gracious as it could so often be, and finds examples spread
over their literature: Tacitus, who wrote that troops sent from Italy to Alexandria
and then home again after a short interval suffered badly from the voyages and were
'long weakened'; Vegetius, who deplored the greed of merchants which encouraged
them to send ships to sea in the dangerous period between mid-November and mid-
March; Synesius, who wrote an agonised account of soldiers standing on deck with
their swords drawn ready to destroy themselves rather than drown as their ship
laboured in a Tramontana of gale force. Horace, Livy, Polybius (who was a Greek,
though Roman in sympathy) and others all raise voices of antipathy to the sea,
and none more agonisingly than Ovid, not quoted by Holland Rose: 'I fear not
death; 'tis the dreadful kind of death; take away the shipwreck; then death will be
a gain to me. 'Tis something for one, either dying a natural death or by the sword,
to lay his breathless corpse in the firm ground, and to impart his wishes to his kindred,
and to hope for a sepulchre, and not to be food for the fishes of the sea.'

The land-loving Romans, with such beguiling lands to love, not only feared the

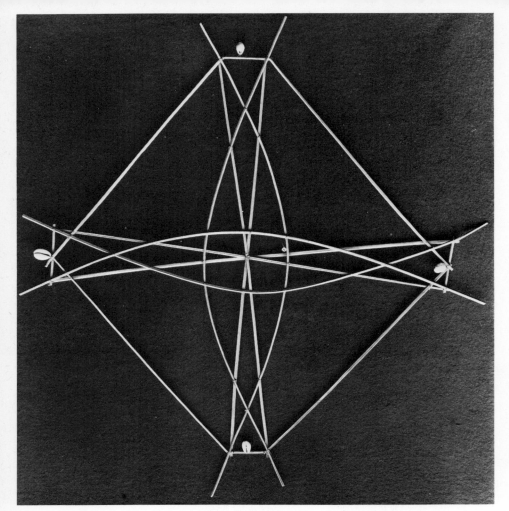

Marshall Islands map

sea, but disdained the commercial operations for which seamanship is the tool; this distaste extended to the seamen themselves, most of whom in the Mediterranean of the *Pax Romana* were Greeks and easterners. But it may be suggested that this attitude, so strong in the Roman, existed amongst most peoples. A certain contempt for seafarers has been widely spread among mankind throughout his history. Professor Holland Rose has pointed out that amongst the seafaring Greek peoples the fisherman did not have the status of the farmer. Throughout history seamen have tended to live on the periphery of their society. It is still so. In the modern ports of the steam-trawlers, you will still find that apartness which existed when sailors dwelled at the end of lanes winding down to little huddled ports where wooden ships lay.

It is in the North, if anywhere, that we find a certain regenerative and mystical approach to the sea, which even the Greeks appear to have lacked – in the *Odyssey* it is written, 'there is nought else worse than the sea to confound a man, howsoever hardy he may be.' When Caesar reached the North Sea coast the seamen he found there were the supermen of primitive races. Further north, by the fjords, the race

90

of sea kings was still in the womb. Later when the Vikings spread south, they came as seamen so deeply impregnated with the spirit of their ships that they seemed a new kind of people. Never in history, it would seem, has the seaman been so completely integrated into his society and culture as the Norsemen. Holland Rose has written: 'Nor did the ancients feel any enthusiasm about ships; and naturally so. For ships were worse than treadmills for the oarsmen and often mere torture chambers for the passengers. Their progress was that of an anaemic centipede, not that of a bird. . . .' But the Vikings, when they took to their boats for the gay pursuit of a perilous quest, rolled down to the water craft with decorative wood-carving of a high order expressive of their deepest feelings.

But the Vikings and their forebears were not typical of the seamen of northern Europe. When Caesar arrived, with Mediterranean galleys which were found to be unfitted for the North Sea, he found seamen and ships worthy of high respect belonging to the Veneti, but otherwise little in the maritime scene of note.

Even so rudimentary a question as what kind of boats the Britons had then cannot be answered with certainty. Was the seamanship of the backward island people confined to operations in dugouts and skin boats? The Celtic boats were no doubt well-developed craft of some size, for the Britons had a high reputation for their basketwork. But did they use oars or paddles as they worked over the turbulent tidal estuaries and bays of their coastline? Did they know how to set a sail? We are uncertain. Whether they had wood-planked boats is purely conjectural. There is no direct evidence that they had, but there is inferential evidence favouring the existence of such craft. Caesar describes in some detail the ships of the Veneti, who roughly occupied the area now known as Brittany and who commanded the carrying trade between Gaul and Britain. There were some British ships from the west of England in the Veneti fleet which opposed Caesar, and as he makes no special comments

Relief maps used by the Greenland Eskimoes

Reconstruction of a ship from the time of the Crusades.
Europe, 12th century. Note the two masts, the double
bonnet on mainsail and the bowlines

about them it is reasonable to infer that these were not markedly different from the
Veneti craft, which were heavy oak-planked and framed vessels with sails.

In his War Commentaries Caesar makes some revealing observations about
Veneti ships and seamanship. The following comes from the translation by John
Warrington.

'These vessels were relatively flat-bottomed, and could therefore ride the shallows
or on an ebb-tide. With their unusually tall prows and sterns they could weather
high seas in a gale of wind; and the hulls, made entirely of oak, were capable of
standing up to any amount of rough handling. The cross-timbers consisted of beams
a foot thick, fastened with iron bolts as thick as a man's thumb, and iron chains
instead of ropes were used to secure the anchors.

'Their sails were made of raw hides or thinly dressed leather . . . probably due to
a mistaken belief that canvas was unequal to the violence of Atlantic gales and
unsuitable for manœuvring vessels of their burden. In an encounter with these ships
our sole advantage was speed derived from the use of oars. . . . Their bulk rendered
them safe against ramming, while their height placed them virtually beyond reach
of our missiles and grappling-irons. Besides, when it began to blow hard and they

92

were running before the wind, they were not only more seaworthy, but could heave-to in shallow water without fear of damage from reefs and jagged rocks; whereas all these factors constituted a serious danger to our shipping.'

There is much of interest to note here. Clearly, the Veneti were excellent seamen, and the tradition of hardy seamanship is still strong in Brittany today. The carrying trade to the Continent was firmly in the hands of the Veneti, and the simpler Celt left the Gaul to it. That Caesar, with his knowledge of the great Roman grain-ships, should have been impressed by these northern vessels is a high tribute to them. The Veneti's opinion of canvas sails may have been wrong, but their use of sail rather than oars is significant. The chain anchor cable can only seem amazing when it is considered that throughout the subsequent ages of sail until the nineteenth century rope cables were used in every vessel, even the largest.

An early three-master. (From an illuminated manuscript of Josephus: *Histoire de la Guerre des Juifs*)

English ship now with a stern rudder. Note the planking up of the space below the platform which is now an integral part of the ship

Opposite page
An ancient 'keel' of about A.D. 1400 found in the River Rother in 1822

It appears that few oars were carried in these ships; for when subsequently the Romans used hooks on the end of poles to catch the halyards and sever them, causing the sail to drop, the ships became helpless.

While the existence of wood-planked boats in pre-Roman Britain is a matter of opinion, there is now a school of thought that emphatically denies the existence there of wood-planked *sailing* craft until about A.D. 700 – over 600 years after the Romans had arrived and some 300 years after they had left. This would mean that the Britons had not been interested in or capable of copying the sails of the Veneti and handing down the practice of using them, with which they must then have been familiar for the last six centuries. This is one of those curious lacunae in the practice of seamanship to be found in various periods and among different people.

94

It would seem that the ships that brought the Frisians, Saxons, Angles and Jutes to Britain during the Migration period, approximately the fifth and sixth centuries A.D., likewise carried no sail. It is even unlikely that sail was being used in northern Europe 300 years later than this; though it may have been found in small craft; or in the Baltic where conditions, so different from those of the North Sea, the Channel and Biscay, may have encouraged sailing. It remains a mystery how it was that the art of handling ships under sail which, in the dawn of our own era, had flourished on the coast of Brittany where there are some of the most dangerous waters of Europe, could have been utterly lost. It is tempting to think that perhaps it was not. Our light on those times in the North plays most erratically over a dim scene.

Professor E. G. R. Taylor has said in *The Haven Finding Art* that 'the Jutes, Angles and Saxons certainly had enough seamanship to make piratical raids on England in large, well-found, oared and sailing ships before A.D. 300.' Perhaps fortunately she adds: 'But about all this period very little is known.' For it now appears almost certain that neither the raiding Anglo-Saxons nor the later ships of the Migration period used sail. The Anglo-Saxons came from homes on the European continent ranging from the Jutland Peninsula and the Baltic coast, Schleswig, Holstein, and down the European coast to what is now Holland. The Nydam ship, remains of which were found in Schleswig in 1863, is considered to be the type of boat in which the Anglo-Saxons went raiding along the British coast and later returned to it as migrants. Another ship, found at Sutton Hoo, Suffolk, is a similar type of vessel. The skill of the northern shipwright, which a few centuries hence was to put into the hands of the Viking seamen such intricately and excellently wrought ships, was yet embryonic. The ability to create out of the awkward oak a ship well shaped for seagoing and able to carry sail was not yet there. Built of broad planks in the northern clinker style, the Nydam ship has no keel but simply a heavy centre-line plank laid flat. The concept of the plank on edge, providing a certain depth of salient keel below the hull, had not yet emerged in Northern shipbuilding. In its absence, hulls lacked the fore-and-aft strength to carry the loading of a mast on the

A ship of the Cinque Ports,
13th century. Stern

bottom and the stresses produced by its rigging. The Nydam ship, furthermore, had sharp sections, those amidships resembling two-thirds of a semicircle. And the hull was narrow, with only 11 feet beam on a length of 76 feet overall. The sectional shape and the small beam produced a craft lacking stability – too crank to carry sail effectively. Not surprisingly, the ship had no mast step and clearly had been propelled by oars alone. And these were very short, indicating that the oarsmen must have worked with a quick stroke that would have been both tiring and not very efficient.

Throughout history the seaman has worked oars in many different ways. He has sat down and pushed them, instead of pulling, or even stood up and pushed them. This was a mode of operation suggested in some early Egyptian representations of ships. The waterman's ways are numerous. But it is difficult to believe that oarsmen pushed, as opposed to pulled, oars over long voyages, and it would seem highly improbable that they stood up for any length of time while rowing.

96

The means by which the migrating Anglo-Saxons reached the shores of Britain throw much light on centuries of Northern seafaring, though the full implications have only lately been realized. The English archaeologist Charles Green has pointed out that the usual view on the migrating peoples was that, 'They were seamen, they had sea-going vessels, so they crossed' the sea; and it used to be generally believed that the Jutes, who inhabited Jutland, made the direct sea passage to Britain from Jutland, the Angles from Schleswig to the Humber and the Wash, the Jutes to the Thames Estuary and the English Channel shore. In a brilliant analysis Charles Green has made a convincing case of the impossibility of this.

It is a reasonable estimate that has been supported by modern seamen with experience of handling oared lifeboats and beach-boats, that the 60–80 foot galleys could not have maintained a higher average speed than 3 knots over a period. The ships of the Migration voyages, loaded with families and belongings – women, children and the elderly – would further have been short of relief helmsmen (though not those of the earlier raiders). A detailed analysis of the cross-sea voyage from Esbjerg to the Humber, allowing for the tides which in places off the English coast run faster than the speed of the ship, and assuming that the ship lay to a sea-anchor during the hours of darkness, but assuming, too, that there was no wind or sea and that the helmsman with his inefficient steering oar maintained a perfect rhumb-line compass course without a compass, shows that the voyage would take eight and a half days. The assumptions made are optimistic. An eight-day period without wind, a seaway or fog, would be rare in these latitudes even in summer. The course steered

Ship of the Cinque Ports, 13th century. Bows. Note the bowsprit not yet used to carry sail, and the platform soon to become the fo'c'sle

Study in contrasts: single-masted square-rigged vessel of the 14th century and the fore-and-aft rig (cutter) of some 300 years later. Note the bonnet and brails on the mainsail of the latter

would certainly be ragged, and the maintenance of even 3 knots over the long period would be unlikely for heavily laden craft. One conclusion reached is that a direct sea voyage would have been impracticable. Making the departure further south, in Schleswig, would slightly shorten the voyage, but still without bringing it within the range of the reasonably practical. The analysis, presented with full navigational details, has a bearing upon all earlier Northern seafaring when the boats were smaller and less adequate than the Nydam type. The difficulties involved in this voyage would apply equally to those from the Norwegian fjords to Scotland. Such direct passages would appear impracticable in other than sailing-ships. The late

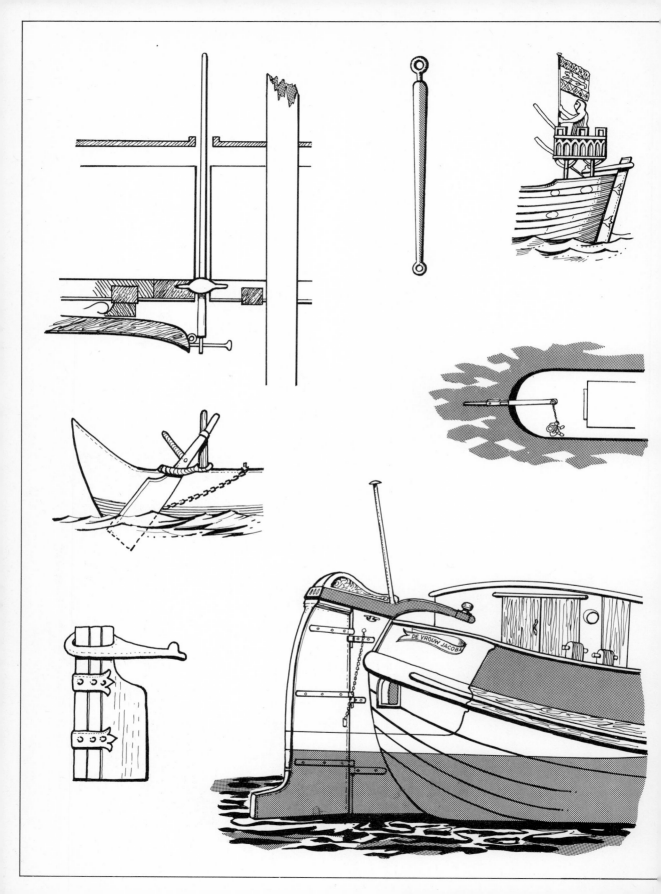

development of the sail in northern Europe would seem to have limited the seamen there mainly to coastal passages.

One can conclude that the Anglo-Saxons rowed down the coast to the Low Countries and thence across to England. A similar analysis of a voyage from Schleswig to the south-east coast of England assumed that one vessel coasted south to Texel, another to Flushing, thereby reducing the length of the open sea passage. Assuming a speed of 3 knots and making some allowance for bad weather, this voyage was shown to occupy a minimum of two months, with anything between two and six months as a reasonable estimate depending on the difficulties encountered.

The absence of charts and even, for many seamen, of local knowledge, when navigating these bank-strewn waters with eccentric tidal sets involved them in dangers that cannot be over-emphasized. A fifth-century writer, Sidonius, a Roman Gaul, wrote to a friend about the Saxon seamen: 'to these men a shipwreck is capital practice rather than an object of terror. The dangers of the deep are to them, not casual acquaintances, but intimate friends.' Such a view, of seamen accepting

A contemporary model of a Dutch nao. *Circa* 1450.

Opposite page
Side and stern rudders and a whipstaff

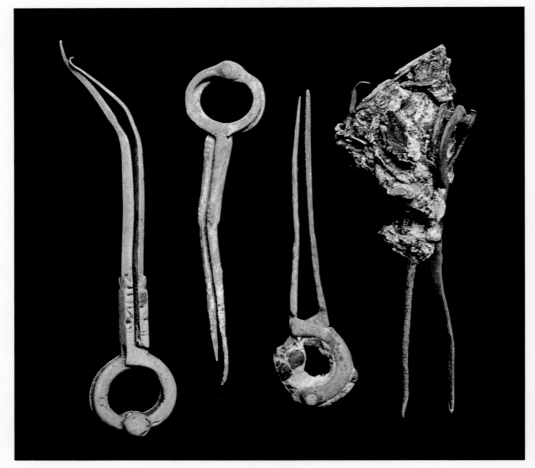

Navigational instruments recovered from the Armada
ship *Gerona*

shipwreck as a frequent inevitability, places early Northern seamanship in its true
light. The losses amongst the galleys must have been enormous, as must the numbers
of seamen drowned. And this was the fifth century, at which time seamanship had
been practised for thousands of years.

In the course of the next 300 years the shipwrights of the North learned to
produce ships able to make efficient use of sail, and to develop the sail and rig which
seamen in the course of unrecorded experiences learned to handle. The seamen of
northern Europe, perhaps the toughest boatmen the world has ever known, found
that the art of seamanship had been given a new dimension.

The art of ship construction, dawdling along the multitude of slow centuries with
scarcely perceptible movements, changes to be perceived only over ages much
longer than the lease of a life, suddenly began hurrying among the Norse during the
period approximately A.D. 500–800. There is the evidence of the Kvalsund boat

which is considered to reveal an early step towards the sailing-ships of the Vikings years later. This boat, says Professor Brøgger, 'can probably be placed about A.D. 600', though this date is yet uncertain and could be later. The significance of the boat lies in the facts that she had an embryonic form of keel and that the earlier loose steering gear had been replaced by the fixed side rudder, the most crucial piece of gear in the ships of the Vikings, and a fundamental reason for their sailing ability. Both the keel and the side rudder were essential antecedents to the development of oceangoing sail. The shipwright's ability to fashion timber, to devise such structural members as a keel able to take the thrust of a mast and provide lateral resistance to the water, and to evolve from the mere steering oar the relatively complex mechanism of the side rudder, governed the kind of seafaring the seamen could evolve. While the link between the shipwright and the seaman was no doubt close in the ages when specialization was only just dawning, the seaman was still dependent on what tools the shipwright had.

The classical side rudders have been considered above. In the North the twin

A traverse board

arrangement was never adopted. The single rudder, man being right-handed, was naturally placed on the right-hand side, which for this reason became known as 'starboard' (steerboard). Preferably a ship would not be brought alongside a jetty with this delicate appendage next to the wall, and subsequently the other side, the port side, received the obvious name; though not, it would appear, until the term 'larboard' had been confusing seamen for a long time. As late as 1789 Falconer in his dictionary was objurgating seamen not to use the word 'larboard' owing to the tendency for confusion with 'starboard'. But in 1580 we find the left-hand side of the ship described as 'port'. This term was already being used for the opening in the ship's hull on the side of the quay through which cargo might be passed.

The side rudder was hung from a heavy oak block fixed outside the hull (well aft) a little above the waterline, where the last internal frame of the hull was specially strengthened to carry it. A hole was bored through the block, planking and frame. The rudder, essentially a short oar with a large blade, also had a hole through it a little above mid-length. A thick withy with a knot at the outer end was passed through the rudder, block and hull, the inner end going through holes in the last frame and being knotted. The rudder bore on the block and also the top of the gunwale, where thick planks were fastened on the outside of the top strakes of the hull, against which the loom of the oar was held by a rope loop with an eye and toggle, passed round the loom and through slits in the gunwale into the hull. The withy was secured slackly enough to allow the oar-blade, lying fore and aft when not in use, to be rotated on its vertical axis, the rotation being effected by a short tiller about 3 feet long, projecting athwartships from the rudder near its upper end. The lashing of rope or braided leather holding the rudder firmly against the gunwale was

Late medieval ship putting out to sea. The artist has given his imagination free play

Ship of 1486

loosened to allow the rudder, which projected well below the keel of the boat, to be lifted when required, a line for this purpose being secured to the after side of the rudder-blade.

Clearly, the side rudder is a sophisticated production showing great mechanical ingenuity. On it, for some 400 or 500 years, depended the finer efforts of Northern seamanship. Captain Magnus Anderson, who sailed a replica of the famous Gokstad Viking ship across the Atlantic in 1893, commented enthusiastically on the ease with which a helmsman was able to control the ship by means of the short athwartship tiller projecting just ahead of him horizontally over the gunwale. What a clear picture you get of the Viking helmsman standing on the slightly raised forward platform in the narrow stern of his vessel, the gunwale, curved into a fine sweep behind him, rising far above his head. There he stands, both hands on the tiller before him, moving it rhythmically forward and aft and swaying himself, while the ship surges forward under the hard-sheeted square sail and his companions lie around in the shelter of the high gunwale on the bottom boards.

The Viking ships of the eighth century were effective sailing craft, though the

105

This rig includes the fore-staysail, or triangular headsail, a fore-and-aft sail of purely north European origin, which in 1607 may have been in use for some two centuries. Here also is seen the gaff instead of the diagonal spritsail

rig was no more than a single square sail, not large for the size of ship, set on a mast stepped a little ahead of amidships. The art of beating to windward had been learned and the rigging arranged accordingly. A vital new dimension had been added to sailing. In rig and hull these vessels had features which were to persist in the ships of northern Europe for four centuries and more; indeed, elements of the rig remained until the square-rig ship had disappeared from the seas. The Vikings' procedures are still anything but unfamiliar.

The first early Nordic sails were of fragile homespun wool which had to be strengthened by doublings in strips, which might be of leather, or it is sometimes thought that a net of rope or cloth bands was secured over the forward surface of the sail to give support. The weak sail would be unable to stand the concentration of load caused by the sheets bent into the clews. In the early days there was, apart from these two sheets, an intricate system of bridles extending along the whole length of the sail's foot, a method of spreading the sheets' load found also in the East. This system, which the modern yachtsman would describe as 'knitting', could be dispensed with when firmer sails of linen became possible. Certainly with baggy sails of homespun anxiously supported and falling under wind pressure into all shapes, the greater refinements of sailing would have been impossible. Improvements in seamanship depended in the first place on improvements in materials. To this extent the seaman has always had to depend upon the inventor.

Once stronger sails had been evolved, sailing performance could be transformed. To achieve some kind of windward performance, the yard had to be swung round

to an acute angle with the centre-line; but then the fore-leech of the sail would tend
to collapse as the sail was trimmed at a fine angle to the wind. Thus came into use a
bearing-out spar, analogous to the whisker pole, or the boat-hook, which a dinghy
sailor will secure into the clew of his jib to bear it out on the opposite side to the
mainsail when running before the wind. The Vikings required such a pole to support
the fore-leech of a square sail when beating to windward. When the yard was swung
to take the wind closer, it was pivoted in a chock at the leeward side of the boat on
the bottom boards about level with the mast; the outer end was forced into a rope
grommet on the fore-leech, and the pole angled forward towards the bow, stretching
the fore-leech and holding it steadily up to the wind. It would seem that two bearing-
out spars may sometimes have been used, in a manner more closely analogous to the
yachtsman's whisker pole, to spread the foot of the sail to its full extent beyond the

A detail view of a spritsail
furled on its yard

beam of the ship, when running before the wind. This spar (Viking word *beitass*) brought a new versatility into sailing.

The purpose of the bowlines, developed later, was the same as that of the *beitass*. These were ropes on bridles secured to the leeches of the sail. With the yard trimmed for windward work the bowline on what was the fore-leech, would be led forward through a lead on the soaring stem and then hauled taut aft, extending the leech up towards the wind. *Beitass* and bowlines were used in conjunction in order to give a lead to the bowline further forward, the spar being fixed to reach ahead of the stem and carry the lead to the bowline at its outer extremity. This was the origin of the bowsprit, originally only a spar to extend the bowlines; thus was taken another step towards the full-rigged ship lying in the future. But bowlines, like *beitass*, appeared to have been used in the eighth century.

Rope and canvas being perishable, less is known precisely about the rigging the seamen had to handle than of the way in which the shipwrights fashioned the hulls. Weather-vanes were fixed at the masthead, beautiful gilded objects though perhaps a little heavy for their delicate work.

The Gokstad ship, which has provided so much of the information we have about Viking shipwrightry, was primarily a galley pulling sixteen oars a side. Her sailing

Mariner's astrolabe, 1585

Opposite
Charles V embarking at Coruna – Flemish breviarum of about 1565. The vessel is of the carrack type

performance, of proved high quality, was of secondary importance. The mast was in a very heavy step rising above the bottom boards, forming a tabernacle with the mast partners open aft. Thus the mast could be lowered by hinging it downwards into the stern, and this was usually done when the ship was under oars. We assume that the mast had no shrouds or stays – there were no signs of fastenings for them in the remains of the hull – and the only support for the mast may have been the halyard, which when the yard was hoisted was taken aft and belayed to form a backstay in the manner practised until the last days of working sail in various types of craft.

We may see, then, the Viking galley as a ship with the minimum of cordage, at least in the period around 900 A.D., but later this may have been elaborated and made similar to that in the trading ships of the *knorr* type. The later and larger galleys

Dutch cutter showing the typical mainsail with long
gaff and no boom

Opposite
Arab dhow (now
in ISCA Museum)
under sail

Portulan of about 1548

pulled more than sixty oars and possibly even eighty. It is unfortunate that there is more practical knowledge about the sailing qualities of the galley than their performance under oars. Only once, and briefly, was the replica of the Gokstad ship handled with a full complement of oarsmen, and little is known about the exercise. The galleys were excellently designed for oar propulsion. The oar ports were close to the waterline, some eighteen inches above it and a little more at the ends of the ship, with the result that the oars made a shallow angle with the water, thereby having their power improved. The oars themselves were made as light as possible, with a slender loom and small narrow blades. They were of various lengths, governed by the position in the ship from which they were to be used, the average length being about eighteen feet. Unfortunately, when the Gokstad replica was afloat in 1893, while plenty of people could be found who knew how to sail a ship, even one practised rowing crew could not be found, where the Vikings raised them by the hundred.

Opposed to the galleys were the trading ships, broader, deeper, fuller lined, in which oar power was sacrificed to carrying capacity and which were dependent primarily upon sail. Though it was a replica of a galley that was sailed over the Atlantic in 1893, the Viking voyages to Iceland, Greenland and Vinland were made in the trading type of ship, of which there were a number of varieties which we may generically call *kaupskip*. High sided and less finely formed for speed than the galleys, it does appear that at least one kind of *kaupskip* had an important feature that improved sailing qualities. The stem and sternposts were carried down vertically to the bottom of the keel, forming an appreciable area of deadwood at either end that was lacking in the galleys, with their end-posts graciously curving downwards into the upward curving keel. These deadwoods were of importance in obtaining lateral resistance in the hull to oppose the side force of the wind on the sail once the yard was trimmed fore and aft for windward work, with the sail held up to weather by the *beitass*.

Depending primarily upon sail, with the middle part of the ship devoted to cargo, and with positions for oars only at the ends of the hull, the rigging became more complex. There may have been two shrouds a side, a forestay and backstay landed on the stem and sternpost, braces from the ends of the yard each with a block and tackle giving a two-part purchase, sheets from the clews of the sail, and the halyard. The latter was led to a simple wooden windlass aft, an early example of a mechanical aid to sail handling. It is uncertain when the bowline came into use, but it was certainly known in the early eighth century, and both *beitass* and bowlines may have been used

Square-rigged ships carrying spritsail, forecourse, fore-topsail, main course, main topsail, mizzen and bonaventure mizzen, both these lateens, and mizzen topsail, not yet set

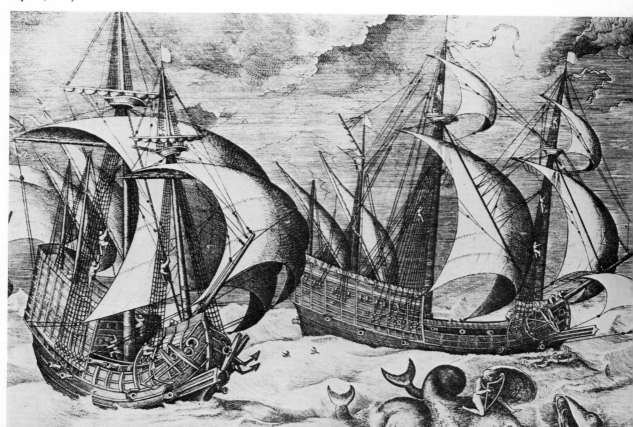

Persian sea
scene,
16th century

together. Another spar may have been rigged as a bowsprit, lashed to the high bows, with a hole or a block at its outer end to form a lead for the bowline as far forward as possible. This became the common mediaeval practice. It is not certain whether the Vikings used reef points.

The compass may have been known by the end of the Viking period, but we must

Three-masted ship with wind on the beam and yards
braced as far fore and aft as possible

visualise them as mainly dependent on the sun and stars for direction. Harald
Åkerlund has written of Viking navigational methods: 'One of the sagas mentions a
man, Oddi Helgason, who was nicknamed Star Oddi, who served one of the Ice-
landic magnates at the end of the 900s as a long-distance pilot. He left notes including
a complete table of the changes in the declination of the sun throughout the year,
expressed in half "wheels", or half the diameter of the sun's height at the meridian
throughout the year. There is also a little azimuth table giving the direction at
various times of the year of the "twilight", which is taken to mean a light streak on
the horizon just before sunrise. . . . It is possible that for this they used an instrument
made on the principle of the pelorus. . . . When on land or at anchor they could
measure the horizon angle between where the sun rose and set, and so obtain an
approximate latitude. Leif Erikson is said to have done this and discovered that mid-

winter's day in Vinland was longer than in Greenland and so realised that Vinland must lie further to the south. The height of the sun was measured with some instrument which we do not know about. An old Faro Island tradition tells of such an instrument: A round disk with a hole in the middle in which was inserted an adjustable peg. The disk was marked with concentric circles; the peg was moved up and down according to the time of the year, and the shadow thrown by the peg showed the height of the sun.'

Whatever their techniques and expertise, the ships of the North seamen were still open boats. The Vikings were supreme boatmen and the instruments they used weak for the voyages they made. From the fjords to Britain, the west coast of Ireland, down the Bay and into the Mediterranean to the Adriatic, and into the eye of the setting sun westward over the Atlantic to Iceland, Greenland and America, they pressed their shelterless, undecked craft with the hardihood of men bred in the lands where the pine and oak swayed in keen and biting air. Despite the extent of their voyages, they kept as much as possible near to the coast, which the shallowness of their ships bereft of some of its dangers. They were tied to the shore in important respects. Only at anchor could the awning be raised and some shelter obtained; only ashore could cooking be done. Inevitably, the season for seagoing was the spring and summer, the ships coming out as the birch buds quickened, and being 'brought to the roller', or run up ashore to their winter berths, as the leaves fell in the autumn equinox. And then a winter would pass before the sails – 'the Tapestry of the Masthead' one of the Sagas calls them – were raised once more.

Another example of artistic imagination, which can so often mislead

ودارابكمين بر روی دریا میرفت اما مولف اخبار و گذارنده اسرار ابوطاهر طرسوسی چنین روایت میکند که چون کشتیها از روی دریا پدیدار شد مطرعوشیه بربالای خطرش آمد و آفتاب درغروب بود که روی سوی ایران کرد و یاد درگشتگان خود کرد و یک نعره بزد و گفت ای عظیم عوشیه از من مبر و باش که دیگر مرا ترا سخن خواهم دید و تو برد لمن جشنودی و بایران شدم ای درنزدیک نوز رنده کانی این سخن خواهی پاداین گفت و خود را از بالای خطرش درانداخت و جان بداد هر قالیس کشته شد که مارا درت خویشتن راز از بالای خطرش انداخت و مرد هر قالیس مارا در ریا گرفت و در کوشک مرد و ماتم او بداشت و را بحال سلیم کرد و درین روزگار که برامد و با دسای میراندا اخبار و گذارنده اسرار ابوطاهر طرسوسی چنین روایت میکند که چون داراب برفت و چهل و سه روز بیوسته برفت که هیچ باسو در ندر روزی در یا بکند و باد مخالف وان سه هزار پاره کشتی بر روی دریا میرفت از دور که عمان پدید شد که داراب گفت عمان رسیدیم کشتیها را بعمان بسلامت رسانیدم بایستی که سجده آورد مرا ی نیا ورد و شادی کرد که کشتی چنین الت و کجل با یران پا ابو در بحر من بایستی که آیا از خدا وند عزوجل بدیدی همه از خود دیدم و قی آفتاب درقطب فلک راست ایستا دبا دی سخت از روی دریا برخاست و یکبار با دبا بهار برافراکشته بدانند کرد و کشتیها را موج بعیق برمی آورد و باز بر زمین فرومی زد جند بار چنین آمد و فرود آمد و کشتیها را برهم زد و همه یکبار غرق شدند

که انان سه هزار پاره کشتی و از ان جندان هزار مرد که دی بماند مگر داراب و معظه طسیه و دایه و داراب کمین دبای همه هلاک شد ندبسبب آن بی شکری که داراب کرد ان جندان نعمت و ان جندان مردم در دریا فرو رفت مگر کشتی داراب غرقه نشد و پنج شبانروز آن کشتی بر روی آب بود و داراب سرسجده بنهاده بود و می نالید درزی

Disaster at sea. A Mughal version

Opposite page
Mughal sea scene

وبال زخم کرفت و در روی دریا آمد و در روی بر یاب شت و هراسب طلب او آمد طرم وسیه راند او و نیزد در رو بی نشت و در رو بی بازد
وبا د لو زند و او را نا مد کرد اما حون مدد کرد در آن نگهبان بش دار بهت مدت شد مدد واران
باب محجل زنگی سوار شند و انه بیرون آمد هراسب و طرم سیه راند بد نشت و بر فراق ایشان کربیت خوان
بروی غالب کشته است اسب را برلب دریا شکیل کرد و او درکشتی در یا آمد و تخت حون دار ب در خواب شد
مردی بود ما هی که همه روز نشت در دریا انداخته بودی حون بش شدی حامدی آن نشت را برکشیدی
وانجه روزی وی بودی هر دی آن بش یا مد مردی را در کشتی دید حفته و اسب از برون سوانگال کرده ما هی کبر
حون آن حال دکفت من بسج صیدی بهتر ز ین یاد مام کن این اب را کبرم و درین جزیره قصبها بسیارت
نجای دکبرم و بفروشم با اسباب من یا حفه خود و باز بخود دانشه کرد که اکر من این اب را با خود حرم خصم او پیدا شود
و در عقف من نپایدد مرا ا دیه آنت که این سن کشتی ا بگبرم و وی نیکی کبرم و آن سن کشتی ا ببره و کشتی با
شمود درکشتی ا در دریا انداخت در عقت آمدن همچنان کرد و آن سن کشتی را بره و کشتی ا در د ر یا خله کرد جون دار به سم
یوسب و دار ب نشت و بر فت دار ب در خواب خوش فته بود تا آنگاه که صبح بد مید و جهان روشن شد و نش شد دار ب حسم
با بر کرد ر بر است خود کوی بی بد وجب در ما جزره و برلب دریا سری دا یسا یی د تا ایت حون فطران سیاه شده
اسطلا بی کرفه و نش خود ش بد یدا شت و ز آن جزیره سلان سار بود و مردمان از بالا فوی شکیل بود ند و بلار
بهرون ور ده بود ند و منهم ها رسکیر و مدد دار ب و دی ا ز آن بهتر کرد و دکفت ای خواجه ی کسی این جزیره راجه خوانند

3

The Medieval Seas

Hitherto the seamen's one navigational instrument had been the leadline. Now, within the space of a couple of hundred years there was to be added to it the magnetic compass and the chart. Between them they revolutionized the practice of seamanship. More accurate means of measuring the Pole Star's altitude than merely estimating its height by eye against the rigging or the figure of a man, were to be adapted from the astronomers' instruments and taken to sea, and at the same time the savants provided a method by which the altitude of the midday sun might also be used for determining latitude. What has been called 'the geometrical seaman' was on the way to conquer new worlds, using ships vastly improved, though still perverse and awkward enough instruments for so grand a purpose. And most of the coastlines of the world were to be surveyed before seamen had any means other than dead reckoning for determining their longitude.

A rig had spread widely over the Mediterranean which was to open up a new kind of seamanship and transform the dangerous art of coastal navigation. Before the land was netted over with roads and railways coastal seamanship played an important role in society, for the seas which flowed in and out of the hundreds of small harbours and estuaries – most now filled with yachts and dinghies, their importance otherwise lost – were the most important links between people ashore. It is revealing that coal should have become widely known as 'sea-coal' by association with the means of delivering it.

The rigs of sailing vessels fall into two generic classes, known respectively as 'square' and 'fore and aft'. All those considered so far have fallen into the first group.

Square sails are the more obvious conception and hence were the first to be evolved. They are set on yards slung at their mid-points on the fore side of the mast. When the wind is not from dead astern, the yards may be braced round to bring one or other edge of the sail, depending on the side of the ship from which the wind blows, up towards the wind. We have seen that the Norse seamen probably, but the Mediterranean seamen never, used bowlines to hold steady the leading edge of the

Portuguese compass
1402.

Opposite page
A telescope
of 1646

sail, an advance in seamanship for which the credit is purely Northern. The fundamental characteristic of the square sail is that under all conditions the wind strikes the same surface of the sail when propelling the ship, but the leading edge of the sail is now one side, now the other, depending on the direction of the wind.

With fore-and-aft sails these characteristics are reversed. The sail is set abaft the mast, not on its fore side as with the square rig, and its leading edge is always the same, as the sail swings on the mast like a gate upon its post. But the wind falls on alternate surfaces of the cloth, depending on which side of the boat it is blowing. A more subtle propulsive power is now derived. It resides in the high and straight leading edge, or luff, presented to the wind, unlike the short and sagging fore-leech of the square sail, which even the bowlines could not steady perfectly when the sail was trimmed at a fine angle to the wind. The fore-and-aft sail gains something of the soaring power of the long and slender wing of the albatross. History finds the first considerable demonstration of fore-and-aft sail in the Mediterranean, though the rig may not have originated there.

By the medieval period the Mediterranean had known many masters: Minoan, Phoenician, Greek, with later all seamen finding themselves working their ships over a Roman lake. Then with the fall of the Empire various peoples, some of them like the Phoenicians being of no great significance on land, became the leading seamen of their day. The Frenchmen of Marseilles, the Spaniards of Barcelona, the republican peoples of Genoa, Pisa, and of Venice as that most astonishing of all

Portuguese carracks

Rigging of an Elizabethan ship

cities rose on its islands, found themselves sharing the Mediterranean with the seaman of a race that was spreading a new religion in the wake of Christianity and a new type of sailing-ship, for the Arabs were well in the forefront of those reaching towards superior navigational techniques.

The lateen became the sail of the peoples called to prayer by the muezzin, and like the crescent it might be regarded as the symbol of Islam.

The Mediterranean during much of the seventh century has been described as a silent lake. By the ninth century the ships of Islam, trading between the East and Spain, had again established a commercial tradition. And for the first and only time in history the main seaborne trade of the Western world was propelled by the fore-and-aft rig. Before it there had been the various square rigs of Antiquity and the classical period; following it was to come the three and more masted square rig evolved by a fusion of the Northern and Southern rigs.

While Baghdad became the centre of learning, Phoenician and Greek shipwrights instructed Arab pupils in the coarser matters of building and navigating ships. And these ships, with their scimitar-like sails, pressed over Eastern seas from the Persian Gulf to Malabar, eastward over the Indian Ocean to Rangoon, southward to Zanzibar, until the Arabs had all but monopolized seaborne traffic and had become middlemen between East and West.

The Arab sail was the settee-lateen, differing from the pure lateen in having a deep luff to the forward edge of the sail, which thus became a quadrilateral in shape instead of a triangle, while retaining the general appearance and qualities of the latter.

Where did the lateen rig come from? Until lately it was thought to have been invented on the Nile in about the seventh century A.D., and then to have spread, displacing the former square sail, in the wake of the Arab conquests. We now see a different picture, and fore-and-aft seamen are discerned, though none too clearly, sailing in perhaps some numbers just outside the narrow focus of earlier historical knowledge. We are able to believe, on archaeological evidence the significance of which was overlooked until lately, that in the eastern Mediterranean of the pre-Christian era there were lateeners sailing on local errands between the tiny harbours

Old English Ship

and creeks where the Aegean islands are sprinkled; that even the spritsail rig, so confidently believed to have been invented by the Dutch in a gust of Renaissance vigour, was in fact sailing in and out of the harbour of Ostia before Cleopatra had fled from Actium.

The lateen, or settee version of it, which became so firmly established in the Mediterranean and in the Indian Ocean, cannot be said to have earned its place through any qualities of easy handling, and it has been uncompromisingly described as the most dangerous rig ever devised by the wit of man. Certainly it needed, and still does need, a more highly acquired skill for its control than any other, and a kind of seamanship only mastered properly by those who have grown up in its ways.

The great yard, made up of two spars lashed together and often exceeding the length of the ship by as much as 30 per cent, provided its own safety-valve by the freedom given it by its weight to drop instantly when the halyard was eased. This

characteristic made the otherwise unwieldy lateen fit for use in the treacherous
Mediterranean weather. The yard was hoisted by a halyard of many parts which
was belayed aft, and the sail was controlled principally by powerful tack purchase
at the heel of the yard, and by the sheet. The settee also has a tackle at the lower fore
corner of the sail. These tackles had to carry the considerable stresses set up by the
yard when it tended to swing and take control in a seaway, and to share the load
there was a vang near the peak of the yard.

An important piece of gear was another tackle by means of which the yard was
hauled aft and round the mast when tacking or gybing. When going about the yard
had usually to be lowered and passed, together with intractable folds of sail, from
one side of the mast to the other, then rehoisted. Lateen-rigged boats needed many
hands, but labour was never a problem along the seacoasts of Islam or in the ports
of the warm Catholic countries, where the rig has persisted until today. Sometimes
when short-tacking, the yard and sail was not lowered but kept hoisted to weather.
Its set was then poor, but acceptable for short legs.

Shrouds and yard
of a Portuguese
carrack. Detail
from pages 122
and 123

Opposite page
The crow's nest of
a Portuguese
carrack. Detail
from pages 122
and 123

The Description of the Cross-Staff.

This Inſtrument is of ſome antiquity in Navigation, and is common-ly uſed at Sea, to take the Altitude of the Sun or Stars, which it per-forms with ſufficient exactneſs, eſpecially if it be leſs then 60 degrees, but if it exceed 60, it is not ſo certain, by reaſon of the length of the Croſs, and the ſmallneſs of the graduations on the Staff.

It should be noted here that the division of sails into the two categories of square and fore and aft makes a line of demarcation that a close study will show to be vaguer than it seems at first. The lateen itself partakes of the character of both. When the clew of the lateen is taken round the mast and the sail is trimmed for a wind astern, it becomes essentially a square sail. There are authorities who will not include the lateen, settee-lateen and the various forms of lugsail which will be examined later, as fore-and-aft sails. We do so. With lug and lateen the wind blows on either side of the sail, depending on its direction, when propelling the ship, but one edge of the sail, the luff, is always ahead of the other, or to windward, whereas with a square sail first one side becomes the luff, or fore-leech, and then the other. Sails of the fore-and-aft character, incorporated in rigs that were to be so extensively developed as the medieval gloom flowered into Renaissance vitality, made coastal sailing and the shorter sea routes more easily mastered. The various fore-and-aft rigs gave seamen a quicker control of their craft and an ability to sail closer to the wind; this meant a little more safety off coastlines which might quickly turn into lee shores. Yet it was the square rig that not only was to open up the oceans during the age that was about to dawn, but was to remain the means of driving oceangoing ships until sail was replaced by mechanical propulsion. Its continuing efficacy resulted from the fact, not yet known to seamen, that over the outer oceans away from the influence of the land there blew the great belts of steady winds, the trades, which enabled ships to carry with them over great lengths of their voyages fair winds from abaft the beam; though to do so it was necessary for them to make their way in wide loops and swoops far from the direct course. The requirements of those who trade along the coast and on shorter sea-routes and of the ocean-going seamen were quite different.

For how long had the power of the lodestone been known? 'That this magnetic stone could attract iron, and that a piece of iron thus attracted could in its turn attract other iron had been a familiar fact since ancient days', says Professor Taylor in *The Haven Finding Art*. But why should the magnetized iron take up a position lying in what we may describe very roughly as a north and south direction? Obviously there was magic here, or what the practical seaman, whose life had been spent working ungainly ships along shorelines and in deeper waters where the clever did not venture, regarded as something mainly unpractical and totally incomprehensible. The magnetic compass was for a long time an *outré* device to the seamen who kept the short sea-routes open and maintained civilization on shore by carrying round the coasts of Europe the trade that advanced the societies of the day.

The Chinese 'south-pointing chariot' has an honoured place in legend and the antiquity of the third millennium B.C. Whether it was a chariot – even whether its south-pointing activity was due to magnetism, are amongst the numerous open questions that hover around the origins of the magnetic compass. The classical Greeks knew about magnetic iron-ore, and the Arabs, and even the Vikings, have

The component parts of Thomas Tettle's cross-staff.
Note the several lengths of transversals

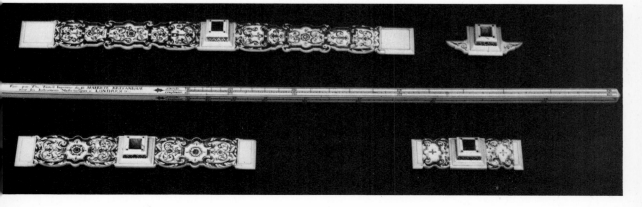

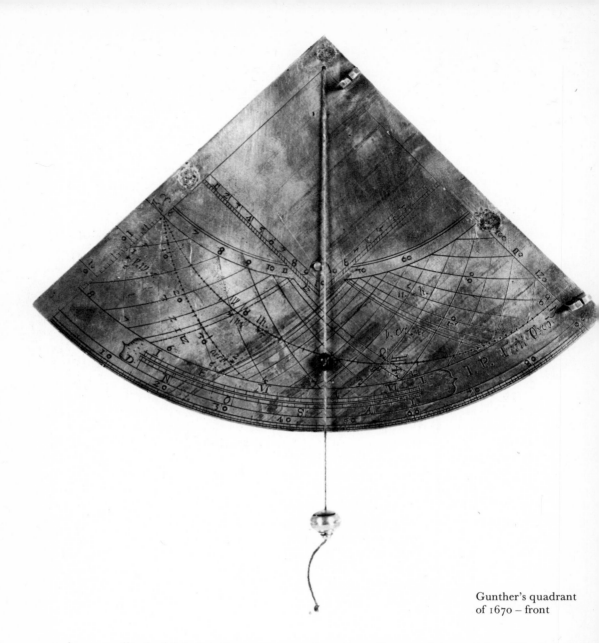

Gunther's quadrant
of 1670 – front

been credited with being the earliest marine users of magnetic attraction. The latter, in their ore-rich lands and with their experience of working iron, may have taken the step of using lodestones afloat, but nothing is known about it. The Arabs, with their lateen rig and ability to sail zigzag courses in some defiance of the wind's direction, certainly would have found a new need for such a direction-finder. What is certain is that when first taken to sea it was a device used not to steer by constantly, but simply for orientation when the older, familiar methods were impossible.

The phenomenon of 'force' acting on another body over a distance and out of contact, and even through an intervening substance, obviously had qualities

130

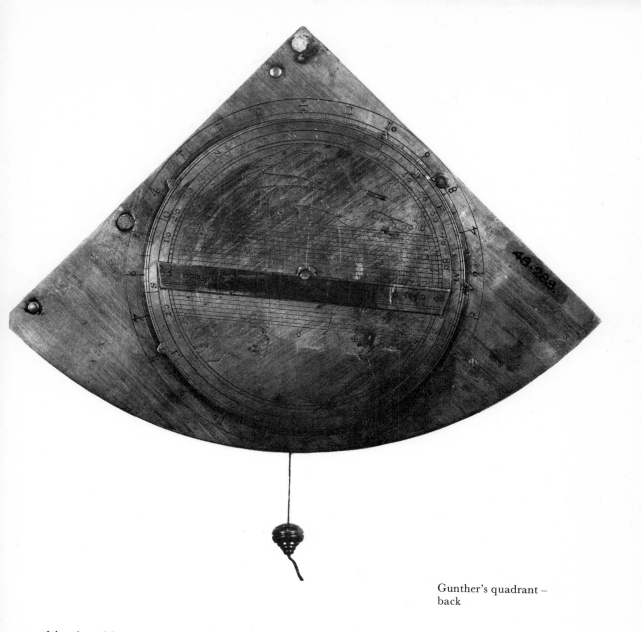

Gunther's quadrant –
back

objectionable to common sense, which so commonly misleads. Today the concept of 'force' has been abolished from the higher physics, but many of the best educated could find it hard to explain briefly what magnetism is, and how, within its limits, the now obsolescent magnetic compass functions. Oceangoing was the space travel of its day and the contemporary public even more ignorant of its processes.

The mariner's compass, as opposed to the magnetic compass, was a means of orientation when there were only the winds and a few stars to guide. In the octagonal Temple of the Winds, built by Andronicus in Athens in the first century A.D., the eight principal winds were shown, which formed the wind-star with eight rays,

Italian compass – 1719.

showing the cardinal and inter-cardinal points. The mariner's compass was originally the subdivision of the circle into these eight winds, which were halved and then halved again until the familiar and long-lived 32 points were formed, the repetition of which in a clockwise direction round the circle became known as 'boxing the compass'. It should be noted that the division of the circle into degrees was unfamiliar, and remained so amongst many classes of seamen in every sea until modern times. The further subdivision of each point, of $11\frac{1}{4}$ degrees, into half-points produced a circle split into 64 parts.

In the North the finer divisions of the circle were not made until later, probably at some time in the latter half of the twelfth century. There is no firm evidence of this being done before 1240, while the first mention of a 32-point system was made by Chaucer even later, in 1390, when writing about another instrument soon to become of importance to seamen, the astrolabe. The eightfold division of the horizon and its further subdivision by halving and halving again the angles between the rays was not the only one used in Antiquity, but the one which spread widely in the wake of the magnetized needle; and in medieval and through to modern times it became the accepted mariner's compass. Its basis was the sailor's lack of arithmetical ability; to halve and halve again angles between the cardinal points was not too academic an exercise; on the other hand it is evident that once the compass rose had been formed of 32 points and 32 half-points, the degree of subdivision achieved, of down to a little more than $5\frac{1}{2}$ degrees, was fine enough to require the use of a magnetic needle.

A soft iron needle magnetized by a lodestone would retain its magnetism for a short time only, and part of a pilot's equipment became the stone with which to refresh the needle. The pivoting of the needle was a secondary stage of development. Originally it was floated in a bowl of water, given buoyancy by sticking it through or into a straw or reed, or placing it on a block of wood. By rotating the stone swiftly above the needle, the latter was made to spin and become slightly magnetized. On withdrawing the stone, the needle would come to rest. The operation was not one readily performed on the deck of a ship at sea. With waves inside the bowl as well as over the surrounding sea, and with the ship heeling or rolling, it must have been exasperatingly difficult to make sure that the needle came to rest, undisturbed or without contacting the sides of the bowl. Equally difficult, as he was soon to discover, was trying to determine from a moving ship the altitude of a heavenly body by means of the astronomers' astrolabe and quadrant. Many refinements were needed before

A deck-head compass
as hung in a cabin

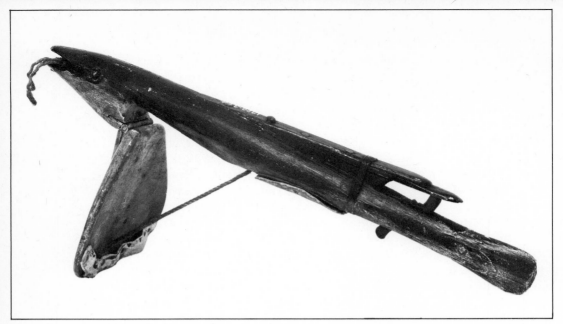

the expression 'steady on course' could mean anything in relation to steering by compass. A star to steer her by could only remain the seaman's preference.

The pivoting of the needle was the first refinement to the compass, followed by the placing of the ancient wind-rose beneath the needle, while at a later date the wind-rose itself was pivoted with the magnetized needle attached beneath it. This may not have occurred until late in the fifteenth century, by which time the card and needle had been enclosed in a box, on which was painted a mark indicating the fore-and-aft line of the ship – the lubber's line – so that the point of the rose lying against the mark indicated the course of the ship. Gimbals came later, perhaps soon after 1500. For some time no allowance was made for variation.

It is possible that the ancient navigators used charts of some form, but history has no knowledge of them, and in the absence of the compass they could only have been productions of a different order from those that began appearing in about the second half of the thirteenth century.

Father of the chart was the long known *portolano*, *leescaert* or *routier*, the last word becoming Anglicized to *ruthier* and thence to the familiar *rutter*. Such compilations of sailing directions, the recorded experience of countless mariners, may be dated back to the classical period. At moments Homer wrote in the style of a pilot book. Very few *portolanos* have survived, which is not surprising, for they lacked artistic qualities or speculative daring, but contained profitable information best kept quiet. As a basis for the marine chart they gave it an advantage over the map, in which un-hindered imagination had more play. Essentially the *portolano* was a list of landmarks recording distances and bearings between them, with perhaps the addition of tidal notes, sea-depths, the character of the bottom and descriptions of special dangers. The inevitably different attitudes of Southern and Northern seamen are reflected in their sailing directions. Northern seamen, operating over the Continental Shelf needed information about its swirling tides, and about the bottom that his leadline could reach. Thus the Northern seamen always remained acutely conscious of the sea-floor with its constantly shifting banks of shingle, while the Southerner was interested in landmarks and bearings.

The early charts were essentially *portolanos* drawn to scale, a process helped by the new mariners' compass, while over them was drawn the criss-crossing rays of a number of compass roses. To any rhumb line laid on the chart might then be found a nearly parallel ray, which traced back to the originating rose would show the course to be steered. These invaluable lines did not appear on the earliest charts; later they appeared in various colours or styles of drafting, making differentiation between them easier. Charts followed maps in becoming to some extent stylized. By the first half of the sixteenth century, to quote Christopher Wood: 'To judge from the monsters then inhabiting the North Sea, it must have been a fearsome place.'

With the multitude of crossing rays on the chart, the compass on deck, and a certain basic accuracy in the information provided on the chart (due to its origin in the older sailing directions) the mariner now had powerful new instruments in his hands. The important principles of projection came later. So long as charts covered a limited area only, errors of projection were manageable. With big areas, or in northern latitudes, the lack of parallelism between the meridians of longitude became exaggerated. True bearings were no longer obtainable from a straight line drawn on the chart, and the length of a degree of longitude would vary noticeably with the latitude. Later, tables were provided to give the variation in scale with latitude, and the projection of Mercator helped towards the production of the plain

Elton's quadrant (back-staff) – 1732

chart on which rhumbs were true courses; but this was not achieved until the latter end of the sixteenth century.

Chart-making was an art rather than a science, and also an honoured and lucrative profession, the results of which were respected more highly by savants than by the general run of sailormen, who inevitably treated the drawings on vellum – the 'sheepskins' – with a certain disdain. Indeed, the practical seamen of the little ships have down the ages shown some casualness towards charts. The British marine artist Norman Wilkinson tells the story of a trawler on naval service during 1915, whose skipper had brought her from the eastern Mediterranean to Malta. 'You got your

Papal galley

Admiralty charts before leaving?' inquired an officer. 'No, Sir, we got no Admiralty charts.' 'Good God, man, how did you get through the Greek islands?' 'Well, Sir, the Mate had an old bible with some quite good maps at the end.'

Along with the more advanced arts of seamanship, chart-making originally belonged to the Mediterranean, with its centres in Italy and Spain. But as superiority in the techniques of shipbuilding moved north so did those of chart-making, which became centred in Antwerp and Amsterdam.

The medieval charts reveal the state of people's knowledge of the different stretches of the European coastline. One made in Genoa in 1548 shows the

General arrangement of a Flemish carrack

Mediterranean with the accuracy that might be expected, but this accuracy diminishes progressively from south to north; while the Spanish and French coastlines show a not inadequate configuration, that of the British Isles is decidedly poor and becomes purely imaginative round the north coast of Scotland.

To use the chart, a pilot needed a straight-edge to lay the course, a pair of dividers, firstly to measure parallelism with the appropriate ray from one of the several compass roses, and secondly to prick off his dead reckoning, derived from the speed, course steered and time sailed. For the last the sand-glass was necessary. The haven-finding art was growing in complexity.

Three instruments were used by astronomers for measuring star altitudes, the astrolabe, the quadrant and the cross-staff, but it was not until the fifteenth century that these were modified for the seaman's use. Neither the quadrant nor earlier astrolabe, which had already been employed at this time for about seven centuries, proved satisfactory maritime instruments and were in due course replaced by the cross-staff, which had the advantage of also being the simplest and cheapest. By 1594, when there had been a considerable amount of experience of these instruments at sea, John Davis – after whom the Davis Strait is named – said in his book *Seaman's Secrets* that unless the sea were smooth it was impossible to make a reliable observation with either the astrolabe or quadrant (navigators would sometimes go ashore to take an altitude with the former), and he added that no instrument 'could compare with this cross-staff for the use of seamen.' Davis himself evolved from the cross-staff (sometimes known as 'fore-staff') the improvement known as the back-staff, or Davis quadrant. Invented in about 1594, the back-staff was still in use at the end of the eighteenth century; the fore- and back-staffs were therefore in the service of seamen for between 300 and 400 years.

The mariner's astrolabe was a simplification of the astronomer's, the rim engraved simply with scales of degrees from zero to ninety, over which could be rotated the sight rule, or alidade, with its two pinhole sights. It was small in diameter, perhaps about 6 inches, heavily cast in brass to encourage its hanging plumb on board a moving ship, but liable in addition to the inaccuracy of errors in the cutting of the degrees scale, where precision had to await upon the mechanical engraving of the late eighteenth century.

Fishing boats of the 15th century

F.

F. is a Turckés man of warr which out sayled the English merchantman
only with her top sailes vpon the Capp. and courses in the brayles

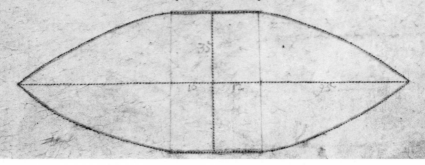

A

A. Is an English Merchantman with all her sayles sett as here
Demonstrated, three poyntes of the sheat vear ___

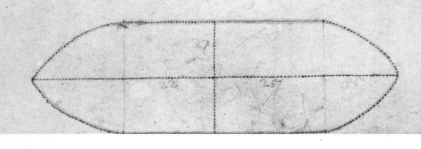

A Turkish warship

Opposite page
Side by side masts were a feature of rig unknown in the West at any period, but not uncommon in the East

Though a more recently invented instrument, dating back to the thirteenth century or a little earlier, it seems likely that the quadrant was used at sea before the astrolabe. It was simply a thin plate of metal, or possibly wood, a quarter of a circle in shape, marked in degrees round the arc and with pinhole sights on one of the straight-edges. A plumb line – a thread or a metal rod weighted – hung over the degree scale from the centre of the quarter-circle. Two men were needed to take an observation, the one holding the quadrant in a vertical plane and sighting the Pole Star through the pinholes, the other reading the scale, which would give the elevation of the star when the observer said 'on'.

It is significant that the mariner's unfamiliarity with the degrees of circular measure sometimes led to quadrants being marked not with these but with the names of familiar landmarks, capes, rivers, islands, ports – the name indicated to the seaman when he was in the latitude of that particular place. He would then know that his ship lay due east or west of this point. Or at least that it was approximately so, for there were a number of sources of error apart from those inherent in the manipulation of the instrument.

A device used by the Arabs may have been the forerunner of the cross-staff. Known as the 'kamal', it was composed of a small, thin rectangle of wood, 'tablet of the Indies', attached to a length of string knotted at intervals. The tablet was held at

a distance from the eye such that with its base on the horizon, the star under observation just rested at its upper edge. The distance was measured by holding the string taut between the teeth, the number of knots left hanging in the excess length of the cord being the measure of latitude. There could be no question here of any closely graduated scale, but the length of cord left dangling represented, by the number of knots in it, the latitude of various ports known to the navigator. A number of kamals were kept each with a different size of tablet, so that the range of angles might be measured.

The cross-staff, so highly praised by John Davis, became the mariner's most important tool for making celestial observations. It consisted originally of no more than a hardwood staff (stave) of square section along the length of which there slid a shorter cross-piece at right angles. To make an observation, the end of the staff was held to the eye and the cross-piece was moved along it until the lower end touched the horizon while the upper end was on the star. When held thus, simple geometry will show that the half-length of the cross-piece – the part on top – divided by the distance between the end of the shaft and the position of the cross-piece was a tangent of half the altitude angle of the body observed. Graduations on the top of the staff enabled the whole angle to be read off directly. The principle was that of the kamal; the practice more sophisticated.

In later years the cross-staff was elaborated, having up to four cross-pieces of increasing lengths, with a corresponding number of scales on the four surfaces of the stave; these enabled a bigger range of angles to be measured. In theory, a correct altitude will be obtained with this instrument only if the eye be at the centre of the staff, in which case the observer would be able to see nothing. In practice, the angle he reads was in excess of the true altitude, and in time it was learned to apply a correction to the observation. But this may not have been until the Elizabethan period.

So we see refinements of technique being applied to the navigational processes which for so long had been hearty approximations.

All this time the impress of the Viking craft, in rig as well as hull, remained strong on north European shipping. But while so much continued as it had been – the double-ended, clinker-planked hull with one steering oar and a single square sail – alterations were occurring that changed the prevalent type of vessel from large boat into small ship.

On the evidence of the Bayeux Tapestry it appears that a portion amidships of some vessels was being planked over at the level of the gunwale top, forming a deck giving shelter beneath it and headroom above the bottom boards of more than 6 feet. Where there was deck, there could of course be no rowing benches; but the under-deck space was available for cargo or shelter. It is not known how usual this form of construction became, but it represents a small step towards the fully decked ship.

This change into a ship better able to carry cargo was made at the expense of oarsmen – and thus the ship was more dependent upon sail. It may have had for a time a less adequate performance under sail than the galley it replaced. With greater beam and freeboard, the growth of bulk was matched, to some extent, by more sail area, but not by any greater efficiency per unit area; and one must admire the sea-

Replica of the 17th century *Mayflower* in which the
Pilgrim Fathers crossed the Atlantic

going skills that coaxed these loaded ships along their short and tidal sea-routes
where head winds would so often be encountered.

It was the introduction of two features, initially intended only to make a ship
more suitable as a fighting platform, that led to structural changes that eventually
transformed boats into ships. The North had not yet reached the sophistication of
developing types of ship specially for war, analogous to the Mediterranean galleys of
great antiquity by this time, which were the warships of the middle sea as opposed to
the round ships of its commerce. Sea war involved hand-to-hand fighting from ships
laid alongside one another, and for this the cargo-carrying ship was converted into a
warship by the addition of temporary end-platforms raised on stanchions above the
gunwale, the platforms being protected by sides cut in the form of battlements. Thus
were formed end-castles, which were first extended in length, then made integral
with the hull by planking in the stanchions on which they stood, so that they formed

what was to become known as the fo'c'sle and poop, with raised decks at bow and stern and accommodation beneath, features which became common to all ships, merchant and naval, above the smallest sizes. This considerable development in design came about between the latter half of the thirteenth century and the first half of the fourteenth, and by the end of the latter century the change would appear to have been general in the larger classes of vessel.

The seafaring of medieval northern Europe was a large and complex business. Dorothy Burwash in *English Merchant Shipping 1460–1540* has identified some forty-three different types of vessel being employed round the coast of Europe at this slightly later period. There has been a tendency to consider the type known as cog to typify the Northern cargo-carrying ship, but the Burwash evidence does suggest the variety that there must have been found alongside the wharfs of medieval harbours.

Cogs were to be found all round the European coast from the Baltic to the Bay of Biscay and the Atlantic coast of Spain, along the Channel coast to the far west, and throughout the North Sea. The name cog is closely associated with the German Hanseatic League. The cities of the League, of which the most prominent were Bremen, Lubeck and Hamburg, have been described as rocks rising out of a raging sea – the turmoil of Europe and that chaotic Empire that has been described as neither holy nor Roman nor an empire. The wide-spreading, loose-trading organization of the League was the greatest manifestation of Northern seafaring so far, and it grew in power and wealth between the eleventh and fourteenth centuries, when it counted ninety cities on its roll.

The medieval cog may be pictured as a double-ended clinker-built boat with castles at bow and stern. The ship was high sided and about three times as long overall as she was broad, with hatches in the one deck for entry to the holds. In one important respect its single-masted square rig differed from the Viking rig: this was the bowsprit which made its appearance some time in the first part of the thirteenth century and was of greater importance than its trifling appearance might indicate. It was not yet used for carrying a stay and a headsail; its purpose was only to give a better lead to the bowlines, extending them beyond the hull and allowing them to support the fore-leech of the sail more effectively. Now, with sails larger in proportion to the hull, which in its turn was shorter in proportion to its bulk, the bowsprit had become necessary to maintain the efficacy of bowlines, and we see an important further step being taken by Northern seamen to increase the weatherliness of their short bulky ships. The spar forming the bowsprit had beneath it a shallow, notched length of timber allowing the bowlines to be set up at different distances outboard according to the wind strength and sail trim. This subtlety in rigging is testimony to the efforts being made to improve sailing qualities.

With the area of sail being increased in relation to the size of the hull, methods of reducing sail in stronger winds became of greater importance. We are not certain whether or not the Vikings used reef-points. A rigged model made in the workshops of the Science Museum, London, carries two sets of points on the striped sail. In the medieval period they were certainly in use, points being perhaps three deep, allowing the sail area to be reduced by about a quarter of its area for each depth as the points were tied. Rather curiously, the use of reef-points became less common after

Goose-winging trim of settee lateen sails

about 1500, and this effective and simple method of reducing sail, by simply rolling or packaging a certain amount at the head or foot of the sail and tying it up in a bundle appears to have been little used again until the mid-seventeeth century.

The other method of shortening sail was by means of bonnets. These consisted of strips of sail which were laced to the foot; letting go the lacing, or 'latchetes', relieved the sail of the amount of area in the bonnet, of which there might be three, analogous to three rows of reef-points. Sir Walter Raleigh mentions bonnets in his *Judicious and*

148

Select Essayes and Observations of 1650, describing them as a recent innovation. This is surprising in a man who had considerable knowledge of ships, for by this date bonnets had been in use for three to four centuries. And they were to remain in use in the smaller craft of northern Europe until the present century. In light weather the sail area might be increased by the addition of a further strip of canvas, known as a 'drabler', laced beneath the lowest bonnet.

Amongst the names applied to north European ships we find balinger, bark, buss, cog or cock, pink, smack, barge, hoy; some of them names familiar in much later periods, but not necessarily then meaning the same thing. The seaman is casual about the nomenclature of ship types, and different names may be applied to the same type simultaneously, or the same name to different types at different periods. But until the appearance of the two- and three-masted ship all types had a single mast and one square sail. It was a rig that survived into the twentieth century, complete with its bowlines, in the Yorkshire keel of Britain; until the arrival of steam, off the Norwegian coast there were many types of single-masted, square-rigged craft to be seen working to windward, their crews hauling the bowlines hard, or shortening sail by taking off a bonnet – practising, in fact, medieval methods of seamanship.

As the size of ships increased, the Northern single steering oar, and to only a slightly lesser degree the twin steering oars of the South, outgrew the limit of what could be achieved with the principle of the side rudder. The rudder hung from the stern on the middle line and swinging on hinges, formed by gudgeons and pintles, like a gate on its post, was needed to control the heavier and higher ships with their growing ability to make some use of other than fair winds. The stern rudder was an essential device to give the ships of the new oceangoing age their necessary degree

A storm at sea

Indian
adventurers sailing
out to colonize
Java. (From the
Sculptures of
Borobudur)

of ocean-going reliability. It reacted upon other features of design: the size, the subtlety of the rig that might be carried, the shape of the hull, and it added to the security with which ships might be controlled under difficult conditions.

The stern rudder came into use in the North between the late twelfth and early thirteenth century. It was, like the bowline, a Northern contribution to seamanship and was one of the factors that finally shifted the superiority in such matters from the Mediterranean to the Atlantic-facing European peoples. It led to other changes in the form of ships. Originally the stern rudder had a tiller curving awkwardly round the still high stern-post. Now the stern-post was shortened, and the double-ended, clinker-planked form of hull, an obvious Viking inheritance, was discarded, the curved stern-post being straightened in order to carry the rudder hangings better, and this led to a differentiation between the stern and bow of a ship, which formerly had been so nearly alike. This differentiation was to become usual in the design of oceangoing ships until the present day.

While the two-masted lateen-rigged ships were common in the Mediterranean, the seamen of the North had been pursuing a quite different development of sail; but the time was approaching when the two lines of development were to merge.

Briefly, while there were two-masted ships in northern Europe, the transition from one to three masts appears to have occurred within the space of half a century. In 1400 Northern ships carried one mast and a single square sail which had been inherited directly and with little change from the Norsemen. By 1500 the largest ships were three-masted and rigged in a way that combined the Northern traditional square rig with elements from the more complex and technically more advanced Mediterranean tradition. The three-masted ship, which Arnold Toynbee was to describe as 'the master tool of Western civilization', had come into being.

Seamen in both the North and the Mediterranean had gained, though in different ways. The single-masted, square-rigged ship of the North remained until its end a heart-breaking vessel to work up to windward, and the best such vessels could do – and a considerable step it was beyond the capability of the ancients – was to carry the wind on their beam, making a course, and considerable leeway, at right angles to the wind. With the three-master the Northern seamen gained powers of weatherliness and manœuvrability beyond the single-master's ability. The Southerner had his closer-winded lateen, but the great swaying yard, having to be lowered and re-hoisted frequently when the wind shifted, was no companion for the western ocean. This became quickly evident on the first voyage of Columbus, when one of his squadron, the *Nina*, set off rigged as a three-masted lateener, but at Las Palmas was converted to the three-masted square rig 'that she might follow the other vessels with more tranquillity and less danger.'

Little definite is known about the short-lived Northern two-masted ships. There were various types, and there seems little doubt that the second mast was sometimes added in the form of a mizzen, astern of the former single mast, sometimes ahead of it as a foremast and sail. Nor is there any certainty of the sail carried on the second

Opposite page
Ship from the tomb of the Carpaneto de Scanzi family
in Genoa

Horizon mirror of Adam's octant

mast, whether it was square or lateen, though it was probably the former. What appears more certain is that the long-established position of the mainmast was not readily changed when the growing size of ships made the addition of more masts and sails essential, with the result that two-masted ships were unbalanced.

The Northern type of single-masted, square-rigged ship began to be found in some numbers amongst the one-, two- and three-masted lateeners of the Mediterranean. It was in the Mediterranean, or possibly in the harbours of the Biscay coast which were the link between North and South, that the three-masted ship, in the form to become known as the carrack, appeared and grew into the largest type of vessel. Essentially the carrack was a ship with a Northern square mainsail and initially a mizzen-mast carrying a Southern lateen, to which was soon added also a small foremast carrying another square sail. Mizzen and foresail were small and had the primary function of balancing the ship and making control easier, rather than of adding effectively to propulsive power. So the Mediterranean returned to the square rig which it had largely abandoned in favour of the lateen, but with the lateen forming one element of the new rig; while the North, which soon adopted the carrack type, chose a rig with an essentially alien lateen element associated with the square rig it had never abandoned. The three-masted ship was born and was to become the basic type of oceangoing vessel. But still the smaller lateeners continued to ply the Mediterranean, and were doing so in the twentieth century, and still the single-masted, square-rigged ship went out fishing and short-distance trading in the North.

While the change to the centre-line, hinged rudder was able to bring larger ships under control than would have been possible with the side rudder, the problem of steering was still only partially solved, the solution, such as it was, proving progressively more inadequate as ships continued to grow. As the deck aft was heightened into the poop, the helmsman at the tiller (secured to the rudder-head) was further removed from where the ship was conned.

This led to the invention of the whipstaff, itself only another partial solution, for it was mechanically inefficient. The staff was vertical to the deck and extended down to connect with the after end of the tiller. It was pivoted at the deck immediately above the tiller on a fulcrum block giving the upper end of the staff, controlled by the helmsman, freedom to be swung athwartships to port or starboard. If the helmsman pressed the whipstaff over to starboard, the after end of the tiller would be turned to port and the rudder to starboard, turning the ship also in this direction. The mechanical advantage in the system became lower as the whipstaff was put to a bigger angle. Not more than about 5 degrees of helm could be applied by this means, and the

Suez fishing-boat. Note the triangular lateen as opposed to the Muslim settee lateen

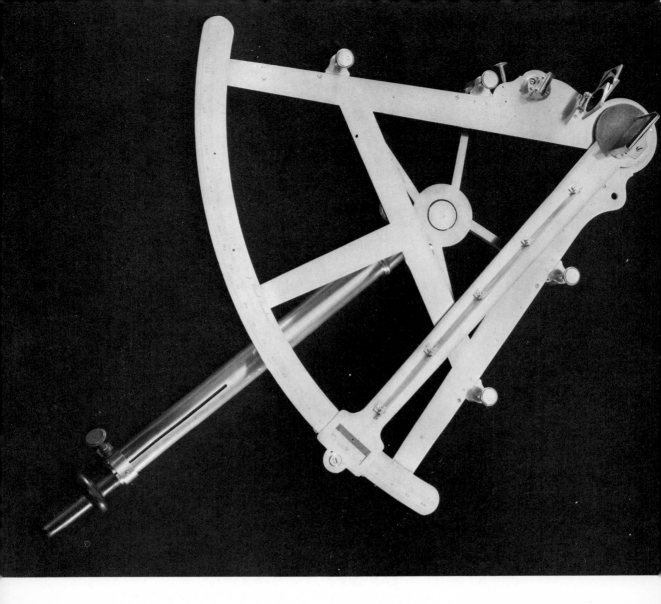

small degree of movement, accompanied by much friction and backlash, could give little precision of control. Indeed, it is generally supposed that the whipstaff could enable the helmsman to achieve little more than keep the vessel moderately steady on course. The helmsman at the whipstaff might still be under the upper deck, depending on the size of ship and the number of decks through which the whipstaff passed in wide slots. In severe conditions and for larger rudder movements, the whipstaff would be abandoned and the tiller operated by means of relieving tackles, with a team hauling on them and under orders from several decks above. The inexactitude of control under these conditions will be evident.

Steering by means of tillers and teams on relieving tackles was still being practised in the largest racing cutters of the yachting fleets during the nineties. Here the

Octant 1775
underneath

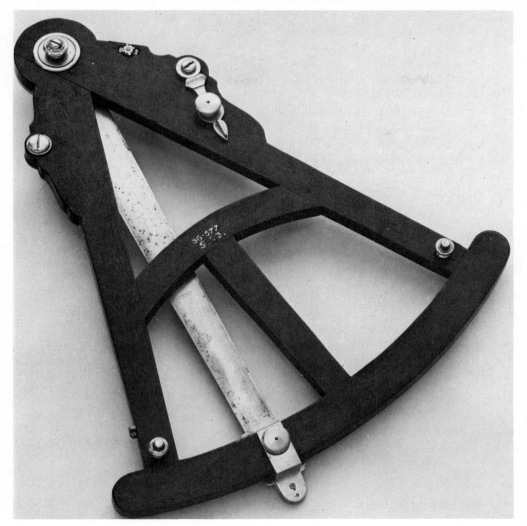

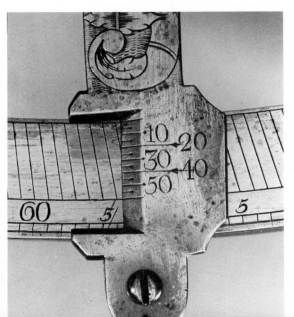

Scale and vernier of 1775 octant. The
vernier became essential for greater
accuracy in reading the scale

Opposite page
A sextant of about 1760 with an 18¼
inches radius for measuring lunar
distances (telescopic sight missing).
The instrument was so heavy it had
to have a frame and belt pole to help
support it when being used

yachts would have been some half as long again as the largest medieval three-masted ships, with more than double the sail area, but appreciably lighter. But the hands on the tackles were in the open, by the skipper, and the yachts were highly manœuvrable.

Uncertainty of steering in the medieval ships had to be mitigated by the use of the sails for control, particularly the lateen mizzen and the small foresail. The early three-masted ships were certainly lacking in that sureness of control that the Viking was able to have over his smaller vessel and single square sail using the side rudder with its short athwartship tiller. The growth in size and complication of the medieval ship was not accompanied by equal progress in the mechanical devices for handling them.

The fore-and-aft rig reached northern Europe tardily, in the early part of the fifteenth century. The Mediterranean had been a sea dominated by the lateen for centuries, but the failure of the lateen to spread northward is not to be attributed only to the stubbornness of Northerners wedded to their version of the square rig, or to ignorance of the Mediterranean rig. It is more likely that such practical knowledge as they had of the lateen with its massive yard had made it clear that such could never be made suitable for the tideways and squalls of the North. This was a verdict that has never been upset. Lateen-rigged ships were never to be more than uneasy visitors north of Biscay.

It was in the form of the spritsail that the fore-and-aft rig initially came to the North. The spritsail was a true fore-and-aft sail, rectangular in shape, set abaft the mast and spread by the diagonal sprit extending from the heel of the mast to the peak

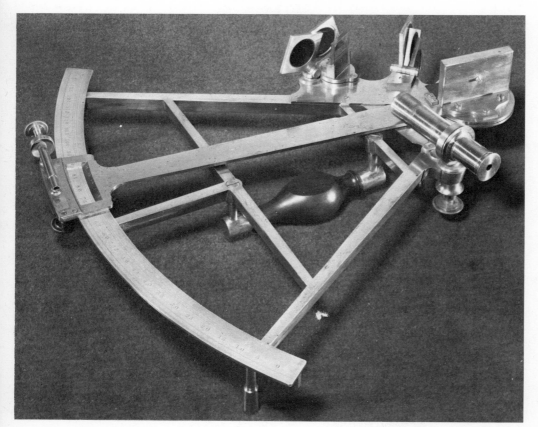

Compare this earlier type of sextant with the one illustrated opposite

Sextant of 1970s

of the sail. Who first devised the rig is uncertain. It used to be confidently described as an invention of the Dutch, possibly as an attempt to produce something with the close-winded qualities of the lateen yet suitable for the mud flats and estuaries of the North Sea. But it is now known that the spritsail, like the lateen, was known to the classical world. It is believed, furthermore, to have come to the Mediterranean from Indonesia, carried thence to the Indian Ocean, where the Greco-Roman seamen found it. It is believed that the lateen, as used in the classical Mediterranean, may have been evolved out of the Eastern spritsail.

All that can be said, without becoming tangled in the more recondite ethnographical problems of rigs – in the rival theories of 'independent invention' or 'diffusion' – is that the lateen rig disappeared out of history's narrow focus from classical times until the rise of Islam and the spritsail rig until the Dutch developed it in the fifteenth century, making it the forerunner of the many later fore-and-aft rigs.

Possibly the Northern adoption of the fore-and-aft rig, certainly its enthusiastic development, owed something to the light of the Renaissance. That intellectual summer shining over the Arno threw its long beams to the Scheldt, where another great race of seamen was appearing.

Increasing use of the compass may have taken some of the urgency out of the attention the practical seaman paid to the sky, but he still had to consult it for another vital part of his activities, the anticipation of weather. The need for this was to some extent in proportion to the weakness of the ships: but the ancients had at least a more predictable climate during the sailing season than had those operating on the edge of the Atlantic and now about to cross it as a matter of routine.

The behaviour of the winds, the appearance of the clouds, of the sun at its rising and setting, of the moon and rainbows, the behaviour of the fish and birds, the feel of the air and the temperature, were the guides that long experience had been able to establish as indications of tomorrow's weather, on which life might depend. Some of the jingles in which weather lore is embalmed must have come down to us from medieval times and earlier. But not such as this:

> First rise after low
> Foretells stronger blow

for it was to be many years yet before the seaman had that essential instrument for scientific weather forecasting, the barometer.

Instead he had highly developed instincts and such lore as

> When the wind shifts against the sun
> Trust it not for back it will run.
> When the wind follows the sun
> Fine weather will ne'er be done.
>
> If the wind is north-east three days without rain
> Eight days will pass before south again.
> If woolly fleeces deck the heavenly way
> Be sure no rain will mar a summer's day.

But

> Mackerel skies and mares' tails
> Make tall ships carry short sails.

The porpoise and the gulls helped the mariner to anticipate:

> When the sea hog jumps
> Stand by at your pumps.

And

> Seagull, seagull, sit on the sand,
> It's never good weather when you're on the land.

Javan proa –
20th century

Opposite page
Javan proa –
18th century

Pharos at Ostia

Opposite page
Dungeness
Fire-tower – early
17th century

And the menace of the lunar halo was appreciated in two lines that rise from jingle to poetry:

> The moon, the governess of the floods
> Pale in her anger washes all the air.

These, and many other easily memorized lines, embalmed the experience of generations, and though we do not know the precise form they took in the medieval period, we may feel sure that the later variations were based upon those older, for they were derived from the same familiarities.

The first barometer is believed to have been made in 1643 on the advice of Galileo. But it was not until the nineteenth century that Robert Fitzroy (1805–65) revealed the value of the barometer for giving storm warnings. He sailed with

Darwin in the *Beagle*, and this was one of the first ships to carry a barometer. Fitzroy showed that it was the amount and rate of barometric change that was of importance in forecasting, rather than the pressure reading of the moment, and though this occurred long after the times with which we are at present concerned, we should complete this subject with Fitzroy's observations: '. . . weather information and particularly barometer readings should be observed and recorded by all ships' captains for comparison and the judicious inferences drawn from them offer the means of foretelling wind and weather during the next following period.'

In an age of immense superstition the medieval seamen no doubt entertained many more esoteric beliefs about weather forecasting and they may even have used as well some relatively sophisticated and now forgotten methods. We may recognize something of their attitude in the methods of the fishermen of Dawlish, England, in the days before the barometer was commonly understood by seamen. In the public gardens at Dawlish there stood a glass tube containing a colourless liquid. When the liquid remained clear good weather might be expected, but should crystals form in it bad conditions were on the way. The character of the crystals was able to suggest the nature of the weather impending, such as wind, rain, fog or snow. No one knew how long this weather-glass had stood in the gardens, but it appears that even after a barograph was provided, the fishermen preferred the older glass and continued to consult it before going to sea.

It is curious that this weather-glass worked at all, since the liquid was sealed in its tube. A few years ago the tube was broken. A chemist of Dawlish discovered an old prescription for the liquid and made this up successfully so that the glass worked again. It was an interesting prescription: potassium nitrate, ammonium chloride, camphor, distilled water and some alcohol, and its efficiency was such that men, whose lives depended on it, regarded it as a reliable means of weather forecasting.

It should be emphasized here that the seaman in A.D. 1500 had not, and would not have for years, any aid to assist man's limited vision. The popular idea of a seaman as one continually looking through some form of 'glass' is very modern in terms of seafaring. The world was circumnavigated, and for thousands of years men had been coasting, and even crossing oceans, without this apparently vital aid.

Nobody is sure who invented the telescope, though it seems not to have been

Beacon at Gangoxuma, Japan – early 18th century

First Linwell
lightship – 1736

Galileo, to whom it is usually attributed. There is little doubt that the invention occurred in the early years of the seventeenth century, and it appears to have come from that nation of seamen, the Dutch. From Holland Galileo heard of it. He recorded his first information about a 'spyglass' (the term 'telescope' was invented some years later) in 1609, but nothing he did benefited seamen until generations later. We return to the medieval seaman, who could only just accept the magnetic compass, let alone a spyglass. He was merely an immensely practical man handling the problems that everyday seamanship offered.

How did the medieval seaman live? That his was a harsh, dangerous life is obvious; though we may feel that the lot of a seaman in a medieval European merchant ship sailing coastwise or cross seas, or fishing over the North Sea banks, was better than that of many workers in the nineteenth-century industrial civilization. Ashore it was a world of 'fields full of folk' raising food and living in villages that were like islands surrounded by seas of woodland, common, moorland and swamp, the dwellings of which were timber-framed, thatched cabins, hearthless and unfloored, containing a single room shared with the animals.

The seaman had only the ship's cat to share such quarters as he could find. But in the numerous smaller ships, single-decked and with the main portion of the hull packed with freight, with fish loaded in an Irish port, with salt, canvas and wool from England, fruit and sugar from Spain, wine in barrels from France, timber from the Baltic, there would have been little space left for the crew other than on deck or under the poop and fo'c'sle. But here at least he was better off than his Viking forerunners, for whom there was neither poop nor fo'c'sle. The seaman had his chest and his bed, the latter item being especially mentioned in the Laws of Oleron; though perhaps for 'bed' should be read 'bedding', which might be spread wherever a few planks of vacant deck could be found that were not under a leak. Though in later medieval vessels some permanent cabins were constructed for the ship's master or a passenger of importance, there were no crew's quarters as such.

The food for a voyage was mainly meat and fish salted in barrels, with bread provided in the hardtack form, also sometimes in barrels, and beer or wine; in English vessels there would be beer for the outward voyage and wine if returning from a continental port. While coasting there would be more fresh stores, and even, as one report has it, 'egys and botter'; and amongst real delicacies were included leeks. But even ashore in those times fresh meat was a luxury, and between harvests a penny's worth of mussels were a feast. The provision list for Southern ships on longer voyages would include salt, flour, rice, vinegar, olive oil, syrup, cheese, almonds, figs, dried fish and salt meat and the usual hard ship's biscuit. Fowl and pigs might be brought on board for killing at sea.

The seaman, absorbed in an intense specialization that likewise produced just a living, had his back turned on his brothers of the soil, yet in some ways he remained close to the land. The medieval fisherman had hands equally for the net or the plough according to the season; but for other classes of seafarer the later seamen's dream of going ashore and buying a farm would have seemed uninteresting. He was too well acquainted with his brother, the husbandman – and in a world that consisted mainly of country, there were no urban yearnings for rural life.

Goodwin lightship – *circa* 1860

The lighthouse
at Ostend – 1814

The employer and employee antithesis was not strong in Northern seafaring, society at sea being too artless to have discovered the delicate arts of class distinction. The Laws of Oleron range from the brutality that a pilot who lost his ship should be hanged, to the ruling that a weather-bound ship's master should discuss with the crew whether or not he should again set sail and accept the opinion of the majority. In medieval seafaring there was great equality between master and man, between ship's master and seaman (who may have owned part of the ship or cargo), a custom that became lost in the backstreets of civilization.

167

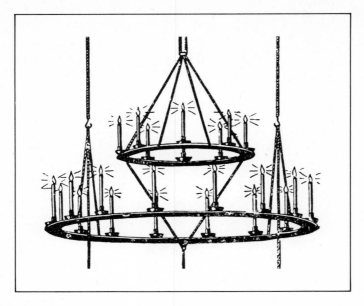

Smeaton's Chandelier

Future ages were to produce press-gangs to man the ships-of-war and periods when seagoing was reasonably described by Dr Samuel Johnson as a bad alternative to going to gaol, but from the evidence it is reasonable to conclude that the medieval seamen of northern Europe may not have found their world so bad. It has, however, to be realized that historians have given much more attention to the husbandman's than the seaman's lot.

Let us look at the medieval seaman as he was equipped in the days just before he set off westward and southward to open up the dark oceans. He had that master tool of Western civilization, the three-masted, square-rigged ship, still in its earliest form, but with the divided sail plan which in association with the stern rudder was able to assure a degree of weatherliness, control and manœuvrability under normal seagoing conditions. The masting and rigging now had a strength superior to those of the Roman corn-ship, though the medieval seaman's vessel was mainly no larger and usually smaller than the Roman's of 1,200 years before. He had the magnetic compass to give direction, but variation was yet unknown and was to cause him great trouble when he ranged far to the west. He had the chip log, but no log and line to provide an estimate of speed. Latitude might be obtained from the Pole Star, and it was about to be shown that the same might be achieved by using the sun's altitude, once the mariner had instructions about the allowance to be made for the seasonal changes in declination. For the known routes he had some rutters and charts, but otherwise for change in longitude he had to rely upon crude methods of dead reckoning that sometimes produced results of astounding accuracy, but more often the reverse.

Soon the mariner was to sail to where different stars swung over the mastheads and compasses behaved queerly; where no generations of experience had enabled sailing directions to be compiled, and only the knowledge of first principles still confined to the savants could add enough to his sturdy basic seamanship to enable him to find the way. It was desirable, now, that the pilot should know the first four rules of arithmetic. But between the adequate pilot and the savant, who with astronomical and trigonometrical knowledge was providing the new navigational technique, the divide was vast; and so, too, between the adequate pilot and the purely practical seaman and ship's master. Around the coast in the dangerous shipwrecking waters the little square-rigged and still single-masted vessels plied their trade, helped by the leadline, the long memories and good eyesight of their masters, and little else.

Near the mid-fifteenth century an English writer mentioned sailors going to Iceland 'by needle and stone'. A seventeenth-century writer said that the crude floating needle was still in use in Northern waters at that time, and much navigation,

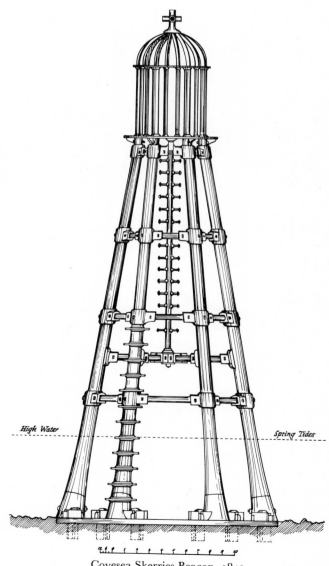

High Water   *Spring Tides*

Covesea Skerries Beacon, 1849

Oostrust. Features of the rig to notice are the spritsail under the bowsprit, the spritsail topsail perilously stepped on the bowsprit, and the lateen mizzen with square topsail

not only coastal, was still by the sounding lead unassisted by chart or magnetic compass. English seamen appear to have adopted a typically sceptical attitude to the clever navigators of the day's *avant-garde*, and Taylor and Richie in their *The Geometrical Seaman* have said that as late as the Elizabethan period Drake was employing Portuguese and Spanish pilots, who would come on board armed with their instruments, sailing directions and charts: 'The Elizabethan seamen scorned the use of charts, or sheepskins as they called them, and would ask the foreign pilot "shooting" the sun whether he had yet struck it!' They were, in fact, very like that twentieth-century trawler skipper who continues unaware amongst the marvels of advancing knowledge.

So it would be a great mistake to imagine that as the Age of Discovery was opening, an effulgent Renaissance dawn was rising over the old art of seagoing, whose practitioners, discarding the crudities of their forebears, embraced new skills and went off to sea enthusiastically flourishing applied science. Celestial navigation formed no part of the master's or pilot's training; mathematics was little taught then; and Samuel Eliot Morison, the modern authority on Columbus, has said of the seamen of the time: 'So simple an operation as applying declination to altitude and subtracting the result from 90° was beyond their powers.'

For most pilots '*l'art & science très subtillez & quasi divine du noble mestier de la mer*' resided largely in a memory stored with past experiences of tides, currents, soundings, the nature of the sea's bottom, and mental images of numerous headlands as they appeared from various bearings and distances. The mathematician Pedro Nuñez, who devised the vernier, which enabled the scale of the quadrant to be read with closer accuracy, writing as late as the sixteenth century condemned with some feeling both the manners and the attainments of seamen: 'Why do we put up with these pilots, with their bad language and barbarous manners; they know neither sun, moon nor stars, nor their courses, movements or declinations; or how they rise, how they set and to what part of the horizon they are inclined; neither latitude nor

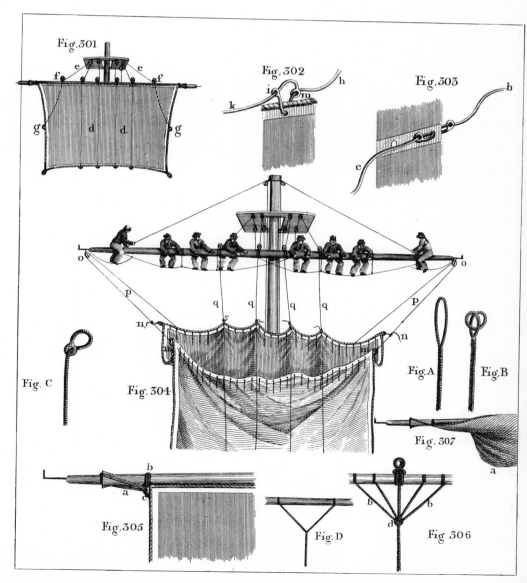

Bending the foresail, etc.

longitude of the places on the globe, nor astrolabes, quadrants, cross-staffs or watches, no years common or bissextile, equinoxes or solstices?'

It is a formidable catalogue of ignorances!

In *English Merchant Shipping 1460–1540* Dorothy Burwash has analysed a few surviving accounts and memoranda kept by shipowners of the period. It may be significant that while compasses, lodestones and sand-glasses figure repeatedly in the lists, astrolabes, cross-staffs and even rutters are not mentioned. However, this does not necessarily mean that these articles were not carried on board; possibly some of the pilots were unlike those castigated by Pedro Nuñez, and provided their own.

The voyages of Columbus, which have been subjected to such detailed historical examination, are suggestive of the conditions of fifteenth-century seamanship, though only of the most ambitious kind in the period. Modern research has tended to minimize the scientific character of Columbus's navigational methods. For example, he did not know how to determine latitude from the sun, but he did use what he thought (sometimes wrongly) was the Pole Star for the purpose, obtaining the altititude with a simple wooden marine quadrant. He did not have a cross-staff; Morison believes that he probably never saw one; also, it is unlikely that he carried an astrolabe except on his first voyage, when it appears to have produced not a single observation. He knew about variation, but not how to allow for it. But variation on his routes was not more than 6 degrees, and in the West Indies was zero.

Out on the ocean, Columbus's knowledge of his position depended upon dead reckoning; that is, upon the continuous recording of speeds maintained over known periods of time and the course sailed during the periods. Course was determined by a magnetic compass with a pivoted needle and no means of damping against the motion of the ship. Gimbals were not yet invented, while the compass card was without numerals or lettering upon it, in the usual style of the day – simply divided into 32 points by triangular markings. Columbus's estimates of speed have been shown to have been highly erroneous, which serves to remind us that here even experienced seamen can be badly mistaken. It is well known how in order to allay the natural apprehensions of his crew as they were carried blindly westward over an ocean they felt might prove to be intermidable, Columbus kept two sets of reckonings, the one he published to the crew being much less than his actual calculation. But it is now apparent that he over-estimated the ship's speed by some 9 per cent, and the phoney estimation of mileage was more nearly correct than the other! In his Journal of the first voyage and under the date Sunday 9 September is written: 'He made fifteen leagues that day [Columbus's league was 4 Roman miles, a league being 3·18 nautical miles] and he determined to reckon less than he made, in order that the crews might thus not become disheartened or alarmed if the voyage were lengthy. In the night he went a hundred and twenty miles, at ten miles an hour, which is thirty leagues. The sailors steered badly, letting her fall off to west by north and even to west-north-west; concerning this the Admiral many times rebuked.'

So we see Columbus grappling with that bugbear of navigation by dead reckoning, inaccurate steering and the consequent difficulty of assessing the mean course. During that night the helmsmen were allowing the *Santa Maria* to wander $22\frac{1}{2}$ degrees off course, while the estimated speed of some 8 knots was good clipping

The flap-surfaced sail

speed for a ship of *Santa Maria*'s length and rig even in free winds, and may have been one of Columbus's over-estimations.

For measuring time Columbus had a supply of sand-glasses which ran through

Wearing under bare poles – scudding

in half an hour, when it was the duty of the ship's boy in the watch to reverse it promptly. But the boy might sleep or be slack, as Columbus often suspected, while the motion of the ship, if fierce, would retard the running of the sand. The effect of this would, as it happens, be to counteract in some degree any over-estimate in the ship's speed when computing the distance sailed. But we see Columbus, and all mariners of his time, dependent upon dead reckoning for determining his position when out of sight of land, while the three elements in the dead reckoning process – the course sailed, the speed and the period of time – were each open to unpredictable and even massive errors.

For plotting his dead reckoning positions Columbus had a chart of the kind described above and dividers, the former with its eastern coastlines – Europe and North Africa, and out to the Azores and Canaries – shown with some accuracy, but with America missing altogether on the western side and the east of Asia grossly misplaced. There were also some hypothetical islands shown; but the chart was at least better than the land maps of the time, whose makers according to Jonathan Swift

> With savage-pictures fill their gaps,
> And o'er unhabitable downs
> Place elephants for want of towns.

174

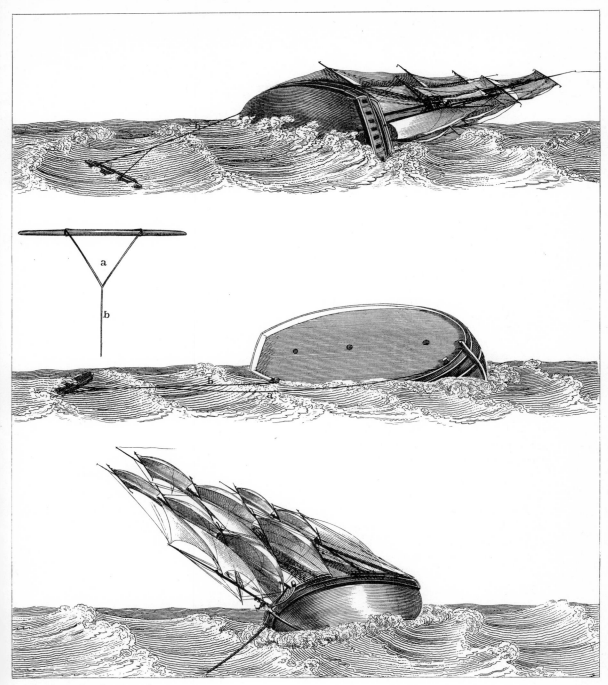

A ship on her beam ends

South Point of Elephant Bay, bearing S. by E. 17 miles. Taken early in the morning when the outline is just visible, and the mountains back of the bay nearly concealed by the fog. Entering the bay you must keep well to the South. When you bear up, take two or three reefs in the topsails, for when you round the point the squalls come over the land with the violence of a gale. Yet apart from this the anchorage is as smooth as a calm, being under the lee of very high hills. The Bay swarms with fish of every description and affords a rare enjoyment both with the sein and line. Anchor a cable and a half from the shore in six fathoms, sandy bottom. The place is not inhabited and the aspect of the country, that of the wildest desolation.

High Red Cliffs to the Northward of Loango, which are distinguished by the mound of trees in the middle

Landfalls, which may provide the seaman's 'moment of truth' – views of the south-west coast of Africa.

For plotting courses when winds forced these to be constantly changed on the return voyages, Columbus had traverse tables. He had leadlines, including some of up to 100 fathoms in length, and frequently used them. Bending two together, he attempted to find bottom in mid-ocean where today we know there to be depths much exceeding 2,000 fathoms. Columbus's celestial navigation was almost invariably unfortunate, a litany of wildly wrong latitudes caused by his mistaking other stars for Polaris. On another occasion, on the homeward passage of the first voyage, we see him again faced by the usual problem of taking star altitudes with a clumsy quadrant. For some days there had been frequent changes of course and he felt uncertain of his dead reckoning, so both astrolabe and quadrant were brought on deck, to achieve nothing, for he was unable to secure a shot from the tossing vessel. Columbus records in his Journal 'he could not take its (Polaris) attitude with the astrolabe or quadrant, as the roll did not permit it'. Then, like those who had sailed the seas of Antiquity, he took an eye shot of the star. It 'appeared very high, as at Cape St Vincent . . .', he wrote. And thus, without an instrument, he gained a fairly accurate idea of his latitude.

178

4

Out to the Oceans

The Phoenicians *may* have sailed anti-clockwise round Africa; they *may* have reached northward as far as Britain, and out into the Atlantic to the Azores. These achievements, or possible achievements, of ancient seafaring cannot be proved, but they are not improbable. That the Phoenicians ever pressed far to the north of Britain or westward beyond the Azores or even to America must be set among the improbabilities; certainly had their ships ever carried them to America it is unlikely that they could have returned against the unfavourable winds. And we have to remember also the large, but unsubstantiated, claims made for the voyages of north European seamen during their Bronze Age period.

Voyages were made down the length of the Red Sea, and southwards round the easternmost point of Africa. India was reached from the Red Sea. The Vikings, we can now have little doubt, reached North America, and may have gone as far south as the Maine coast. Recent support favouring the old claim for the Vikings being the discoverers of America appears in the map found in 1965, which shows Greenland and also an island where America ought to be – the Vinland of the Vikings? If the map is correctly dated as 1448, the claim for the Vikings is much strengthened.

The first rounding of Africa and crossing of the Atlantic encouraged no successors and left no legacy of knowledge. They were events lost to the awareness of medieval seafaring. But then, at the close of the Middle Ages in the brief span of thirty-six years (1486–1522) or about half a lifetime, a series of ocean voyages was made in quick succession, breath-taking in comparison to the slow-moving centuries of semi-mythical exploits before them. True our more certain knowledge of this period may add to the impressiveness of these feats, yet these voyages did differ from all previous ones in that not only was each a tremendous venture, but it opened a door on to the oceans through which the many followed in a process that is still continuing.

The geography known by enlightened people in the mid-fifteenth century was far removed from reality and so bewilderingly different to what was known at the end of the century that even modern man accustomed to the rush of change, must sympathize.

After some 2,000 years of debate, the educated now accepted that the world was round, but there were widely varied opinions about the size of the spheroid world. People's ideas about the shape of its land masses were essentially Ptolemaic, and so rather more than 1,000 years old. There was no America. Africa reached southwards in the vast and spreading broadness of the unknown to merge with the great southern *terra incognita* that extended from Africa to Asia and made a lake of the Indian Ocean, in which India was hardly a promontory and Ceylon an enormous island.

179

Dutch *kuff*

There was, of course, no Pacific, nor any room for one on a globe so much of which was occupied by the land masses of Europe, Africa and Asia. The area of the oceans was much under-estimated. Had seamen been aware of the distances they must sail perhaps they would not have set out so blithely. We are concerned with their voyages only in so far as they reflect the expanding capabilities of seamanship.

In 1487 Bartolemo Dias sailed south from Lisbon and found the southern extremity of the African continent, thus crowning the efforts of earlier Portuguese mariners who had been pressing further and yet further south. He rounded the Cape of Storms, which on his return was tactfully renamed the Cape of Good Hope. Five years later on a night of high winds, Columbus with his squadron was rushing down on what he did not know was a lee shore until he saw a light 'like a little wax candle rising and falling'. The light may have been imaginary, but shortly afterwards the moonlit squadron had come in sight of the coral island now called San Salvador.

The year 1498 saw doings that would have appeared marvellous beyond reason to a seaman of one generation earlier. In this year Vasco da Gama, having sailed from Lisbon, rounded the Cape of Good Hope, worked up the East African coast to Mombasa and then crossed to India with the monsoon that had carried earlier mariners thither from the Red Sea. Columbus made his third crossing of the South Atlantic, taking a more southerly course than hitherto; he sailed with six ships in the week of May that saw Vasco da Gama reach Calicut. Also in that May John Cabot sailed from Bristol, England, with five ships on his second voyage across the Atlantic, both the end and object of which are uncertain. He was presumably not trying to find a north-west passage to Asia, since he did not know America existed and believed that when he had made a landfall in the previous year (somewhere between the southern coast of Labrador and Nova Scotia) he was in Asia; only where was the great civilization, the silk, spices, seaports and trade? The end of the expedition is also a mystery: it is not known whether any of the ships returned, but considered unlikely that all five failed to do so.

1498 was a particular year and one of the most memorable in the history of Europe. It was the year of expansion in which a Portuguese found a route to Asia by sea and the Spaniards and English made the accidental, and at the time unsatisfactory, discovery of a new world apparently much poorer than the old. Seamanship had never impinged upon the destiny of man so powerfully. Disinterested

Dutch *sneck*

Gustaf III. A Swedish East Indiaman setting out, 1807

exploration played the smallest part in the triumphs of seamanship at this time or, indeed, for centuries to come:

> Home is the sailor, home from sea;
> His far-borne canvas furled
> The ship pours shining on the quay
> The plunder of the world.

Seamanship was practised, as hitherto, for money. Why else should practical men take such risks, and imaginative men risk such fortunes? Asia and profit were the goals of the voyages of 1498, just as they had been of those undertaken earlier and for years to come.

The small size of the ships in which the great Renaissance voyages were made are often held up to wonder. In fact they were some of the best ships for their purpose available, for in those days expeditions were often backed generously in the financial terms of the period.

We are approaching the time when ships began growing rapidly in size and in the elaboration of their rig, as they have done ever since. Some that were put afloat were the wonders of their day, but their ever increasing size was due to prestige rather than sound seamanship. The *Great Michael* of 1511 may have had a length from stem-head to stern-post of 240 feet, and the Swedish *Elefant* (1532) is believed to have been about the same length. They were thus some two and a half times the length of the Roman corn-ships. But size need not mean oceangoing ability.

Little is known individually about the ships of the early oceanic voyagers because the vessels were ordinary small merchant ships of the period, remarkable only in what they achieved. The *Santa Maria* is believed to have been some 95 feet overall, and Columbus disliked her not only for her dull sailing qualities but because he believed her draught was too large for exploration. He lost her on his first Christmas day in the New World, when she ran aground. His favourite ship in the squadron was *Niña*, a smaller craft of about 70 feet overall. Magellan's ship *Trinidad*, in which he was to become the first circumnavigator in 1519, was about 75 feet overall and perhaps 21 feet in beam. The *Golden Hind* (formerly named *Pelican*) in which Francis Drake circumnavigated in 1577 was again about 75 feet in length, and she was the largest of the squadron. Her tonnage was about 100; other ships in the squadron were of 80, 50 and 30 tons. The *Golden Hind* was about half the length of some of the larger ships involved in the battle between the British fleet and the Spanish Armada in 1588. For comparison, it might be added that the length of a three-masted trading cog of about the middle of the fifteenth century might be about 100 feet, and that of the stately trading carracks 100–135 feet overall. John Cabot's three-masted *Matthew* was a typical small trading vessel. From the Bristol Customs Records one may gather an impression of the busy passage-making of such an ordinary little ship in the course of her routine service. On 20 December 1503 *Matthew* was reported as leaving Bristol for Ireland. On 5 May 1504 she returned to Bristol from Ireland, having, we may guess, been coasting there after discharging her original cargo. On 13 June

Entering Ostend
Harbour, 1814

she sailed for Bordeaux, whence she returned on 12 August, only to sail again a little more than a fortnight later for Spain. There is no Odyssey here, yet in a few humdrum trading voyages the little ship may have sailed further than Ulysses.

We should look in some detail at this small type of three-masted ship that had become the instrument for opening up the hitherto mysterious oceans. There were three masts and five sails: main course, forecourse, lateen mizzen, main topsail and spritsail. The rig was now both divided and balanced, split into units disposed so that the sails might be trimmed to produce a directional equilibrium without the use of excessive helm under average conditions. Contrast it with that of the Roman corn-ship of the second century A.D., which had a hull longer and heavier than many of the three-masted ships of the fifteenth and sixteenth centuries, but with the sail plan split into two units only, one relatively small, set on two masts, so that good balance was impossible.

The chief source of drive in the ship-rigged medieval vessel was the main course, very much larger than the other sails, set on a mast longer perhaps than the ship and with a yard exceeding the length of the keel. There would be two bonnets for this sail, whose size shows how it was devised from the single sail of the earlier northern ships. The value of the other additional sails was out of proportion to their areas. The lateen mizzen was a crucial unit of this rig. Exactly as introduced from the Mediterranean, it brought to the rig a fore-and-aft element that was of the greatest value for manœuvrability and for keeping the hull up to the wind when the main course was trimmed round and hardened with the usual bowlines led to the bowsprit. The forecourse was a relatively small sail, the partner of the mizzen. The 'sprit-sail', which is spelt thus to distinguish it from the fore-and-aft sail about to come into prominence and known as 'spritsail', was an innovation. Up to date the bowsprit

Rotterdam. Note that two topsails are the only square sails set

Frederica of Gefle, 1852

had never carried a sail, but now it was crossed by a yard beneath it on which a square sail was set, faintly reminiscent of the Roman *artemon*, which augmented the forecourse in producing equilibrium between the fore-and-aft canvas. It is possible that the sail first came into use in the two-masted ships which initially carried only a main course and lateen mizzen. The lack of counterbalancing sail forward would have been an obvious fault, which the sprit-sail on the hitherto sail-less bowsprit helped to mitigate. Later, or at the same time, the addition of the foremast and fore-course remedied this defect. The spritsail, set beneath the bowsprit and close to the water, was not an ideal spread of canvas, being liable to pick up the waves: the triangular fore-staysail, which was to become so important to the performance of the square rig had possibly not yet been devised and certainly was uncommon. Later, of course, this fore-and-aft element additional to the lateen which was already an established part of the basic square rig, contributed most to increasing the efficiency of that rig. The square topsail was important for additional drive rather than balance.

There was now considerably more gear than in the single-masted ship. The lifts and braces of the main yard were repeated on the foreyard; likewise its sheets and bowlines, while the spritsail also had its pair of sheets. Owing to the width of the mainsail, the sheets and the braces, which were tackles running through single

Shipping in the Thames Estuary

blocks giving a power of two – disregarding friction – had usually to be led in through the hull planking, while the falls led aft to where they could be handled, thus further increasing friction. Sheets for the main topsail had to be led through blocks placed towards the outer ends of the main yard, and thence back to the mast and down to the deck. Excluding the gear for the lateen mizzen, there were thus four pairs of sheets and three sets of braces (assuming that the main topsail had no braces for its yard) required for trimming the sails, and also the bowlines. For the lateen mizzen there were braces close to the upper end of the yard, and a topping lift of several parts leading from bridles on the spar, with the hauling parts led forward to the mainmast and down to the deck; there was also the tackle at the heel of the spar, which had to carry so much weight once the sail was full of wind.

When the main halyard was let go and the yard and sail came down – provided always there was no jam anywhere in ropes that swelled with the wet and blocks which twisted on their rope strops – other gear was required for gathering in the sail, and to get down the yard the lifts had also to be let go. To lower the main course, one group of men would cast off the halyard, another ease away on the yard topping

186

lifts, while a third would haul down on the clew lines, which led from the two lower corners of the square sail up to a block on the yard and thence down to the deck. This would draw the sail up the yard. Then, to gather in the bunt of the sail there were martinets, later known as leech lines, leading from a little way above the mid-point of each leech up to the yard and down again through a block, these helping to keep control of the sail as the canvas flogged with the lowering of the yard. With the yard partly lowered, members of the crew would be climbing the ratlines and going out along the yard to pass gaskets round the canvas and make a tight bundle of it.

The standing rigging necessary to support the spars had inevitably increased in elaboration compared with the single-masted ship. For the lateral support of the mainmast there might be from five to thirteen shrouds on each side, depending on the size of ship, with correspondingly lesser numbers for the main and mizzen. Their multiplicity reflected the need to spread the load of the mast when under a pressure of sail, for the shrouds were of highly stretchable rope, with great stretch, too, in the lanyards by which each shroud was set up through deadeyes.

Here the practices of the seamen of the North and Mediterranean differed. The latter did not use deadeyes but block and tackles for setting up the shrouds, and the shrouds were not rattled down in the Northern fashion. There was instead a rope ladder abaft the mast for going aloft. There were forestays for the main and mizzen, the latter leading from close beneath the top (the lookout's perch) to near the heel of the foremast, the former to the bowsprit.

The single-masted, square-rigged ship, descendant of the medieval cog and her kind, continued to sail, but even among smaller craft the addition of masts and sails was common by the mid-sixteenth century, and topsails and studding sails became not unusual. In the Mediterranean and on the Portuguese and Spanish Atlantic coasts, where Arab influence persisted, lateen-rigged craft with from one to three

English type of brig

masts remained the principal coasting vessels, generically known as caravels (*caravela*).

One weakness of the lateen rig was that the tremendous length of yard required for a large sail, automatically limited the size of the ship itself. This was circumvented by adding extra masts, but while the two- and three-masted lateen-rigged caravel (*caravela latina*) with its close-winded qualities and ability to eat into the wind, was accepted as the best coasting vessel and also made some of the pioneer trading and exploring voyages down the West African coast, square elements began to appear in the lateen rig, as lateen elements had joined the Northern square rig, to produce a better oceangoing vessel. The lateen paid heavily for the weatherliness conferred by the long, rigid leading edge of its swaying yard. In coastal waters handling a two-masted lateener, hoisting the sails, tacking, furling the sails up to the yard, were operations that one acute Western observer recommended 'as an experience likely to bring life to any jaded soul seeking sensation'.

The ships which Prince Henry of Portugal – 'The Navigator' – sent on the series of voyages southwards along the coast of Africa, which culminated after his death in Vasco da Gama's voyage to India by this route, were probably two-masted lateeners, though the later ships may have had three lateens. But after this various combinations of square and lateen sails were evolved, ships carrying square rig on the foremast with lateen main and mizzens, or permutations of square and lateen on four masts. These ships were logical efforts to combine the advantages of the square rig when running down wind in deep water with the close-windedness of the lateen for coastal work.

Caravels were built or converted to carry three masts with square rig on the fore and main and a lateen mizzen, *caravela rotunda* as opposed to *caravela latina*. These vessels were thus normal square-rigged ships like the carrack, only smaller and with the caraval's finer lines and greater speed. Columbus's *Pinta* was a *caravela rotunda* when she sailed on the first voyage, but she may earlier have been converted from a *caravela latina*. Columbus's favourite *Nina* set forth rigged either as a two- or three-masted lateener, but was converted to the ship rig at the Canary Islands. Both *Nina* and *Pinta* were favoured for their sailing qualities under the ship rig, in contrast with the similarly rigged carrack *Santa Maria*.

It may have been in a *caravela latina* that Bartolemo Dias achieved the rounding of the Cape of Good Hope, but Vasco da Gama's vessel was ship rigged; and though explorers leading a small squadron might include in it a *caravela latina* for inshore work, seamen discarded them for ocean work.

As seamen began making all the oceans their parish, they became aware of various new problems of navigation. Underlying them all was that of determining one's position after many days out of sight of land, the old problem now magnified.

Position in the north–south direction might be found, with differing degrees of imprecision, by means of quadrant and cross-staff observations, but there were no means of finding one's east–west position once it had been mislaid; thus, when this occurred, it became a question of whether a safe landfall could be made before disaster overtook one. When land had been dropped astern, knowledge of one's position thereafter depended upon dead reckoning. It is appropriate that this form

of navigation had in its name an undertone of doom only too easily realized. The expression is actually a contraction of 'deduced' reckoning. For generations the deductions he had to make were the harshest test of a navigator's skill.

Dead reckoning is the process of determining a ship's whereabouts by a continuous record of courses steered and distances run on each course, with allowance made for the vessel's leeway and any current. Since all the factors involved in the estimation were subject to errors, sometimes gross, the result of dead reckoning over a prolonged period could be no less drastically wrong. Since the east–west position, or longitude, is a simple function of time – one minute being the equivalent of 15 minutes of longitude – the mariner's problems would have been largely solved had they been provided with a reliable watch. Isaac Newton himself wrote in a tone of some hopelessness about the impossibility of making a timepiece able to maintain accuracy to within a few seconds during the rough-and-tumble, and the temperature and humidity changes of an ocean voyage. 'I could easily give you hundreds of instances in which a vessel's ignorance of her longitude led her to swift destruction . . .', said Rupert Gould when lecturing in London on maritime timekeepers. And he

might have added that there are hundreds more instances hidden in the record of missing ships.

It is too easy to find examples of seamen in unweatherly sailing-ships being lost to their true positions by hundreds of miles after weeks at sea. More impressive an example of the perils inherent in dead reckoning is the error made during less than twenty-four hours in one of the best-charted and best-known seas by navigators who were both well educated and equipped with the finest equipment. During the battle of Jutland (or Skagerrak) in 1916 two parts of the British fleet were about to make a rendezvous in the North Sea having left English ports some 200 miles apart eighteen hours earlier. There had, in the course of those hours, been a number of changes of course and speed by both parts of the fleet, and one section of it had been in action. But the navigation was in the hands of specialists, the ships were the most powerful steam-driven vessels afloat, the weather calm. When the two parts of the fleet made visual touch the combined error in their dead reckoning positions amounted to 10 miles. One part of the fleet was about 4 miles to the south-east of reckoning, the other about 6 miles to the west. That such an error was possible enables us better to appreciate the difficulties confronting earlier mariners.

In the fifteenth and sixteenth centuries the compass was perhaps the most reliable piece of navigator's equipment, though its use was inevitably bedevilled by inaccuracies of steering, due not only to human error but also to the mechanically crude helm arrangements of ships and the uncertainties of courses held during bad weather. There was also the question of compass variation, which became a formidable one as ships began sailing seas where changes in variation were considerable. There were two conflicting ideas about variation: one practical, the other academic – and both wrong. There were seamen who denied that variation existed, and attributed the resulting steering errors to unknown currents and errors in dead reckoning. What could be more reasonable? The more scientifically inclined believed that variation might hold the secret of determining longitude; that it might change in some regular and ultimately predictable manner with longitude. Nothing might seem more reasonable than this, too. And what a tidy scientific solution it was! Such ideas persisted until about 1620, and, meanwhile, the course indicated by the compass remained subject to doubt.

The traverse board enabled some record of the doubtful courses steered to be kept. The board showed the 32 points of the compass, and along the rhumb of each point were eight holes to take a wooden peg, radiating outwards and representing each half-hour of a four-hour watch. The eight pegs indicated the mean course steered during half-hour tricks at the helm. It was the navigator's problem to interpret these judgements in terms of northing–southing and easting–westing, bearing in mind that while his cross-staff observations might serve as a check on his dead reckoning in the north–south direction he had none for easting and westing. The pegged recordings of courses and times on the traverse board could be converted

Left
The search for economy in the early
19th century led to better lines and
greater speed

into distances made good to the northward or southward by means of tables provided in the sailing manuals, but it was not until some time in the sixteenth century that similar tables were provided for easting and westing. By the latter half of the sixteenth century the use of the traverse board appears to have become fairly common in ships which were not 'caping' (i.e. sailing within sight of land from cape to cape).

Coasting voyages might include considerable periods out of sight of land, such as one from Portugal to the North Sea, when a ship would be driven to make a sweep out into the Atlantic in the face of the prevailing northerlies. On such passages ships might still be without any form of chart – the British continued to despise their use – and dead reckoning and an alert lookout was all that could keep them off the shore when the ship was put about to work towards the land again. William Bourne in his *A Regiment for the Sea*, published in 1574, wrote: 'I would not any seaman should be of the opinion that they might get any longitude with instruments, but (according to their accustomed manner) let them keep a perfit accompt and reckoning of the way of their shippe, whether the shippe goeth to leewards, or maketh her way good, considering always what things be against them or with them: as tides, currents, winds or such like. . . .'

Compasses began to be mounted on gimbals during the late fourteenth and early fifteenth centuries, and were illuminated at night. At some time in the later fifteenth century the lubber's line made its appearance on the bowl of the compass – a short vertical line which, when the compass was in the binnacle, was precisely on the fore-and-aft line of the ship. The coincidence of the lubber's line and a point on the compass card indicated the course being steered. The lubber's line, which became to later generations as familiar a part of the compass as the card itself, reflected the growing size and elaboration of ships, in which the helmsman might himself be unable to see and line up the masts or stem-head with the point of the compass on which he was meant to be steering. An element of precision was thus entering into the techniques of the mariner, but so slowly in that age of dawdling change and leaving so much in the arena of huge and often tragic imprecision, that the flair and instinct of the experienced, intelligent, but probably most unacademic ship's master or navigator remained the best assurance of safe conduct afloat.

It was not until some time in the latter part of the sixteenth century that there was any better method of measuring speed than experienced judgement or the Dutchman's log. While, as the poet suggested, long experience may attain to something like prophetic strain, it is certain that navigators with long familiarity of assessing speeds were able to make great errors. This was inevitable when so many and various conditions might be encountered, including the times of severe weather and darkness during which an estimate of mean speed would be beyond the most seasoned judgement. The Dutchman's log was no more than any small floating object thrown overboard and timed during its passage between two marked points along the length of the ship a known distance apart. A simple multiplication would then give the speed. But with no watch available for determining the time, and with

the sand-glass unsuitable for such work, usually rhythmical counting had to be resorted to for measuring time. The few navigators who possessed one would have used a watch, which, however useless for keeping time over long periods, would at least have been capable of measuring periods lasting only for a minute or so. All measurements involved in navigation were widely approximate. In the Peabody Museum, Salem, Massachusetts, there is a Dutchman's log-timer, but this is no more than a brass tobacco box with various charming but irrelevant engravings on it, including what is believed to be the head of Amerigo Vespucci, and a table for converting times into speeds, though with no great precision. 'But it sufficeth our Seamen to find the way [i.e. speed] of their ship in Leagues or Miles.' This was written in 1624, while the log-timer which was made by Pieter Holm, who ran a navigation school in Amsterdam, is dated 1729, or about a century and a half after the invention of the log and line, or chip log.

The latter passed through various developments, and in its ultimate form provided a means of determining accurately the speed of sailing-ships. The chip was a billet of wood weighted to float upright and so offer resistance to the water. It was attached to a light line and thrown overboard astern while the line was allowed to run out for a fixed period. Then the line was hauled in and the length run out measured in fathoms, assumed to be equal to the width of the arms' stretch. Such initial crudities were refined. A half-minute sand-glass was used for measuring time, and knots were tied in the line at intervals of 7 fathoms, or 42 feet. A stray line was attached to the log billet itself with no knots in it, and this was allowed to run out first so that the billet was 20–30 fathoms astern of the ship and in relatively un-disturbed water before the first knot passed over the rail and measurements began. The number of knots going outboard during the timed period was then assumed to be the speed of the ship in nautical miles per hour, a nautical mile being regarded as the length of a minute of latitude.

Several typical navigational approximations were involved here, reasonable enough when set among all the other unavoidable ones. The implicit assumption was that the distance between the knots bore the same relation to a nautical mile as the measured time bore to an hour. The nautical mile was measured with con-siderable accuracy in the middle of the seventeenth century under the direction of Colbert, and was found to be 6,111 English feet. Owing to the plane of a meridian being slightly oval, a minute of arc varies between 6,046 feet at the equator to

Admiral
Cunningham's
telescope

Opposite page
Harrison's number
one timepiece

6,109 feet at the poles. Conventionally the nautical mile is now considered to be 6,080 feet, or the mean of the two measurements. But if a log line with knots spaced at 42-foot intervals was run out for half a minute, the relationship between time and distance was not accurately preserved. The distance was too short.

In the early part of the seventeenth century there were suggestions for reknotting the line, but in the latter part of the eighteenth century the old line was still often used, while many sailors – particularly, it appears, those of Spain and Portugal – did not even use log and line, but still stuck to the old empirical methods of judging speed. Eventually the knots were spaced at 47·25 feet and a 28-second sand-glass used, which is the correct proportion for a nautical mile of 6,080 feet. But while seamen were moving slowly towards acceptance of this, a ship's speed over any length of time, like her course, was never more than an approximation. In the first quarter of the seventeenth century, some traverse boards had an extra space provided for pegging the speed for each half-hour of the watch, the speeds being derived from log and line measurements made at longer intervals, perhaps two-hourly.

With longitude depending upon the erratic evidence of dead reckoning, navigators evolved a technique which was employed until at last the chronometer was produced in the eighteenth century. This was to sail to the latitude of the ship's destination, which it was possible to determine at sea and, having reached it, to proceed east or west along that latitude. All that was necessary to know, having reached the required latitude, was on which side of the intended landfall the ship was. If the destination was a small island, the initial courses would be arranged to bring the ship well to the east or west of it so there could be little doubt on this score. The procedure, both of sailing to the latitude and then sailing along it, had to be

Lienen off Naples, January 1865

Bahrain pearling
dhow – 20th
century

modified to allow the ship to make the best use of the prevailing winds. This process
of running the easting or westing down further added to the length of sea voyages,
already liable to be made considerably longer than the direct course by foul winds.

The working of the tides was an everlasting preoccupation of the seaman who
operated inshore, and grounding owing to faulty prediction a continual hazard. And
it was not only the oceangoing seamen who suffered from lack of timepieces in the
days when there might not even be a town clock in the ports (if there were one it
would probably be in error by an hour or more, for which reason it was most
sensibly equipped with only one hand!). In the thirteenth century the monks of
St Albans produced a tide-table giving the times of high water at London Bridge in
terms of each day of the moon's age, but such compilations could not help seamen
without a clock.

It became the practice to keep a record of the compass bearing of the full and
new moon at the moment of high water at various ports. This information was known
as the 'establishment' (rule) of the port. There would be two bearings for every
port, indicating the morning and evening tides. For Dover the establishment was
north and south, making high water during full and change at noon and midnight,
which is in good agreement with modern tide-tables. At other phases of the moon
the time of high water had to be worked out from the daily retardation of the tide,
which was approximated as three-quarters of an hour in the twenty-four hours.

Working the tides, or 'tiding over' was an art and often it was itself enough to
enable ships to work down Channel from the continental or English coasts – down
that 'Sleeve', as it was called, where the prevailing south-westerly winds lay in the
teeth of ships bound round Finisterre or out over the Atlantic. A ship might leave

The octant, which followed the back-staff and preceded the sextant, each representing further refinements in measuring altitudes

the Downs, a roadstead off the coast of Kent just south of the Thames Estuary, encouraged by a favourable SE. wind just abaft the beam, which would carry her to a point where perhaps the Isle of Wight, showing darkly through mist, lay to starboard; there the wind would turn into the familiar westerly quarter, dead foul. And thus it might remain for some days, while the ship, unable to sail closer to the wind than some 75 degrees and faced by the short, steep seas, would be unable to make good any distance to windward while the tide was foul. Progress was only possible by anchoring while the flood tides ran, getting up the anchor as the ebb started and beating to windward against wind and sea, making little to windward through the water, but mercifully being carried, though slowly, on the huge body of the ebb until the slackening tide and the young flood made it necessary to anchor once more. These were the conditions that made 'down Channel' too often synonymous with discomfort, delay and frustration.

The three-masted vessel, having five sails all square but for the lateen mizzen, was the prototype of the northern oceangoing ship which in a process of continuous change became the square-rigged ship of the end of the sailing era. Initially, the

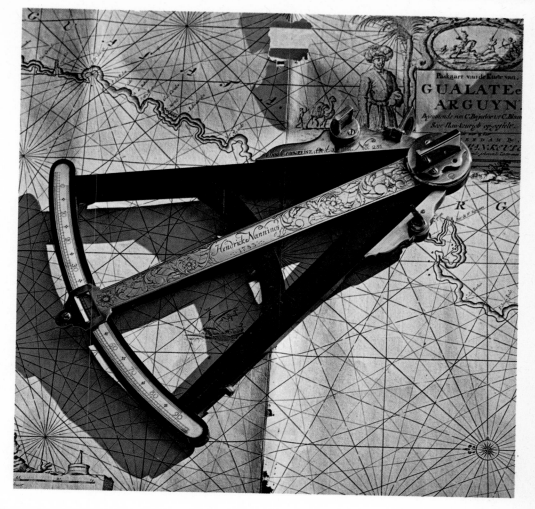

main course, direct descendant of the one sail of the single-masted ship, was much the largest in area, the other sails being in the nature of auxiliaries. Then the size of the forecourse and main topsail were proportionately increased to give a more nearly equal division of the rig. With increase in size of ship came additional sails, thus avoiding intractable size in any one sail. But inevitably each additional sail had to be attended by lines and tackles to handle it, and by standing rigging to support the increased sparring, and this meant more complication.

A new sail to appear was, logically, a fore topsail to match the main topsail, but it may have been before this that a second mizzen mast was added, the bonaventure mizzen, which also carried a single lateen sail. The three-masted vessel with five sails thus grew into a four-masted vessel with seven sails. Bonnets were now fitted to the foresail and sometimes to the spritsail as well. To take the sheet off the bonaventure mizzen it was necessary to fit an outrigger, later known as a bumpkin, over the stern, a spar also found sometimes in three-masted ships. By 1540 the biggest of ships, such as the *Henry Grâce à Dieu*, carried an array of sails as numerous and complex as any yet set afloat. There was a topgallant on the mizzen, as well as a topsail on the

Out on the yard

bonaventure mizzen. These mizzen topsails were all lateens. Such a rig was, however, freakish. It has been estimated that half this colossal ship's sail area was in her main course. This is an early example of the seaman's love of fancy sails, of setting canvas wherever possible and by means of remarkable ingenuity. We still do not know how the lateen topsails were set. The increasing agglomeration of ropes in these complex rigs must have caused fearsome problems of handling; it was, too, the frequent cause of gear carrying away. The intricate network of running rigging that was accumulating aloft included bowlines for the topsails and possibly the square topgallants as well.

The latter part of the sixteenth century saw the appearance of the sprit-sail topsail, a sail that might seem to be a kite of the most eccentric kind, yet it was to become common. The spritsail topmast stood on a small platform at the extreme end of the bowsprit. The platform carried the shrouds, and the insecure mast was crossed by a yard for the topsail, which can only be described as a curiously un-seamanlike sail to have persisted for more than a century, during which time the seamanlike fore-and-aft fore staysails were being carried. Sir Alan Moore has said that the persistence of this sail can only suggest 'a regard for square canvas that is almost numinous'. Very much more rational were the studding sails, which appear to have been introduced perhaps in the first half of the sixteenth century.

When Philip II of Spain received news of the disaster to his Armada, sent against England in 1588, he is understood to have said: 'I sent my ships to fight the English, and not the wind and the waves', with suitable resignation, adding, 'Praise be to God'.

That the Armada achieved nothing was ultimately due to the weather. This must not disguise the fact that those July and August days of 1588 saw the new and the old ideas of applying seamanship to war in conflict. The old lost, and the lee shore of the Hebridean and Irish coasts, where the Armada's bones were cast, became their graveyard.

The Armada campaign was a revelation of the new seamanship. It was fought only seventeen years after Lepanto, which was a little more than 2,000 years after Salamis. During those two millennia war at sea had been chiefly a matter of galleys, of ramming and boarding and soldiers grappling on the insecure planks of the galleys' decks, all within sight of the shore. Propulsion was by slaves at the oars.

At Lepanto the Marquis of Santa Cruz had commanded the rear of the galley fleet, and in the last stage of the battle had brought up his squadron at a critical moment and completed the victory. It was Santa Cruz who in 1586 made the first plans for the Armada against England, and in the fleet he envisaged were forty galleys. By the time the Armada sailed two years later, all but four of the galleys had been eliminated. It was a revolution in the military ideas of seamen, and it may be regarded as a tribute to the vision of Spain's fighting seamen in the sixteenth century that they dropped the galley, of such honourable antiquity, more readily than soldiers of the twentieth century dropped the horse and adopted the tank. But unfortunately the change of ideas, swift though it was, had come too late.

In so far as the fighting ship had become a sailing-ship it had until 1570 been in the nature of a floating castle manned by soldiers. The revolution in essence was one of sailing seamanship, the production of a sailing-ship with good speed, able to sail closer to the wind, having adequate manoeuvring qualities, and with fighting power independent of soldiery. The fighting galleon that emerged was a finer-lined vessel than the floating castle, with less freeboard and windage, and her offensive power lay in her guns, with which she could fight at some distance, and which were used to their best advantage by the tactics only her good sailing qualities made possible.

Note the spritsail topmast being used simply as a
flagpole; also the lateen yard of the mizzen

This new type of sailing warship had appeared in 1570, having been suggested by Sir John Hawkins, Treasurer of the Royal Navy in England, and in 1587 in Cadiz harbour Sir Francis Drake, with a few galleons armed with ship-killing guns, was able to master a dozen galleys bravely led by Don Pedro de Acuna. The galley may have had a power of free movement denied to any square-rigged sailing-ship; but fragile in construction and unable to bring any broadside fire to bear, the masters of 2,000 years of warfare on sea proved that they were formidable only to other galleys and incapable of dealing with ships carrying heavy guns that could hold them at a distance.

The galley did not pass out of naval warfare in the sixteenth century. In the Mediterranean, so often windless, they fought their last action in 1717. In the sea-going conditions of the Baltic, where coastlines ragged with islands and rocks emphasized the disadvantage of the large square-rigged sailing-ships' lack of free movement, the galley survived as a warship until the late eighteenth century; there were even a few in service at the time of the Russo-Swedish war of 1809. This, however, was the last of oar-power in warfare.

Before Drake had revealed the superiority of the heavy-gunned, manœuvrable sailing-ship, the advisers of Philip II had been expressing their doubts about the ability of war galleys to make the sea voyage from northern Spain to the English Channel. The Armada, as planned by Santa Cruz, was to have had the forty galleys as the spearhead of its fighting power. Then the composition of the fleet was revised, the onus was transferred to the heavily gunned galleons and great ships, but with little time left in which to prepare and without the experience that had led the English to devise the faster and more handy type of galleon, these Spanish ships were inferior to many of those in the opposing fleet. All four galleys which sailed with the Armada failed to reach the Channel. They began straining and leaking in the waves of Biscay, and in a gale off Ushant they finally became separated from the rest. One stranded while making port; the other three just managed to save themselves.

Also with the Spanish fleet were six galleasses. The galleass was an attempt to retain some of the galley's power of free movement while enjoying the sailing ship's endurance and ability under sail. It was a compromise similar to that when ships were given auxiliary engines, though still carrying a considerable area of canvas. Neither had a long life, for the more advanced method of propulsion quickly superseded the other. The galleass had more beam and draught than the galley, thus gaining some of the strength and some of the carrying capacity of the sailing-ship, though losing some of her previous speed and manœuvrability, but she could not carry the effective rig of the sailing-ship. Even in northern Europe fully rigged fighting ships were built with some twenty-eight oars a side.

Originally the term 'galleass' was applied in the Mediterranean to oared-cum-sailing vessels used for carrying freight. These were long-voyage merchantmen in which a return was made to the classical method of handling the oars, these being

Opposite page
The later iron sailing-ships had iron spars, the longest of which weighed 2 tons or more. When storms or squalls inflicted damage, such as the crew of *Tillie E. Starbuck* are here seen clearing away in 1884, it could not be repaired at sea as it would have been in the previous age of wooden ships and wooden spars.

VIS. VIN

The end of the *Herzogin Cecilie*

placed in a single line with several men, up to a total of five, pulling on each. Every summer the great galleasses, more than 150 feet in length, would arrive from Venice and Genoa in such northern ports as Amsterdam and Southampton, loaded with exotic freight from the Orient. With their low, slender hulls six times as long as they were broad, their two-pieced curved lateen yards swaying from two or three masts, they must have looked exotic themselves as they passed among the high-pooped, square-rigged ships and the small, round-ended robust craft which carried spritsails, or perhaps even the new gaff mainsails and the triangular foresails of the newer mode of seagoing. By the end of the seventeenth century the galleys and galleasses which North Sea seamen had so heartily despised 100 years earlier, were on the verge of being accepted in northern Europe; but in the end the earlier view prevailed.

The disappearance of big-oared ships from the main seaways of the world was one of the more comforting developments of seamanship; the realization at last of that vision of the prophet Isaiah, who foresaw his people restored to 'a place of broad rivers and streams wherein shall no galley with oars . . . pass by'. For the Israelites in captivity had known, like uncountable thousands before and after them, the terrible toil of the oars, which was one of the worst inflictions that the sea ever laid upon man. The harnessing of the wind, passing through its phases from crudity to ultimate subtlety, never succeeded in banishing the 'melancholy of the sea'. But it did relieve man of one kind of slavery.

Mention has been made of the ship's master's competence, or incompetence, in matters of navigation. By this time the two classes of 'common navigator' and 'grand navigator' had become accepted. The former might be a master and part owner, or even owner of his ship, though he might be unable to sign his name, but he would be a capable navigator in the old manner, using compass, leadline, perhaps a chart, certainly a memory stocked richly with the prominent marks of the coasts round which he sailed. The grand navigator had knowledge in addition of the basic mathematical and instrumental techniques of what was still the new navigation.

In either case a ship's master had to be more than a navigator of either kind. He was responsible for the safe conduct of the ship and all in it, and the handling of the ship under all conditions, part of which function entailed handling the crew. While there remained much of the medieval egalitarianism between crew and master, especially in the smaller ships, the master's power increased with the scope and importance of the voyages now being regularly made. The organization of a ship's crew became more specialized. In the smallest ships the master might be his own pilot, mate and purser; in the larger these would be separate officers.

Second in command was the mate, or chief mate if two were carried, a man who also might be a part owner of the ship. Ideally he could perform all the functions of the master, and if young would be on his way to becoming a master and at least a common navigator if not already capable of being one.

The bosun was in direct control of the crew, and when no mates were carried he was the second-in-command. He was responsible for the maintenance of the ship and gear, work which, whether performed by a mate or bosun, was the most exacting on board. Xenophon once described the internal management of a Phoenician merchant ship. His description shows how close the seafaring of the fifth century B.C. was to that of the fifteenth, sixteenth and seventeenth centuries A.D.

'I think that the best and most perfect arrangement of things which I ever saw was when I went to look at the great Phoenician sailing vessel; for I saw the largest amount of naval tackling separately disposed in the smallest stowage possible. I have never seen gear so well arranged, or so many coils of rope and tackles stowed so neatly. A ship needs a large number of spars and warps when she enters port or puts to sea; much rigging when under sail, and contrivances to protect her against enemy craft. She carries a stand of arms for the crew, and each mess needs a set of household utensils. In addition she carries a cargo which the captain sells for profit. All gear necessary for these several functions was contained in a small store not more than fifteen by twelve feet. I noticed that each article was so neatly stowed that it was

Departure of an English East Indiaman

The paddle steamer *Caroline*. Here sail and power are
approximately equal partners in the propulsive scheme

ready to hand; it had not to be searched for, and there was nothing to cast off and
cause delay when anything was needed in a hurry. I found that the bosun knew each
particular locker so well that he could, even when on deck, say exactly where everything was stowed and how much there was of it. I saw this man in his off-duty time
carefully inspecting all the stores most likely to be needed. I asked him why he did
this. "Sir," he said, "I am looking to see that all the gear is properly stowed, nothing
foul, nothing missing. For when God sends a storm at sea there is no time to look for
what is needed or clearing it if foul. God threatens and punishes careless sailors and
you are lucky if you escape with your lives. You are fortunate if, even with good
seamanship, you arrive safe in port.'''

The intricate character of the Renaissance sailing-ship meant that the Renaissance bosun or mate needed to be even more methodical and pay even greater
attention to detail than his predecessor.

Other ranks on board ship were the quartermaster, who was not himself the
helmsman but supervised the steering, being the link between the perhaps totally
illiterate and tough rather than intelligent hand at the helm and the compass and
steering generally. Big enough ships, such as the well-manned carracks and their
later counterparts, carried a purser, who was the representative of the owner, and

performed the commercial tasks which in smaller vessels would fall to the captain. The office of pilot might be that performed today; but the pilot might also be the member of the crew responsible for navigation throughout the voyage. In naval vessels, where officers might be gentlemen rather than seamen, the pilot's situation was not unequivocal.

Seamen in all ranks tended to be young, perhaps because 'few grew to grey hairs'. As far as inevitably chance statistics can reveal – statistics not providing what in the mathematics of probability we would now regard as a good random sample – we find in the fifteenth and sixteenth centuries the greatest numbers of seamen in the age group between twenty and thirty, while those who rose to the rank of master did so between thirty and forty, if not earlier.

With their multiplicity of gear, cumbersome, grinding with friction, and with only inefficient, low-powered tackles to provide any mechanical advantage, and so many operations – even under the simplest of three-masted rigs of five sails – requiring simultaneous attention when manœuvring, ships were greedy for man-power. Despite the fact that on shore unemployment and poverty were general, no country had enough seamen, while it would seem that the ordinary seamen, those Sons of Martha of the days when indifference to the general well-being was the habit of society, did not have the strength and resilience of those who are cared for and well fed. The skeletons recovered from the Swedish warship *Wasa* (1628) when she was raised from the bottom of Stockholm harbour revealed a smallness of stature and proneness to disease we have no reason to believe was other than widespread among seamen at the time.

In those days the sea was a wild, lawless place where pirates abounded and ships had to be manned for self-defence. On the longer voyages a ship's complement had to be large enough to withstand the appalling wastage due to accident and illness. To go to sea undermanned was, according to a contemporary, 'perilous and foolish thrift'.

The Romans had ranked seamen as the lowest of social classes. In this respect conditions had improved, though the fact that sailing-ships were so hungry for man-power attracted to them many of the footloose and downright bad. They drew, too, from the closed fishing communities, which were to remain so stubbornly apart even when fishing was done in steam and subsequently motor vessels. When in non-Catholic countries the old faith that restricted the Christian's diet to fish through all the forty days of Lent, became a memory regretted or damned, the eating of fish had to be encouraged by more secular means in order to maintain the reserve of seamen that these fishing communities were. By then, however, seamanship had become a means of getting on in the world. Seagoing was a career open to talent. Respectability and more were to be had from the sea.

Early in the sixteenth century those who were opening the ocean ways encountered a new obstacle which was to remain for the next 300 years the curse of all long sea voyages.

After a period at sea that might be as long as six months or as short as six weeks, men would find that patches of their skin were becoming as 'hard as wood', and then turning pimply and bleeding. They would have pains that were the result of internal

A three-masted ship with the fore and main courses
clewed up in the bunt and the spanker brailed into the
mizzen-mast and yard.

bleeding. Their gums would swell and blacken, their teeth become loose. After a
period, during which an increasing sense of exhaustion would lead to total incapacity,
death would come perhaps in the form of a heart attack. The disease – scurvy –
which so easily might be fatal without treatment, could in fact be cured quite simply;
but for 300 years there was no general agreement on what the correct treatment
might be. During this time more naval seamen died from scurvy than were killed in
action, and ships might be lost because they did not have enough fit men left to
handle them. In Anson's voyage round the world, after a year at sea 626 of the ships'
crews totalling 961 had died, and after crossing the Pacific there were only 71 able-
bodied men in the single ship that remained of the fleet.

Detail of the forecourse

DE HAVEN VAN OOSTENDE.

H.M.S. 'BASILISK'
(Common paddle)
Length extreme
190 feet
Breadth extreme
34 feet 5 inches
Tonnage 1030 tons
Power 400 h.p.
Armament 6 guns
Engines by Messrs
Miller Ravenhill
& Co.

Towing stern to stern each vessel exerting her utmost power in opposite directions.
This trial of power between the paddle wheel and screw

It was scurvy rather than storms that became the terror of long sea passages. Earlier seamen, when ships were unable to remain for long periods at sea, were spared that at least. Columbus had no scurvy on his voyages, but it has been authoritatively said that between 1500 and 1800 no extended sea voyage escaped the curse, and it attacked seamen frequently during the nineteenth century also. It has not been unknown in the twentieth.

We are now aware that scurvy is a deficiency disease caused by lack of ascorbic acid in the diet. It so happened that seamen's rations tended to be lacking in the foods containing ascorbic acid. In the British Navy the official scale of rations per head per week between 1622 and 1825, comprising 7 gallons of beer, 2 pounds salt

H.M.S. 'NIGER'
(Smith's screw)
Length extreme
194 feet 4 inches
Breadth extreme
34 feet 8 inches
Tonnage 1072 tons
Power 400 h.p.
Armament 14 guns
Engines by Messrs
Maudslay Sons
& Field

took place in the English Channel on 20 June 1849,
and lasted one hour, in which time the *Niger* towed the
Basilisk at the rate by patent log of 1·466 knots per hour

pork, 4 pounds salt beef, 6 ounces butter, 12 ounces cheese, 3 pints of oatmeal, 2 pints dried peas, contained no ascorbic acid at all. In addition, the seaman's life was one liable to cause rapid absorption of the acid which is accelerated by overwork and exhaustion.

By the end of the sixteenth century there was a certain awareness that such fruits as oranges and lemons and such vegetables as lettuce and watercress were excellent anti-scorbutics, yet even by the end of the following century there was still no general agreement about the cure. It was in 1697 that the British Physician to the Fleet said, 'this is a disease left without a remedy at sea'. Admiral Rodney's fleet in the West Indies, where the anti-scorbutics grew in profusion ashore, had in 1781 a sick list of

1600, mainly scurvy cases, out of a total strength of 12,000 men. Among the cures used for scurvy were an aromatic sulphuric acid known as 'elixir of vitriol', which contained no ascorbic acid, and Captain Cook, who is commonly regarded as the seaman who conquered scurvy, believed it was best countered by plentiful fresh water and personal cleanliness. That Cook's long voyages in the Pacific were remarkably free from scurvy was largely due to the unrecognized virtues of the provisions he obtained. On the way out during the second voyage, Cook's ships *Resolution* and *Adventure* lay for a time in Table Bay: 'During this stay the crews of both ships were served every day with fresh beef or mutton, new-baked bread, and as much greens as they could eat.' The last was crucial, and the year was 1772.

But lying off Cape Town in the previous year Cook had encountered a more typical situation: 'An English East Indiaman sailed for the port of London, who had buried above thirty of her crew while she was in India; and at that time had many others severely afflicted with the scurvy. . . .'

During the seventeenth century the Dutch East India Company, after trying and failing to grow such excellent specifics against scurvy as lettuce and watercress on board their ships, made settlements in South Africa where the fresh fruit and vegetables might be raised for delivery to ships that called. But useless remedies

218

The leeboard in a Dutch cutter.
This feature and the rig are both
indicative of efforts to obtain the best
possible degree of weatherliness

continued to be used, none with greater persistence than lime juice. In its fresh state lime juice has a small ascorbic acid content; in its preserved state, as usually taken on board, next to none. Though in 1514 a Dutch physician of Gouda correctly prescribed scurvy-grass, watercress and oranges as a cure, widespread confusion about the causes combined with the fact that other diseases were sometimes wrongly diagnosed as scurvy, meant that this curse of the oceanic routes hung over generations of seamen and took a greater toll of them than the sea itself.

Salten of Bod∮

The period 1400 to 1700 witnessed the introduction of the new fore-and-aft seamanship peculiar, so far as we know, to the Atlantic-facing peoples. It has been suggested
that the lateen, the fore-and-aft spritsail rig, perhaps the lug rig, were known in the
classical Mediterranean and had arrived there from somewhere else further east.
Perhaps every sail and rig devised in the age of seamanship since the Renaissance
could be related, if we knew enough, to something that had already been invented
in principle, somewhere, sometime.

Whatever their remoter origin, the various types of fore-and-aft rig now being
evolved in the seas north of the Mediterranean and the Biscay coast owed much
more to the Dutch than to any other nation. The new seagoing people of the mud
flats and estuaries made a fresh approach to the creation of small craft for their
shallow, turbulent coastal waters and for working over the North Sea banks where
the sea bottom and the coast are always near and menacing.

There is pictorial evidence that the spritsail rig was in use in Dutch waters by
1420. In the early fifteenth century, therefore, and perhaps before, there was in use
in the North Sea – and about to become common – a rig that had been seen in the
Mediterranean of the first century though apparently it had never prospered there.

It was possibly also during the first part of this century that the most important
and versatile of all fore-and-aft sails, the triangular staysail, or sail set upon a stay,
made its appearance. Our growing knowledge of prehistory entitles us to think that

the ethnological rig types may have come to the sea peoples of Western Europe from very long ago and far away, but the splendidly efficient staysail would appear to be a purely Northern sail of comparatively recent origin. There was clearly a need for a form of headsail to improve the ability of boats with single spritsails set on a mast right forward. Such a sail if it were to fill the space available between the forestay and the mast had to be triangular. When it first appeared, the craft with a spritsail and a fore staysail set ahead of it was perhaps the handiest one afloat. In a painting of Antwerp by an unknown artist made between 1518 and 1540 there appears among the square-rigged ships and Mediterranean lateeners sailing off that many-spired town several small sprit-rigged craft with staysails. This valuable sail found its way into the square-rigged busses, greatly to improve their handling qualities, and later – surprisingly much later – into the square-rigged ships. It was one of the great inventions of sailing seamanship and was to travel far, being later set in lateen-rigged craft, in boats of the Pacific and Far East, and sometimes bringing an Occidental air to the junk. It is possible that the staysail was developed before the sprit-sail (that is, the sail set on a yard crossed beneath the bowsprit), but the latter can never have been other than inconvenient to handle in small craft, and for it the staysail provided a substitute.

The Dutch were also using in their smallest craft a rig in which, according to a contemporary observer, the 'sails stand like a pair of tailor's shears'. This may have been a Northern development of the lateen, a lateen with the yard stepped directly into the bottom of the boat instead of being hung from a mast. The yard, in fact, formed the mast, and as it was stepped at a big rake the sail set on it took almost

Munin of Göteborg

Note the reductions in canvas in the two ships

the form of an isosceles triangle. And while it had none of the unhandiness of the long, swinging lateen yard, it retained the latter's flexibility, the mast being unstayed and the sail loose-footed. As a triangular sail set on a mast, it resembled the mainsail of the modern yacht, though the origin of the latter was quite different.

This early Dutch triangular sail presents us with some of the most awkward problems of sail ethnography. Its appearance in northern Europe may have been the result of diffusion rather than independent invention. Sails of a related type are known to have existed in the Pacific, and a Peruvian triangular sail was illustrated in G. de Spilbergen's book published in Leiden in 1619. The accuracy of this drawing has been questioned, but Professor G. F. Carter has said that there is a literary record of the Incas having traded with people who came from the Pacific with triangular sails. If such a sail was used, Spilbergen's drawing was not the only means by which knowledge of it might have come to Holland. As Richard Le Baron Bowen has pointed out (*The American Neptune*, vol. xix, p. 168) Spain was well established in Peru during the sixteenth century, and the Spaniards had close links with Holland. Perhaps nobody will know whether the triangular sail travelled half

222

round the world, from the Pacific islands to the Peruvians and thence to Holland via Spain or whether some Dutchman one day had the idea of stepping a lateen yard directly into the bottom of his boat.

The important thing is that during these formative years the seamen of northern Europe were evolving, whatever their origin, essentially new kinds of fore-and-aft rigs that led directly to those which remained in use until the end of the commercial sailing-ship. These rigs gave new powers of speed, control and closewindedness, and a firmer command over wind and sea than any before.

An important step forward was the invention of the gaff, first known as the half-sprit. The spritsail, with the long sprit crossing the rectangular sail diagonally, always on its starboard side, had not wholly eradicated the weakness of the lateen, the one suffering from the length of its sprit, the other from the length of its yard. A rectangular gaff sail would have emerged simply by the process of cutting off the projection of the lateen's yard forward of the mast, together with the sail beneath it, and then providing the fore end of the shortened yard with a jaws able to abut the mast and ride up and down it. Or the gaff may have developed from the sprit: or

223

Bremerhaven. Some sail on the square-rigged foremast still
allied with steam propulsion

from the very short curved gaff used by the Dutch which was in effect no more than a small headstick on an essentially triangular sail. However it came about, the gaff qualifies as a brilliant invention in that it transformed the fore-and-aft rig. Though the gaff sail did not become common until more than 100 years later, it was in existence by 1523, on the evidence of an illustration of the siege of Stockholm in that year.

In 1675 a most interesting comparison of the rival merits of the gaffsail and sprit-sail was made by Samuel Fortree in a manuscript *Of Navarchi*. Fortree admits that the length of the yard was a weakness of the spritsail, and also the fact that when the sprit was to leeward the sail would bag against it, losing its fair curves, and also be difficult to furl in a high wind, being pressed hard against the spar. He pointed out that the gaffsail was able to sail closer to the wind and was much easier to tack. But it was not so good when sailing before the wind, while the fact that the gaffsail was 'spritted aloft' caused the ship to heel more, which resulted in the vessel griping and carrying weather helm.

With the exception of a few notable types of craft, of which the Thames barge was one of the best known, the gaff rig eventually replaced the spritsail. The triangular headsail, or staysail (considered below) and the gaffsail, were fundamental to the evolution of modern fore-and-aft seamanship. They were unlike anything that Eastern fore-and-aft seamanship had produced. The next to appear was the boom to extend the foot of the sail and then the additional triangular headsail. The boom, which came into use early in the seventeenth century, was unquestionably an Eastern spar. With both gaff and boom the Northern fore-and-aft cutter's mainsail was complete. Later this was used for the mainsail and foresail of schooners, for the mainsail and mizzen of ketches, as well as for the mizzen of the square-rigged ship when eventually the lateen was discarded for this purpose. Thus by the end of the seventeenth century the way was open for the development of the many new types of sailing vessel.

It has been said that the battle to sail to windward efficiently has daunted seamen since the dawn of maritime history. It has, incidentally, been won only in the eleventh hour of sail, in the best modern yachts. Efficient weatherliness depends upon hull as well as rig, and the best form of hull for the purpose may not suit its other functions. The Dutch, devising new fore-and-aft rigs and developing those already old, led the way, and here their use of the leeboard was one of their triumphs. How could craft be made weatherly which were also full-bodied enough to carry great loads, and shallow enough to operate where the sandbanks strewed the estuaries?

In 1702 the *Dictionnaire de Marine*, published in Amsterdam, gave the following description of the leeboard: 'The leeboard is made of three boards laid over one another and cut in the shape of the sole of a shoe, or a half oval. . . . If one wishes to sail close-hauled the leeboard which is on the lee side is lowered into the water, and thus prevents the vessel from falling off.' This was a device unknown to the ancient Mediterranean, but leeboards had been fitted earlier in Chinese junks and in the balsa rafts of the Pacific, so it is likely that the idea came to the Netherlands from the Pacific.

The really decisive change in the rig of the three-masted ship was made some time in the middle of the seventeenth century. For more than 200 years these ships had been suffering from lack of efficient head canvas. They carried their sprit-sails, and for the last half-century the larger ships had had clumsy spritsail-topsails perched on the bowsprit end, but the only fore-and-aft element in the rig of the bigger square-rigged vessels was the lateen mizzen. Yet ever since the mid-fifteenth century the smaller craft had been setting the triangular forestay sails, which added so much to their weatherliness and manœuvrability. The addition of more fore-and-aft sails, in the forms of staysails and jibs, to the basic square rig, was a crucial step in improving its efficiency.

The fact that staysail and jibs had been known for so long but not adopted in the bigger ships is a curious example of marine conservatism. A fore staysail may first have been set as a jury rig following damage, when a lateen mizzen was unbent from its yard and secured to a main forestay. Its effectiveness must have been quickly apparent. By about 1650 forestay sails were in use, to be followed by foretopmast staysails, thus giving the square-rigged, three-masted ship two fore-and-aft sails right forward, and the lateen at the stern, where they were best placed to improve balance and control. Then followed the jib, the outermost of the staysails, set from the foretopmast head to a light spar extending the bowsprit, known as a jib-boom.

These new sails involved adding to the rigging. Hitherto the bowsprit, a stout

225

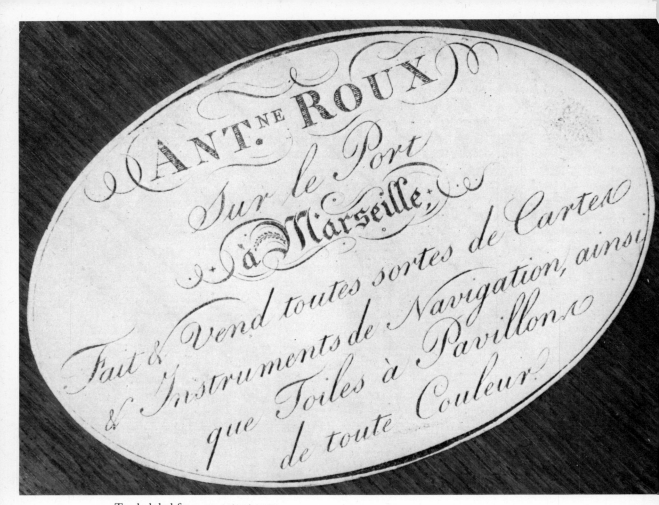

Trade label from an octant case

spar stepped well inboard forward, had no support from beneath, and the depressing action of the sprit-sail assured that it would not be lifted. But this was precisely what the triangular headsails tended to do, to the benefit of sailing qualities but the danger of the bowsprit. The bobstay was thus devised, a piece of rigging running from the end of the bowsprit down to the stem. At first a light member of the rigging, it increased in strength as more use was made of staysails and jibs, until heavy wire or chain was being used. As these sails became more efficient a dolphin striker (martingale boom) was added to the bowsprit rigging to form a truss of the bobstay; subsequently martingale guys and bowsprit shrouds were added, so that the bowsprit became as well stayed and important in the rig as a mast.

The awkward sprit-topmast had been eliminated in all but the largest warships by the early eighteenth century, and soon in these also it survived only as a flagpole. A more important change was the revival of reef-points. It has been seen that the Vikings may have used these, and medieval seamen certainly did so to shorten their single square sails. Then their use curiously became less common. The renewed use of reef-points, especially in topsails, led to a change in methods of ship handling. Formerly, in worsening conditions, the unreefable topsails had first to be furled, followed by the bonnets being taken off the lowers; and under the worst conditions a ship would scud under forecourse alone. With the reintroduction of reef-points, sail would be shortened by first furling the lowers, and in strong winds a ship would be handled under reefed topsails. This was one more step forward in maintaining control of a ship in storm seas. In such conditions the fore-and-aft staysails and jibs played an important part.

Navigators were not the only ones who worked with broad approximation and rule of thumb. Early in the seventeenth century it was written that it was rare to 'see two ships builded of the like proportions by the best and most skilful of shipwrights, though they have many times undertaken the same'. Now shipwrights, like seamen, were being required to study geometry and mathematics, the one to build satisfactorily the larger and more complex ships that were appearing, the latter to conduct them safely over the longer voyages now becoming habitual.

Some light has been thrown on the sailing qualities of seventeenth-century ships by the performance of the replica of the Pilgrim Fathers' *Mayflower*. This vessel typified the ocean-going three-masted ship of modest size carrying the basic ship rig of lateen mizzen, mainsail, main topsail, foresail, foretopsail and sprit-sail. The reconstruction was based on research by the American naval architect William A. Baker, Curator of the Francis Russell Hart Nautical Museum in Massachusetts, and the ship was built in Brixham, Devonshire, England. The dimensions were 104 feet overall, 79 feet on the waterline, 25 feet beam and 12 feet 6 inches draught when fully loaded, and she had the high and rising poop – that mass of windage aft – associated with ships of her period.

The *Mayflower*'s performance was rather better than would formerly have been expected for a ship of her type and time. She proved capable of sailing within six

Compass made by the firm of Roux, Marseilles. The degrees are in the quadrantial style commonly used before the 0–360 degree system

Sun compass. By means of the shadow cast by the upright central style on forenoon and afternoon altitudes, the value of variation might be derived

points, or about 70 degrees, off the wind, which is closer than many other ships of her day; and showed a highest average speed, maintained for twenty-four hours in a good fair wind, of 7 knots. But her average speed on the 5,420 miles Atlantic passage was only 4½ knots, which however is higher than that attributed by good judges to the *Santa Maria*, a ship of similar size and rig. This may indicate that some progress had been made in hull design and sail setting during the 130 years between the two voyages.

An impressive feature of her performance was her ghosting ability. Today's yachtsmen, used to handling close-winded craft which, to some extent, pay for this virtue by a sluggishness when their hulls of deep draught and sails of high weatherly qualities are set to run before the wind, would be expected to notice this. The modern yachtsman, able to set balloon spinnakers so big that the boat could be wrapped up in them, can compensate for this weakness. These immense, fairy-like windbags of today are the latest version of all the fancy kites hoisted by seamen in the past to catch light following winds. But the earlier vessels, thanks to modest draught and sails not badly shaped to make effective use of winds from astern, were able to make good way in light conditions.

It is of interest to read what Captain Alan Villiers wrote about the prospects of sailing the replica of the *Mayflower* across the Atlantic while the vessel was still under construction. His is the attitude of an experienced twentieth-century seaman versed in the sailing practices of the last square-rigged ships and also of contemporary lateen-rigged Mediterranean craft.

'One of the differences between this new *Mayflower* and the original is that the new ship has head-room in her 'tweendecks, which the old ship certainly had not. Her 'tweendecks were for cargo stowage, and the inconvenience caused by lack of clearance for their heads was just something her hundred-odd passengers had to take in their stride and suffer. Head-room in small ships is a new idea, and there is evidence that mariners were smaller men a century or two ago, or even less than that. Look

Walker's meridional compass, 1793

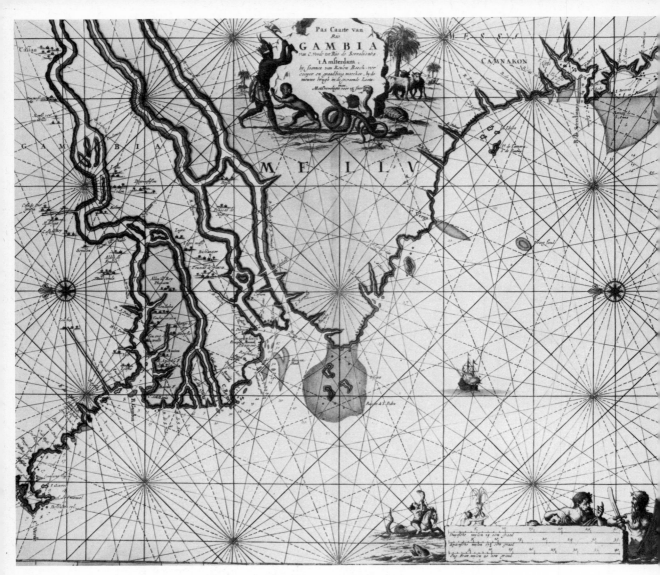

Part of the West African coast depicted in a portulan
of 1683

for example in the forecastle of the old clipper *Cutty Sark*, in her new berth at
Greenwich, and you will find no head-room for moderns at all. Perhaps the theory
was that sailors were so tired when they were sent below in the old sailing-ships that
they just stretched out, and the matter of head-room did not arise. In the case of the
new *Mayflower* the matter is different, for she is to be an exhibition ship, after she is
handed over, and Americans are tall. They dislike bumping their heads on ships'
beams.

'I hope this matter of head-room will not affect her sailing qualities adversely.
She will certainly have a higher hull out of the water than the original, and her after-
castle – a narrow, two-decked poop structure – will tower an amazing height. And

230

Opposite page
The same coast in a modern chart

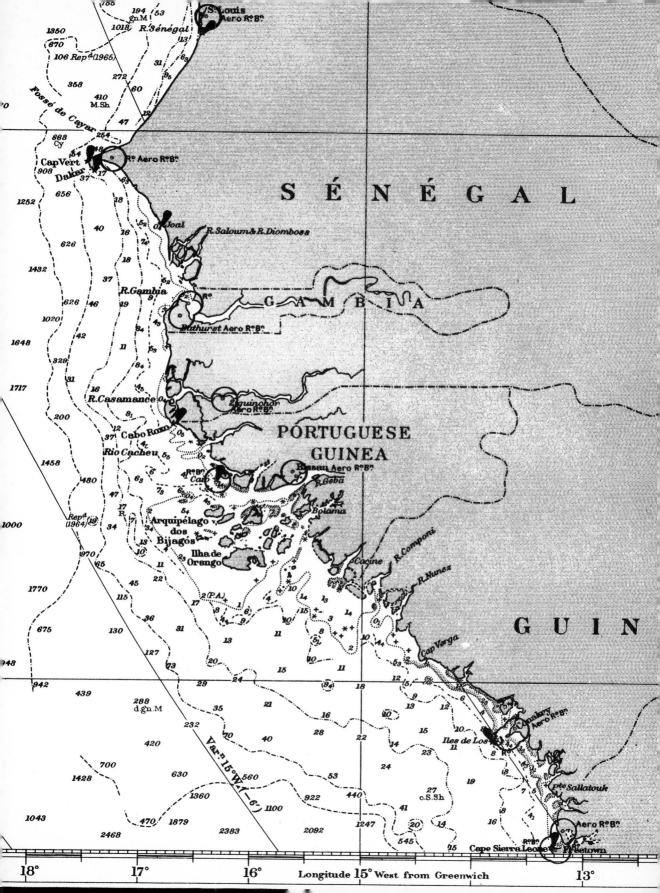

I should think, catch more than enough wind, which there is only a sprit-sail to balance. I cannot say I care much for that spritsail, never having been along with one, nor for the lateen mizzen either, though I have been with lateens enough during the years I was sailing with the Arabs. That is, indeed, just why I do not like them for North Atlantic conditions. The Arab dhows could swing their lateen yards easily, and the mast was raked forward to simplify that manœuvre. On an Arab lateen mast there was no standing rigging, the shrouds being set up by means of tackles to windward every time the sail was shifted over. But the *Mayflower* has standing rigging, and how a lateen can be effectively manipulated under such conditions remains to be found out – by me, at any rate. Just how permanent the standing rigging was meant to be, three centuries ago, I do not know either, but it is perhaps significant that there were no splices in it at all – a fact which the Gourock Rope Company's researches (they are making the cordage for all the rigging, standing and running) has unearthed.

'Despite her spritsail and her lateen, the new *Mayflower* – she is ninety feet by twenty-six, with a depth of eleven feet – ought to be handy little barque. Her rig is low and snug and ought to be controllable, since the course yards lower on deck, and the topsails gather into her commodious tops. In our big sailing-ships, all the square sails had to be handled aloft, and the deuce of a job it could be at times. That particular headache will be absent anyway, and I do not doubt that the ship will be handy. I do not doubt, too, that the hull will slip along very nicely in anything of a sailing breeze at all: it is just that towering after-castle that worries me. It cannot be too bad: after all, such constructions survived at sea for a good many hundred years. Maybe they helped the old ships to lie-to, without any canvas set, and apparently the *Mayflower* did ride out a blow or two in that manner on her historic crossing. She probably also made a lot of leeway.

'Leeway or not, I do not doubt that little ships of that type sailed quite well. We are inclined to forget that *all* the commerce of the world was carried on in such ships for at least three centuries, from the discovery of America until the beginning of the nineteenth century. Improvements in sailing-ships came slowly, and the really big steel "windjammers" were a very late development. What bothers one slightly about the new *Mayflower* venture is not the voyage, for after all she is a plain little barque, to be handled as such – a little barque with nice underwater lines and a snug rig. No, it is the awkward sails – or the sails which may prove to be awkward – like that spritsail and the lateen mizzen which cause me a passing headache, and the fact that all the rigging is of cordage. Hempen shrouds were long gone from seagoing ships when I first went to sea. There must have been a lot of "give" in them. I can remember really old salts talking of pretty little wooden ships which they spoke of as being "alive" – alive because they were built of wood (which, according to the old-timers, was a much more shipshape material than metal could ever be) and because their cordage rigging "lived" with the ship, accepting all the movements in a natural manner.

'Maybe. I do not know. We will find out, I expect. But I do know that our cordage is all best hemp, laid up especially in Scotland by a ropework which knows its business. All the stout hempen shrouds have been stretched properly: every

Compass by David Napier, 1847

lanyard, every ratline, every tack and sheet and brace and halliard is good stuff, to be relied upon. The sails are best Scots canvas, too. They will stand, all right. The really awkward thing about the rigging is its apparently unnecessary complication. All of us who have known the Cape Horners of our time are used to utility rigging – the bare minimum of stout wire (and even chain) which could do the job. The *Mayflower* type of ship bristles with awkward leads and cumbersome complications, like that steeved-up bowsprit, braces led to stays, and so forth. It will be difficult to accept all this, knowing (from our modern knowledge) how the whole rigging could be improved so easily. Yet we shall accept her as she is.'

A typical small merchant ship such as the *Mayflower* may be expected to have had a better sailing performance than larger ships, and particularly warships, with their array of masting and cordage and weight of guns. Seventeen years after the *Mayflower* had sailed, the three-decker, *Sovereign of the Seas*, famous for her size and elaborate decoration, was completed. With a length of 232 feet her speed, if it corresponded to the *Mayflower*'s best average, would have been some $10\frac{1}{2}$ knots, but it may be questioned whether her gear could have withstood the wind needed to reach this. It is doubtful whether the larger seventeenth-century ships of the line were able, while maintaining a reasonable speed, to lay a course within eight points, or 90 degrees, of the wind; they could thus never reach a coast lying in the eye of the wind, but had to wait for the wind to shift. As late as Nelson's day the ship of the line, if not as big as it was shortly to become, had reached the acme of its sailing performance, but yet it could make a course of only about 75 degrees on either side of the wind. Sailing performances fell off steeply in a seaway, and the ocean-going ship on a long voyage would suffer in both speed and weatherliness from the accumulation of weed on the underwater hull.

Slowness was the curse of ocean voyaging. Even had it been possible to maintain a direct course the physical conditions involved in driving a ship through water under the power that might be harnessed from wind could only produce speeds tiny in proportion to the distances involved; while in practice, for reasons of navigation and ship design, courses had often to be heartbreakingly far from direct. The fact that the square-rigged ship was unable to sail on courses occupying from 40 to 50 per cent of the compass does throw into relief the importance of the various fore-and-aft rigs being developed in the coasting and fishing fleets. In these, single-masted, square-rigged ships of the older type were still in use, but as their sails were braced by bowlines they would have been able to hold a better wind than the three-masted, oceangoing ship with its clutter of windage in rigging and hull. The lateeners and other fore-and-aft rigged craft might have sailed within 60 degrees of the wind under the best conditions; the small square-riggers not closer than 65 degrees. Compare this with the modern yacht, the highest development yet of fore-and-aft rigged craft. The most refined types of inshore racing yacht may claw up to windward within 40 degrees of the wind, and offshore racing yachts within 45 degrees. The pilot cutters and schooners of the nineteenth century, which persisted well into the twentieth, the most weatherly working craft afloat, were able to hold a course within 55 degrees of the wind. But the performances of all craft fell away when it was most needed, when the wind came in off the sea and increased, raising the short, steep waves of shallow water and drastically reducing the performance of the little ships, which had to battle to evade the clutches of the lee shore, battles that were too often lost. At such times it was preferable to be sailing on the wider oceans with longitude mislaid by several hundred miles.

The period of seamanship with which this section has been concerned extends to the early decades of the eighteenth century. Towards the end of this period Samuel Pepys, who like Colbert is amongst the greatest naval administrators of history, deserted his desk to make the voyage from Plymouth to Tangier and back with a squadron of naval vessels. The comments of this alert, observant man vividly illustrate the conditions of the most advanced seamanship of the day.

Magnetic compass, a device seamen had to do without
during thousands of years of voyaging

On the evening of 26 February 1684 the squadron set sail from Cadiz for the
return to England. By nightfall on the following day the *Grafton*, flagship with Pepys
on board, in company with nineteen warships and nineteen merchantmen, had a
strong south-westerly wind on or a little forward of the beam. The *Grafton* was a new
ship of the most advanced design, a two-decker of 1,153 tons carrying 380 men and
62 guns. As night came on she was being driven under the two lower sails and the
lateen mizzen. In the early hours of the morning the mizzen was split, to be followed
an hour and a half later by the mainsail.

The sails of the period, it should be noted, were of a fairly baggy cut, the canvas
being gathered up by the sailmaker when stitching it to the bolt rope, which was
shorter than the breadth of the sail to which it was sewn. There was involved here a
rudimentary idea of aerodynamics, but an unfortunate one. It was considered that
the resulting baggyness of the flax canvas would hold the wind and derive the
maximum thrust from it before the air escaped over the lee-leech. While sails of this
cut might be reasonably effective when the wind was from astern, it was the worst
form possible when sailing to windward, as Pepys's squadron was to learn from bitter
experience during the next few weeks, if they had not known it already.

The ship lay hove-to while the *Grafton*'s crew bent a new mainsail and mizzen.
During the succeeding day she beat up and down in the heaving seaway gathering

together the scattered squadron, which then put into Tangier and under the shelter of Gibraltar, more than 50 miles to the south of their point of departure. Here the squadron had to make repairs, sailing again nearly a week later with a fresh southerly wind astern to help them on their way. But soon the wind backed into the west and the squadron was unable to claw northward of Cape Spartel or lie close enough to the wind to clear Cape Trafalgar. On one tack the flagship would be heading for the outlying dangers of Cape Trafalgar, on the other losing distance to the south. So the squadron was brought to anchor under Cape Spartel, still no further north than when it had left Tangier. With feeling, Pepys recorded in his memorandum book the baleful effect of cross-winds on ships at sea, and how little this was understood by landsmen. Clergymen were particularly criticized: 'Our want of prayer for a good wind do enough show how little our churchmen make it their business to go to sea.'

When the squadron again put to sea it was to encounter a gale that made the March of 1684 memorable. The mainyard of the *Grafton* became sprung near the slings – the point where the spar would inevitably be weakened by the fastenings of this ironwork – and the repaired yard, fished together, broke again two days later.

Horizon mirror octant – 1859–76

Three days were needed to repair the damage. The wind was NNW., the seas heavy, and the ship was handled under foresail and foretopsail, the valuable staysails set ahead of these, and with the main topsail set in place of the mainsail. With the wind where it was, the ship was inevitably set to the south and west while endeavours were made to work out into the Atlantic and to the northward. Three weeks after departure for England, the squadron was still struggling off the African shore, further from its destination than when it had sailed from Cadiz.

The squadron, becoming reduced as the ships were scattered, struggled northwards when the winds gave them a break. With nothing in sight but washed-down decks, swaying yards and the sea all moving hills rushing before the wind, Pepys noted that 'nothing can give a better notion of infinity and eternity than being upon the sea in a little vessel'. And when later, in another gale, six men were washed from the mainyard and three of them drowned, he reflected on their lot with some insight into one of the curiosities of seafaring: that certain men may be driven to sea by nothing more than desperate necessity and yet continue 'with a resolution to live and die in it and so make it their intent to make themselves masters of it by learning and doing and suffering all things'.

Throughout the voyage Pepys had taken particular interest in the navigation. On the passage out he had found that the several people on board able to keep navigational reckonings produced remarkably different results by the time the ship had reached the vicinity of Cape Finisterre. Shortly afterwards they sighted the Burlings which were not to be expected to be within 25 miles; it was found that the various charts on board did not even agree about the position of the islands. Pepys acidly observed 'that it is by God's Almighty providence and the wideness of the sea that there are not a great many more misfortunes and ill chances in navigation than there are'. The return voyage, after the constant head winds and violent weather, ended in the flurry of navigational dissension that was the typical approach to landfalls. When soundings had shoaled to 65 fathoms and the lead brought up small white shells and sand, some believed the ship was to the west of the Scillies, others to the east of them; while yet others thought that she was so far to the east that the next likely event would be stranding on the coast of France. Pepys was caustic about the navigators' disputes; particularly the way in which 'soon as ever we see land all difference is forgot, or any desire of recording the truth, but on the contrary, everybody endeavours to make himself be thought to have been in the right, and not thinking also that they shall ever come to the same loss in the same place again. Hence it comes that the science of navigation lies so long without more improvement'.

The plane chart was proving inadequate for long voyages. Improved now with tidal information and the drawings of coastal features to aid identification, it remained an effective tool for coastal and short sea passages. 'For the coasting of any shore, or country, or for short voyages, there is no instrument more convenient.' Yet it is worth noting that Michael Coignet writing in 1581 made no mention of charts, even of the plane variety, as an aid to navigation. Had the writer been an Englishman this would have been more understandable, for the English were still backward in the higher arts of seagoing; but Coignet was a Fleming, the people on whom the skills of the Mediterranean chart-makers had descended.

Once the area covered by a plane chart became large, the fact that no allowance was made for the convergence of the meridians meant that a straight line drawn on the chart no longer gave a correct course unless this was due east or west. In northern latitudes the error became more pronounced. A further error was caused by lack of allowance for variation. The unacademic seaman was faced with the curiosity that if two ships, sailing along the same compass course without error, started a given distance apart, they would gradually draw closer in spite of the fact that according to the compass they were sailing parallel with one another. The plane chart also produced gross errors when used for plotting the results of astronomical observations. The projection devised by Mercator, published in 1569, for scholars rather than seamen, provided the basis of the true chart, and during the seventeenth century this came into general use for long voyages. The projection had a feature, at first distracting to maritime users, that the parallels of latitude were not a constant distance apart, but increased progressively to the north and south of the equator. To seamen, who had learned that while the length of a degree of longitude changes, owing to the convergence of the meridians, that of a degree of latitude is fixed, this characteristic of the new chart could only seem confusing. In fact, the spacing of the parallels was made with a progressive and proportional error from north to south which compensated for the changes in the spacings of the meridians; with the result that at any point on the chart the north–south and east–west scales corresponded. A straight line drawn on the chart gave a true course.

That such a rhumb was still not actually the shortest distance between two points when great distances were involved, was realized by some navigators. Great circle sailing – proceeding, that is, along a course represented by a thread stretched taut between two points on the surface of a globe – was apparently practised in the early part of the seventeenth century, with navigators presumably using globes. To determine a great circle course on a Mercator chart, on which it appears as a curved line swinging, in the northern hemisphere, to the north of the straight rhumb, involved the use of trigonometry, and is an indication of the skills now being brought to sea in the cause of the higher navigation. That a great circle was the shortest course became visually apparent when demonstrated on a globe, and such people as John Davis, inventor of the backstaff, held globes in high esteem as navigational instruments. But that the curved line of a great circle, as it appeared on a Mercator chart, in fact represented a shorter distance than the straight line could be made equally evident if distances were scaled with allowance made for the scale of this projection changing with latitude. Davis made it clear that a navigator who practised the refinement of great circle sailing, entailing constant changes in course to maintain arc, must not be tempted simultaneously to alter course to make the best use of a favourable wind. Great circle sailing was a technique that demanded long periods of fair winds.

The true chart was mated with Davis's backstaff, replacing the former cross-staff,

The gyro compass, independent of magnetism, underwent its first sea trials in 1907, and was originally devised for use in the Arctic, where a magnetic compass becomes hopelessly erratic. It since became, in all larger ships, the mariner's principal means of maintaining direction, though the magnetic compass, requiring no source of power for its operation, remained as standard equipment in all ships

An azimuth compass, used to obtain a magnetic bearing of the sun by means of the shadow cast by the wire attached to the rotatable sight rule. From this variation could be derived. This form of azimuth compass replaced that shown on page 228

to produce a new standard of precision in oceanic navigation. During its many years of use the cross-staff had undergone various modifications, but two outstanding weaknesses remained, which the backstaff eliminated. The observer still had to maintain a back- and arm-breaking posture while taking a sight, but with the back-staff he was able to stand with his back to the sun and so avoid blinding glare; secondly, he did not have to observe heavenly body and horizon simultaneously. Instead, by manipulating the staff, or quadrant as it effectively was, the sun's light, concentrated by a pinhole into a bright spot, was brought into coincidence with the horizon, viewed through a slit. This refinement of the trusted cross-staff was a step towards accuracy in navigation that may have seemed over-delicate at the time when position at sea was a complex of so many approximations; but it was an advance towards the age of commanding sail which was on the incoming tide.

By the early years of the eighteenth century the matter of compass variation was put into better order by Edmund Halley's map on which was drawn, from the evidence of observations made during a long sea voyage, a series of isogonic lines – lines connecting localities of equal variation. Since the amount of variation, which had been so much discussed and misunderstood and caused so many disasters, changes with the distance of a compass from the magnetic pole and the size of the angle, as measured from the compass, between the magnetic and true poles, the isogonic lines followed none of the tidy laws which had sometimes been ascribed to them. The fact that variation also altered with time had been appreciated by a few in the sixteenth century, and by the middle of the seventeenth was established — though practical navigation lacked yet the precision for the pilot to be much interested in the phenomenon.

Man had by this time taken the wings of the morning — faltering though the wings might often be — and had flown to the uttermost parts of the sea. Edmund Halley also made a study of the steady oceanic wind systems. Until invention of a chronometer provided the means of determining longitude, ships were compelled to go far from their direct rhumb-line course in order to sail down a parallel and so pick up the longitude that had been lost. But until the last days of oceanic sail, when the old problem of longitude had been solved, the ships still had to sail far from their rhumb line because they lacked the weatherliness to sail close to the wind. Their courses over the oceans still made great loops and swoops as they followed the trade wind belts. Halley increased the knowledge of these, their extent and variations. Samuel Purchas, who is believed to have assisted Hakluyt in some of his work, wrote of the sea in his *Pilgrims*: 'Man would lose half his inheritance, if the art of navigation did not enable him to manage this untamed Beast, and, with the bridle of the winds and the saddle of his shipping, to make him serviceable.' Possessing ships that could not sail effectively with the wind much forward of the beam, it was the more predictable movements of the air masses over the oceans that give power to the bridle of the winds.

5

Commanding Sail

The savant had long played a crucial role in one department of seamanship – that of navigation. Here significant advances usually owed little initially to the seamen themselves. The fact that the atmosphere and demands of life afloat were inimical to speculative thought also had its effect on the design and structures of the ships seamen had to use, but here the possible usefulness of help from erudite landsmen was doubted even while the intellectual activities of the eighteenth century were expanding.

If science be regarded as the correlation of experience with concepts, it may be claimed that the century was well advanced before science had more than touched the ship. Ignorance about so fundamental a characteristic as a ship's ability to remain upright is an illustration in point. After the integrity of her buoyancy, the maintenance of a ship's stability is the next essential. The fact that under sail the force that propelled was also one that tended to capsize made a knowledge of stability the more urgent; while the various conditions of loading under which a ship might go to sea, and the many attitudes she would assume in a seaway, combined to make the question of her ability to return to the upright when forced from it a vital one of infinite variety. A seaman might develop a second sense about his vessel's stability, an instinctive reaction to her manner of moving, her sluggishness or quickness when rolling, her manner of hanging at the end of a roll or reacting with excessive violence against it; but these instincts could easily mislead. Today, when the science of ship stability is a well-explored branch of naval architecture, it is recognized how fallible are the most experienced instinctive judgements in this matter.

Considering the chaotic state of theory up to the mid-eighteenth century seamen cannot be blamed for their lack of knowledge of the subject. A common belief was that for a ship to be stable the centre of her weight (centre of gravity) must be below the centre of her displacement (centre of buoyancy). This, incidentally, *is* the condition of stability for a submerged submarine. It became evident, however, that most ships, with their crowded spars and towering hulls had a centre of gravity far above the centre of buoyancy; yet they remained stable and able to return to the upright from considerable angles of heel. That they did so was a fact that the seaman could only accept as a grace, and pass on to more practical matters; but even mathematicians, who in the eighteenth-century manner were sceptical of grace, were unable for a while to account for this fortunate behaviour, or equally to explain the physics of the occurrence on the many unhappy occasions when a ship rolled over. The French mathematician Le Père Hoste, whose work *Théories de la Construction des Vaisseaux* appeared in 1697, gave an explanation, but not a satisfactory one, of why a vessel with the centre of gravity well above the centre of buoyancy could neverthe-

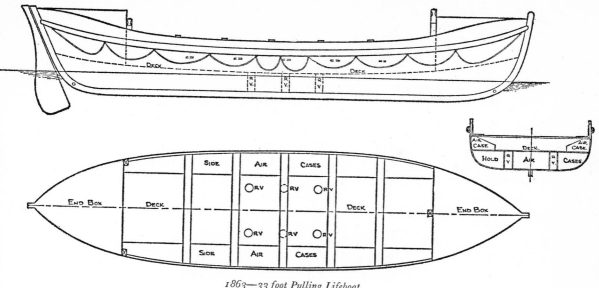

1863—33 foot Pulling Lifeboat

less be stable. The matter was not resolved until Pierre Bouguer evolved his theory of the metacentre, and it was some time later that this was put into a form that was useful to ship designers. By this time it was the last years of the eighteenth century. Ship stability, however, still was a matter with dangerous areas of doubt. As late as 1870 the British turret battleship *Captain* capsized in a summer gale in the Bay of Biscay owing to faults in design which were the outcome of misunderstanding the facts of stability. And it is to be noted that distinguished seamen had earlier reported favourably on the vessel.

That landsmen could have useful ideas about ships or even improve their performance, was a matter still regarded as questionable in 1870, let alone a century earlier. The last days of sail and the awkward transition period between sail and steam showed how dangerously fallible were seamen's ideas about improving the ships they knew well enough how to handle. As in former centuries, it was landsmen who had put the tools of scientific navigation into the hands of often reluctant seamen, now the time was coming when landsmen were going to design better ships. But their first eighteenth-century efforts to do so could not encourage confidence.

The first important efforts by eminent mathematicians to solve specific problems involved in seagoing ships were made in France. In Britain the work was minimal, though the superior sailing qualities of French ships of the line and frigates during the Revolutionary and Napoleonic wars was frankly recognized by the enthusiasm with which captured French ships were incorporated in the British Navy and copied in design – a tribute to the superior French work in scientific seamanship. The Académie des Sciences gave money prizes for papers offering solutions to problems of ship design. In 1766 one such was awarded to Bourde de Villeheut for his paper studying the loading of ships. In it he pointed out that at each point along the length

MALACCA LIGHTHOUSE
— Erected 1874 —
George Wells & Cᵒ

of a ship the weight and buoyancy should be as nearly equal as possible. Another author elaborated the principles thus:

(i) Every part of the ship should be loaded with a weight proportional to its displacement.
(ii) The lightest loads should be placed at the ends of the ship.
(iii) Permanent loads should be stowed amidships, the consumable stores at the ends.

Prior to this Pierre Bouguer had won a prize from the Académie for a work on the masting of ships. He observed the dangers of excessive stability, in that the quick periods of rolling led to loss of masts. He made studies of the strength of ships, thus tackling, from the mathematical and theoretical point of view, a problem that practical experience had been unable to solve. The seamen had 'undergirded' St Paul's ship, which was otherwise in danger of opening up in the seaway; and while the wider distribution of rigging stresses and better dispositions of timber in the construction of hulls had produced ships that by comparison were strong, ships still suffered weaknesses, accentuated now by the greater stresses produced by sailing closer to the wind; while wooden ships continued to have a liability to 'hog', or droop at bow and stern — one facet of the above imbalance between weight and buoyancy.

In the middle of the eighteenth century seamen obtained what Sir Isaac Newton and many lesser men had believed to be verging on an impossibility — a timepiece able to withstand the rigours of conditions at sea whilst retaining an accuracy in the order of three seconds per day or better. '. . . By reason of the Motion of a Ship, the Variation of Heat and Cold, Wet and Dry, and the Difference of Gravity in different Latitudes, such a Watch hath not yet been made', wrote Newton, and since the average watch of the period was accurate only to some five minutes per day, it seemed to need a horological miracle to produce one.

Meanwhile the ever-growing amount of ocean voyaging brought increasingly into prominence the losses of ships and men due to navigators' failure to keep track of their longitude. The London shipping interests made a petition to the Government asking that it should concern itself with the problem of longitude, as a result of which a committee was formed. There followed the establishment of the Board of Longitude, and considerable financial awards were offered for the invention of any means of determining longitude at sea. If such a means enabled the longitude to be determined to an accuracy of 60 geographical miles, after a voyage of six weeks, the award was to be £10,000; for an accuracy of 40 miles, £15,000; for an accuracy of 30 miles, £20,000. To achieve the last degree of accuracy using a timepiece, it would have to be correct to within three seconds per day during the six weeks' period. Other seagoing nations offered similar though smaller awards; the eighteenth century became what someone described as intensely 'longitude conscious'.

But when Captain James Cook was on his first voyage during 1768–71, the chronometer, though now invented and with a proved accuracy of an astonishing one-tenth of a second per day, was still among the rarest of instruments, and Cook sailed without one. He derived his longitudes by the technique of lunar distances. Provided the moon's position could be predicted with great accuracy in relation to some standard longitude, such as that of Greenwich, lunar observations by sextant from a ship would enable the difference in longitude between the standard and the ship's to be derived from tables. Captain James Cook, that most exceptional of seamen, acquired great skill with lunars, which were essentially an astronomer's problem owing to the fallibility of the tables. On his first voyage Cook had with him, among the many savants crowded into the little ship, an astronomer from the Observatory at Greenwich. He and Cook took lunars off Cape Horn and, from the deck of a vessel in violent motion, obtained a position that proved to be a mile out in latitude and 40 miles in longitude, a remarkable achievement in the circumstances. When the *Endeavour* reached home again, anchoring in the Downs on 13 July, it was the first time that a ship had made a long voyage with a nearly precise record of all her movements at sea. The year was 1771.

But without a chronometer this would have been beyond the capabilities of other seamen. Cook wrote of the chronometer after his second voyage: 'I must here take note that our longitude can never be erroneous while we have so good a guide as Mr Kendal's watch.' This watch was a copy by Larcum Kendall of the fourth time-keeper made by John Harrison with which he won the prize of the Board of Longitude (though it took him a long time to extract all the money from them).

'He [Harrison] had made the world then believe that Man could make a machine which could keep time at sea so very accurately that, by its means, he could determine a ship's longitude . . . that was a service to humanity in general, and to seamen in particular, which it is almost impossible to exaggerate.' Thus wrote Commander Rupert T. Gould in *John Harrison and his timekeepers*.

Harrison's was the ultimate triumph, but forerunners had shown the way. A Flemish astronomer, Rainer van den Steen, had suggested the use of a portable time-keeper for determining longitude. The great Dutch scientist, Christian Huygens, actually made several marine timekeepers in the latter part of the seventeenth century, but their mechanism depended on the pendulum and they were useless at sea. Following Harrison's work, seamen found themselves with the essential time-piece. By this time they also had that ultimate refinement of the quadrant, the sextant. It had been the practice of taking lunars that had encouraged the greater standard of accuracy that the sextant represented over the quadrant. Four dates are outstanding in these later developments in marine navigation: 1701, when a world chart of magnetic variation was produced; 1731, when Hadley's reflecting quadrant became the forerunner of the sextant with telescopic sights, vernier and other refinements; 1767, when reasonably reliable lunar tables were published for the determination of longitude; 1779, the end of Cook's second voyage, when the chronometer had been put to the fierce test of the voyage and proved itself. The navigator was equipped with instruments that have not essentially changed since then, and reliance on which is only now, in the later twentieth century, being modified by the developments in parabolic navigational systems.

The ship chosen for Cook's first voyage, and almost certainly chosen by Cook himself, was one of the smaller, simpler merchantmen of her day, a Whitby (York-shire) collier, 98 feet in length. Despite the simplicity and ordinariness of the vessel, which was like numerous others engaged in the coal trade, she was as good for the

Old Lundy Island
lighthouse

new purpose as any type of vessel then afloat. As Cook wrote, the qualities required 'are not to be found in ships of war of forty guns, nor in frigates, nor in East India Company's ships, nor in large three-decked West India ships nor indeed in any other but North-Country-built ships such as are built for the coal trade. . . .'

Like the great explorers of the medieval period, Cook wanted a ship no bigger than was essential to carry the required number of people and the stores, as simply rigged as possible, strongly built but of light draught. Seaworthiness is not a function of size, which may indeed be inimical to certain seagoing qualities and certainly to handiness. *Endeavour*, which the ship was renamed, was about the same length as the *Santa Maria*, and like her rigged with three masts. The draught of 15 feet when loaded for six months, was possibly less than the *Santa Maria*'s. She was not a fast type of ship, but thanks to the refinements of rig produced in the course of the 300 years separating the two ships, her sailing qualities were much superior.

Partly this was the result of greater sail area and the area being more subdivided. Where the *Santa Maria* carried four square sails, *Endeavour* had eight, with a course, topsail and topgallant sail on the fore- and mainmasts, and on the mizzen a square topsail, while like the *Santa Maria* she carried a spritsail on the bowsprit. Where the *Santa Maria* had a lateen mizzen, which was the sole fore-and-aft element in her rig, *Endeavour* carried five fore-and-aft sails, one of them the spanker, or gaff mizzen. Apart from this were a jib and staysail and between the main and foremasts a main topgallant and main topmast staysail.

These differences in sail plan between two fairly ordinary vessels of their respective periods may appear as little progress after three centuries of ocean seamanship. But the differences in the handling qualities of the two ships was considerable, thanks partly to the fore-and-aft sails, and particularly the jib and staysail, and the easily handled spanker. Lack of fore-and-aft canvas condemned *Santa Maria* to clumsiness. The greater area of canvas carried, the splitting up of the area into tractable units, produced a more complete rig of superior power. But compared with the larger ships of her own day, *Endeavour*'s rigging was simple, with her single topsails and topgallant sails and small mizzen-mast carrying only a spanker and topsail.

Cook completed a standard Admiralty questionnaire on the sailing qualities of the *Endeavour*. The questions themselves as well as the answers are able to reveal some of the attitudes to ship handling at the time. In the following the questions are given with Cook's answers in italics (originally in his handwriting).

1 How she behaves close hauled and how many knots she runs under the following conditions:

    In a topgallant gale. *Steers well and runs about 5 knots.*
    In a topsail gale. *Six knots*
    Under her reef topsails. *Keeps her full tack and she goes as well as with whole topsails.*
    Under her courses. *She behaves as well under her courses as most ships.*
    How she steers and how she wears and stays. *Steers and wears very well.*
    Whether she will stay under her courses. *I do not remember that this was ever tried.*

New Lundy
Island lighthouse

2   In the circumstances above mentioned (in sailing with other ships) in what proportion she gathers to windward, and in what proportion she forereaches, and in general her proportion of leeway. *We never but once had the opportunity to try her with other ships. Her proportion of leeway is a point or a point and a half.*

3   How she proves in sailing through all the variations of the wind from its being a point or two abaft the beam to its veering forward upon the bow-line in every strength of gale especially in a stiff gale and a head sea; and how many knots she runs in each circumstance; and how she carried her helm. *Her best sailing is with the wind a point or two abaft the beam. She will then run 7 or 8 knots and carry a weather helm.*

4   The most knots she runs before the wind; and how she rolls in the trough of the sea. *Eight knots and she rolls easy in the trough of the sea.*

5   How she behaves in lying-to, or a-try, under a mainsail and also under a mizzen balanced. *No sea can hurt her under a mainsail or mizzen balanced.*

The remaining questions concerned the draught and trim of the ship under various conditions.

Launched in 1888 as a purely pulling craft, she was later fitted with a petrol engine. In service for fifty years, the *Bedford* was called out forty-two times

By the time Cook was making his second voyage (1772–5), one object of which was to discover whether or not there was a great southern continent to balance the northern land masses, he could reasonably have been described as the first 'complete seaman'.

He had the widest, most valuable kind of experience in basic seamanship and ship handling, coastal and deep sea. This he shared with many; beyond it was a dedication to study and a flair for the arcana of his work which made him the pattern of the 'grand navigator' as opposed to the 'common navigator'. The astronomer knew more of astronomy than he, and the mathematician more mathematics; but Cook was able to combine a greater knowledge of these subjects than had ever before been associated with the practice of seamanship. He had trained himself in survey and became, thanks to unrivalled opportunities which he grasped so competently, the greatest cartographer of any time. Finally, on his second and third voyages, he carried the newly invented chronometer, and now used lunars, in which – as in spherical trigonometry – he was an adept, mainly to check the rate of the chronometers.

Thus late in the history of oceangoing sail the complete seaman made his appearance. Not until the latter end of the eleventh hour of sail, only three generations before regular steamships routes were being established in growing numbers, did

250

seamen find themselves fully equipped for the business of ocean voyaging. But from the date of Captain Cook until the development of wireless telegraphy, leading to the navigational systems of today, changes in the methods of navigation were in the nature of refinements only.

It happened that this most finished practitioner of Western seamanship was able, while voyaging through the island groups of the Pacific, to see still in daily use the practices and instruments of the earliest seamen. He was able to look at the origins, as earlier had the Dutch and Spanish explorers among the islands. It was not always certain whether a group of islands had been discovered before or not, their positions having not necessarily been accurately recorded, while empty seas might be found where islands had earlier been reported.

Six days after leaving the Marquesas and running before a fine easterly wind they came upon a string of low islets and later other islands among which they moved for some days. The people's 'instruments of war were clubs, spears and stones. Besides the vessels of war there were one hundred and seventy sail of smaller double canoes, all with a little house upon them, and rigged with a mast and sail, which the war canoes had not. These were designed for transports and victuallers; for in the war canoes was no sort of provisions whatever.'

This may recall the fact that in the classical Mediterranean the sails and rig of the oared fighting ships were left ashore before battle was joined. On Cook's third voyage (1776–80) it was recorded of other native canoes that they 'are of simple structure, but to appearance well calculated for every useful purpose. Even the largest, which carry twenty people or more, are formed of one tree. Many of them are forty feet long, seven broad, and about three deep.'

Neither double-hull craft nor those with a hull and outrigger on one or both sides had ever been developed by the seamen of the Mediterranean or Atlantic. It has been observed that such types, belonging to a different boat-building culture, tend to be found mainly amongst islands. Experiments with them by Westerners, who learned of them in the East or Pacific, were not pursued with any determination, and perhaps partly for this reason were never successful. One double-hull craft built for an Englishman in the reign of Charles II disappeared in the Bay of Biscay, and while ships of this type very occasionally appeared even in the steam age, a distrust of them has remained inveterate among the technologically most advanced seamen.

In about 1840 Dr Thompson wrote revealingly about one aspect of Pacific seamanship: 'Over tempestous seas the war canoes ride like sea-fowl. Should a wave throw a canoe on its side, the paddlers to windward lean over the gunwhale, thrust their paddles deep into the wave, and by a curious action, force the water under the canoe. This makes the vessel regain her equilibrium.' Captain Cook measured one of the big single war canoes. It was 68½ feet long, 5 feet broad and 3½ feet deep. Basically it was a substantial dugout with a single deep plank added on each side, increasing the depth by about a foot. In areas where the trees were big enough to ensure stability in a single canoe, this was the type of vessel adopted, and it has been recorded that in high winds several such canoes would be lashed together to ride out the seaway, with their bows kept up to the wind. Cook wrote of a fleet he found at

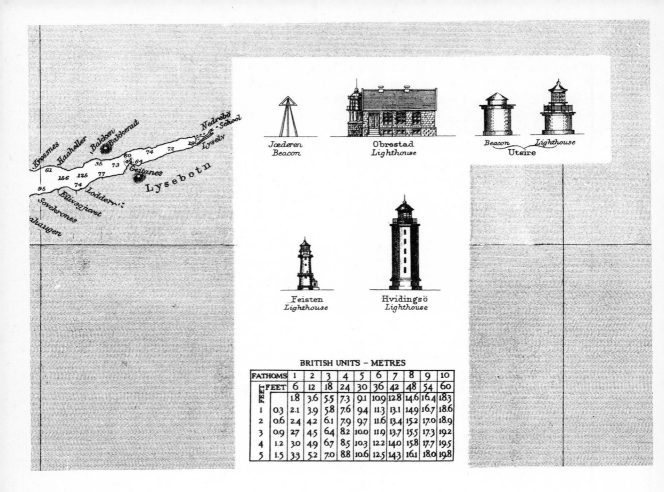

Jœderen Beacon — Obrestad Lighthouse — Beacon / Lighthouse Utsire

Feisten Lighthouse — Hvidingsö Lighthouse

BRITISH UNITS – METRES										
FATHOMS	1	2	3	4	5	6	7	8	9	10
FEET	6	12	18	24	30	36	42	48	54	60
	1.8	3.6	5.5	7.3	9.1	10.9	12.8	14.6	16.4	18.3
1	0.3	2.1	3.9	5.8	7.6	9.4	11.3	13.1	14.9	16.7	18.6
2	0.6	2.4	4.2	6.1	7.9	9.7	11.6	13.4	15.2	17.0	18.9
3	0.9	27	4.5	6.4	8.2	10.0	11.9	13.7	15.5	17.3	19.2
4	1.2	3.0	4.9	6.7	8.5	10.3	12.2	14.0	15.8	17.7	19.5
5	1.5	3.3	5.2	7.0	8.8	10.6	12.5	14.3	16.1	18.0	19.8

Tahiti 'of 160 large double canoes, very well equipped, manned and armed. . . .

It was in three generic types of craft that the seamanship of the Pacific was practised: (*a*) single dugout canoe; (*b*) double dugout canoe; (*c*) single dugout canoe with outrigger. In the second group was a type of craft in which the two hulls were of unequal size. Modern yachtsmen have shown a remarkable enthusiasm in the course of the last few decades for the various types of multi-hull craft, and one of this kind, though built with a sophistication far beyond the Pacific islanders, has recently been raced across the Atlantic. The present writer said of her shortly afterwards in *The Observer* (London) that she 'is one step further than the catamaran and trimaran towards the utterly alien in western concepts of seagoing sailing craft. What can the successors of the Vikings and Drake think about a marine vehicle having no definite bow, stern, port or starboard, but which goes with first one end leading then the other; and in which everything, including the rig (which is placed on one side of the ship not on the middle line) together with the mind of the skipper has to go into reverse every so often?'

Faced with essentially primitive single- and double-hull or outrigged craft and populated islands in the wastes of Oceania, Cook and his companions were confronted with a problem – essentially one of seamanship – of how the islands had even become inhabited. The problem has not yet been definitely solved. Primitive seamanship, and the earliest experiments in navigating out of sight of land, took place in sea areas whose boundaries were extended coastlines. Such was the early seagoing of the Aegean, the Mediterranean, the Baltic, the North Sea. The seamen of Europe had a coastline extending from northern Scandinavia to the south of Africa lying behind them when they set off over the Sea of Darkness. It is quite different among thinly scattered oceanic island groups where, even if a sense of direction is retained, there can be little confidence in regaining shore.

While he was among the Tonga Islands Cook noted some facts about the islanders' methods of navigation: '. . . The sun is their guide by day and the stars at night. When these are obscured, they have recourse to the points from which the waves and winds come upon the vessel. If during the obscuration the winds and waves should shift . . . they are then bewildered, frequently miss their intended port and are never heard of more' (Cook, 1784, vol. 1, p. 376).

It is now considered that the Pacific islands people came from Indo-China, Malay, even Formosa and the Asiatic mainland. The Polynesians, perhaps from Burma, migrated through the chains of Caroline, Marshall, Gilberts and Ellice island groups to the Samoan Archipelago. It is considered unlikely that they came

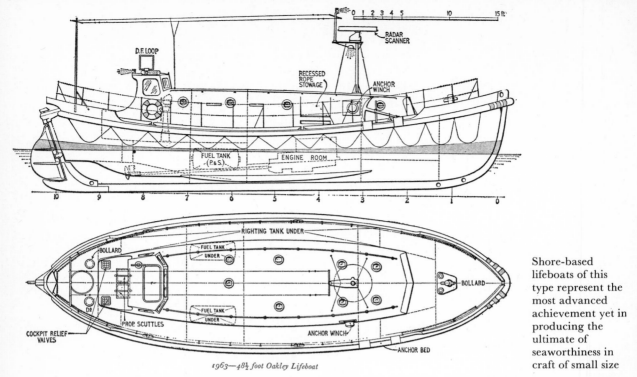

1963—48¼ foot Oakley Lifeboat

Shore-based lifeboats of this type represent the most advanced achievement yet in producing the ultimate of seaworthiness in craft of small size

from America, which was the idea inspiring the famous Kon-Tiki Expedition. The migrations (if the word is appropriate in this connection) may have been occurring at just about the time when the Mediterranean was a Roman lake and the highest expressions of seamanship were represented by the seasonal voyages of the great corn-ships between Egypt and Rome. Earlier Pacific peoples may have come from Indonesia and passed through the Fiji and Tonga groups, reaching as far as the Marquesas.

But when we speak of these people 'pushing out' and 'following the islands' and 'spreading', what is meant in terms of seamanship? We are not concerned here to discuss the origins of such peoples as the Polynesians, Melanesians, Micronesians and so on. It is a complex problem involving the study of their cultures as revealed in their languages, their customs, tools and weapons, including their boats, which may suggest different origins. The central fact of seamanship is that peoples using craft that were rudimentary in construction though of some sophistication in design, spread over the Pacific, where the sea was enormous and the islands were assuredly not 'dust upon the sea', as those of the Aegean have been called; nor like the latter held within the frame of three continental coasts placed at distances great enough, no doubt, but trifling compared with those involved in the Pacific.

After 200 years of discussion, two principal and contradictory theories of the migrations are held; the voyages were mainly accidental; they were mainly intentional. The latter theory must incorporate the idea of a past age in which was practised bold and skilful seamanship which would appear to have become a lost art by the time the seamen of Europe entered the Pacific and found islands peopled by 'noble savages' and those not so noble, by hearty cannibals, by uninhibited children of nature, and by other children whose habits made even earthy eighteenth- and seventeenth-century Europeans feel uneasy.

Captain Cook himself would appear to have supported the idea of accidental rather than intentional voyages. The former theory has been aptly summarized by Andrew Sharp originally in a publication by the Polynesian Society. The colonizing of the distant islands was not achieved because the people had vessels that *'were good enough to take them to such islands but because they were not good enough not to'*. The concept here is that the long Pacific voyages were not the result of deliberate maritime enterprises but the merciful endings to near disasters, which led to accidental settlements.

Cook's Tahitian interpreter had encountered on the island of Atiu, 600 miles from Tahiti, three of his countrymen. They alone survived from a canoe carrying twenty people which had set off from Tahiti many years earlier on a passage to an island about 100 miles distant. A gale had taken them off course, they had lost the island of their destination, they had drifted helplessly while all but four of the canoe's complement had died, and eventually the four survivors were cast up on Atiu. Captain Cook believed that this event typified how many of 'the detached parts of the earth, and in particular, how the South Seas, may have been peopled . . . '. It is an opinion with the weight behind it of Cook's knowledge of seafaring.

It is to be noticed that he speaks in a general sense of 'detached parts of the earth'. The theory of discovery or settlement resulting from unwilling voyages is able to throw a disconcerting light on many achievements that are conventionally regarded as triumphs of early seamanship. May it even be extended to the Vikings reaching Iceland, Greenland, America? It is believed that the Phoenicians may have reached the Azores, and this is presented as the outcome of seamanship of the highest order. If they were ever in the Azores, it may equally be regarded as the result of the stranding of a helplessly drifting vessel.

The vision of an early, great colonization period in the Pacific is able to raise tempting visions of superb seamanship being practised by men without instruments and using the methods, examined by Cook in the Tonga Islands, which were essentially similar to those adopted by the early seamen in the Mediterranean – 'the sun their guide by day the stars at night'. If this idea is correct, we must accept the fact that on the broad back of the Pacific, and using dugouts and outriggers, there was once a race of seamen with a confidence and ability unattained by any seamen in a similar state of development elsewhere.

When the Europeans reached the Pacific in the square-rigged ships equipped with compasses, quadrants, and manned by those with some knowledge of cartography and astronomical principles, though still without the means of determining longitude, they were frequently in doubt about their positions on that ocean with its immensity, emptiness and unknown currents. Islands were commonly being found and then lost again, to reappear at some later date in positions quite different from those first reported. Islands, indeed, were being mislaid as late as the nineteenth century.

In the light of what is now known about the history of seamanship, we can reasonably only suppose that in the Pacific until the coming of the European deliberate voyages were confined to sea gaps of 100 to 300 miles in the seamen's local groups of islands. These were indeed achievement enough, requiring an accumulated lore about currents and weather. And when this failed, when the currents became the master in light winds or the winds became the master while the sky was shrouded in cloud, the canoes lost their tiny island landfalls, and while countless thousands never made a landfall again, the few stumbled upon an island, and one more little step was made in the dispersal of mankind.

Dr Malinowski in his *Argonauts of the Western Pacific* has provided an erudite study of the way in which certain islanders, especially of the Melanesian people, organised a system of commerce and communication over great areas, of which there was no counterpart in the seafaring history of Europe when its people were in a similar state of development. We may see here, without becoming too visionary, an age of seamanship whose details are lost. The islanders had the advantage of splendid trees and fibre for the production of boats. Their homes were set amid an ocean often calm, with a fairly predictable climate and in areas of constant wind. Voyages of several hundred miles from isle to isle, aided by the navigational and meteorological lore examined by Captain Cook, could under these favourable conditions have become routine ventures. The unanswerable question is what length were the voyages that became routine? All we may be sure of is that certain of the islanders, such as the Polynesians, had a deep love for sailing and the so often gracious sea which encompassed their homes.

Seamen have always endeavoured, though usually in vain, to avoid unduly slow progress, but it was not until late in the history of seafaring that there was any deliberate, sustained pursuit of speed in ocean-going ships. There was too much of prior importance to be achieved.

In what were nearly the last days of commercial sail the finest merchantmen afloat, also the largest and those employed in the richest of all trades, were the ships sailing to India and China, on the routes that earlier generations had discovered after such great endeavours. The East Indiamen were built on the lines of naval ships. After 1800 ships of over 1,000 tons were built in this class, and in them long sea voyages under sail reached the highest level of comfort and safety yet attained. The discomfort and danger still remaining was enough for most people. There were the minor inconveniences of cabins little bigger than cupboards, or no cabins at all for the majority of passengers; food that deteriorated as the voyage lengthened, possibly leading to scurvy; the dangers of shipwreck, fire and foe. In that day of ocean sail, when so many thousands of people made the voyage to the East, the sea should still have been for the adventurous.

The East Indiamen varied in sailing qualities, but their common characteristic was slowness. Built to carry the maximum of freight and people, the bluff fullness of their lines precluded high performance at any time, and the method of their handling, by the best seamen of their day, but ones trained for a prosperous, monopolistic service, was the essence of caution. Slow days on passage were followed by slower nights, often hove-to.

It was in these last days of sail that there appeared for the first time a kind of ocean seamanship focused on speed. Smugglers and revenue cutters chased one another in small, over-rigged ships, pilot cutters raced one another to the incoming ships; these were small craft in coastal waters. About 10 knots was the maximum speed ever reached under sail until the clipper ship era of the nineteenth century, and none but the larger vessels under exceptional conditions could attain this.

The Americans showed a flair for obtaining speed under sail which for a while made them outstanding. Several reasons accounted for this: there was the Civil War and the need for blockade runners (precisely similar reasons led to the rapid development of high-speed planing motor-boats in the days of the U.S.A.'s prohibition in the 1930s, and a type of seamanship was first practised more closely related to the technique of the airmen than to former seafaring men); there was the slave trade and the ships needed to curb it; there was the prosperous opium trade to China, when a knot might mean the difference between a huge profit and a loss; and here the Europeans as well as the Americans cashed in on fast craft. There was the tea trade, too, bringing a golden cock for the masthead of the first ship home and profits in richer gold for the first cargo. Commerce and romance met. Owners were sometimes ready to spend more money to assure the speed of their ship and her arrival home first than they could recoup on the extra profit for an early cargo. In the U.S.A. this attitude was particularly pronounced.

The new great nation caught the spirit of speed, the spirit of the new age, for better or worse, caught it before the others and were led by it in their ideas about one of man's oldest endeavours – harnessing the wind to drive ships.

The leading American historian of sail, Howard I. Chapelle, has written: 'The mania for speed had slowly been infecting American seamen and shipbuilders since 1790. Fast passages made by driving the old packet type unmercifully were evidence of the disease that had appeared in the '30s, even earlier. The wild tales of these hard-driven ships seized the imagination of the public and shipping men alike. The result was an accentuated importance placed on such passages and a great deal of publicity for them in the newspapers. As a result of the interest aroused, a reputation for being very fast brought cargo and passengers to a ship; fame for her captain and owner, but Hell for the crew.'

It was not only in the clipper ships but also in the later steel sailing-ships, such as those in the wool trade to Australia, that something approaching a transformation occurred in the handling of ships at sea, and it was remarkably different to the philosophy that governed seamanship in the East Indiamen. Since square-rigged ships were forced, by their limitations of weatherliness, to direct their courses along the belts of the oceanic fair winds, far from the direct route, their speed of voyage depended on scudding before these winds. As winds increased they maintained their course, reducing sail by an amount that depended on the temperament of the master, but not heaving-to. Conditions were thus introduced that had not affected smaller, less fine-lined, slower ships in the past, with speeds appreciably less than the following seas and incapable, owing to their limitations in helm control and strength aloft, of being kept running under canvas in storm conditions. Cautious seamanship led to heaving-to at an early stage; or if caught by quickly rising winds, a ship would be forced to run before it under bare poles, and perhaps with warps streamed astern to reduce the speed.

In the later sailing-ships, however, ships were liable to be kept running beyond the point when rounding-up and heaving-to were practicable. Having hung on to

canvas and the maximum speed as long as possible, the seaway running up astern would have become too heavy to allow the ship to be rounded-up, an operation during which she would have to pass through the possibly fatal pause of lying broadside to the waves, while endeavours were made to bring her head up to the wind. So the ship would be kept running under reduced sail in conditions that made it clear why the prime abilities of the practical seamen were 'to hand, reef and *steer*'. Only the best men could then manage the helm.

The ship now faced the twin dangers of being pooped by one of the following seas, or being forced into an uncontrolled broach, when she would drive herself off course against the helm and lie with the wind on the beam, all canvas alive and flogging, broadside to the seas. While running under severe conditions the ship would all the time be yawing heavily – a respect in which some much admired ships were better than others, but which in all was unavoidable to some extent – while a number of men on the helm fought against the yawing which could so easily lead to the broach, the knocking flat of the ship, the loss of masts, of deckhouses and the ship itself. And all the time the seas would be coming up astern, unseen by the helmsman, which might roll over the poop and down the length of the ship, taking with it all that was within its power.

To experience these conditions, once common to the larger ocean-going sailing-ships, was the penalty attached to the most advanced skills of shipbuilding and seamanship, a penalty of progress. Speed is inimical to every other quality required in a ship. The lines of hull that made high speed possible reduced carrying capacity, while the maintenance of high speed induced stresses in hull and rig that resulted in ships being driven for part of the time on the verge of mechanical failure or beyond it.

Speed is a quality that is unfailingly attractive in ships. Possessed of it, the ugly are forgiven and the unseaworthy have their most graceless faults overlooked, or are encouraged to wear them proudly. Possessed of enough speed, a reputation is assured that will keep a ship's name sweet when others just as worthy have joined the many unremembered. Who today can think offhand of the name of a single East Indiaman? But has anyone forgotten *Ariel*, *Thermopylae*, *Lightning*? Who recalls that an *Aquitania* was contemporary with the first *Mauritania* on the North Atlantic express passenger service? Yet there was only the little matter of a knot or so between the two, and the former ship was the more comfortable.

More mendacious claims have been made about speeds than anything else connected with ships. How fast were the ruthlessly and often brilliantly handled clipper ships? The subject has been examined in detail by the late Captain James Learmont, who was at one time master of the iron clipper *Brenhilda*. His observations cut to the roots of clipper seamanship.

He first stresses the fact that by the time people became interested in accurate records of speed, the larger sailing-ships had passed into history and first-hand evidence was scarce. Nor might such evidence be worth much when found. 'It is not generally recognized', he writes, 'that the "record runs" claimed by various sailing vessels in the nineteenth century *were never checked*.' (The italics are mine.) Captain Learmont takes a number of days' runs recorded in *Lloyd's Calendar*, and proceeds to demolish their claims. They all involve day's runs exceeding 400 miles, and the ships are the famous American clippers by Donald Mackay, which were built speculatively

Modern Bermuda rig. Note the tall narrow mainsail
and overlapping headsail, products partly of the
aerodynamic knowledge and partly of the measurement
rules governing yacht racing

for the British market. Learmont points out that the conditions under which the ships were built and sold inevitably encouraged excessive claims of speed. Secondly, the method of measuring speed through the water with a Yankee log and a sand-glass, used under the formidable conditions of wind and sea inevitable at times of fast sailing, was amenable to the grossest error, which Learmont estimates even as high as 5 knots.

'In my experience,' he says, 'it has taken three apprentices, the officer of the watch and myself to haul in the line at 12 knots. In the conditions that would prevail in a ship going at a much higher speed, it is doubtful whether a master could have spared the hands to be used for such an inessential job.

'This recording of the hand-log . . . was just an elaborate scheme of window dressing, expected by advance agents . . . who did not miss an opportunity for getting full publicity for box-office purposes.' The author proceeds to show how the speeds obtained from heaving the log cannot always be reconciled with the records of the chart, and concludes: 'From every angle, taking my long experience in sail into account, I do not believe that any ship ever exceeded or even reached 400 miles in 24 hours under sail. I believe that the best day's run (noon to noon) ever to have been made under sail was that of the five-masted barque *Preussen*, when she made 370 miles under Captain Petersen in the South Pacific.'

This, it may be noted, is a speed of a little less than 15½ knots. Whatever the periodical bursts, average speeds over long voyages were inevitably undistinguished and provide the true index of sails' weakness. The most famous voyages of the tea clippers on the China route produced average speeds of a fraction under 6½ knots. When on the Australian wool trade the *Cutty Sark* made a voyage at an average speed of 8 knots, but on this route respectable average speeds were just over 6 knots. It was then in the eighties of the last century. When the last wool fleets sailed, as late as 1925–9, average speeds were a fraction under 6 knots. Though it cannot be proved, it is reasonable to believe that by the eighties of the nineteenth century something close to the limit of performance had been reached in ocean-going sailing-ships of a commercially useful kind, and had steam never gone to sea, future improvements could have been marginal only. In the later days of the sailing-ship, one improvement was able to produce fractionally better performance. This was the use of iron trusses or brackets, for slinging the yards on the masts. Trusses held the yards further ahead of the masts than the chain slings formerly used, allowing the yards to be braced further round to the beam in foul winds, and so improving the weatherliness.

The battle for weatherliness was already old when in the pre-Christian Mediterranean the first kinds of fore-and-aft rig appeared; the scientific enthusiasms of the Arabs found in the lateen rig one means of gaining hitherto unequalled weatherliness; in Dutch hands the north European versions of close-winded rigs saw their first stages of evolution; and the climax of these was reached when revenue cutter chased smuggling lugger in the nineteenth century. In terms purely of sail-handling virtuosity such canvas-loaded craft represented the highest expressions of that kind of seamanship ever attained outside the esoteric realms of the later yachting.

As a sailing machine – and as opposed to an ocean-going square rigged ship of the kind considered immediately above – no craft was more highly developed than the

HAMB. FÜNF MAST VOLLSCHIFF "PREUSSEN" CAPT. B PETRSEN. 1909.

The five-masted ship was a late and rare development only reached when sailing-ships attained their largest size

Balloon spinnaker, a sail of extremely light cloth (now
nylon) big enough to wrap up the yacht carrying it, and
unlike anything formerly evolved in the ages of sail
until 1866, and not developing the full balloon form
until the 1920s

French luggers of the *chasse-marée* type, which became so well known as privateers
during the Napoleonic struggle. For mackerel and long-line fishing, trawling and
cargo carrying, vessels of the *chasse-marée* type were commonly used, but they were
refined to its highest pitch for privateering and smuggling, in which speed was the
first quality required.

The *chasse-marée* in full flight was tremendously canvassed on three masts, a mainmast nearly amidships, raked sharply aft, a foremast at a lesser rake stepped in the eyes of the hull, and the mizzen no less extreme in its position hard up against the transom. Immense spars, bowsprit and bumpkin totalling in length not much less than the hull, extended beyond the stem and stern. Sails comprised mainsail, foresail and mizzen, with topsails, and the main and fore possibly with double topsails. All these sails were standing lugs, with the tack of the lower sails close to the heel of its mast, so that it was a relatively narrow band of canvas ahead of the mast. The mizzen was sheeted far outboard to the end of the outrigger, and forward was a large jib tacked down to the long bowsprit.

Notes on the handling of the French lugger appeared in the *Manuel de Jeune Marin* by J. Noguès (Paris 1814). Below is an extract, with some notes following:

'The jib and mizzen are the first sails to be set in getting under way.

'When all the lower sails are set, if one is to make a series of short boards the foresail and mizzen should be set to windward of their masts; then when the ship goes about one needs only to haul over the fore and jib sheets and shift the *foule*. The tacks of foresail and jib are not touched at all; the mainsail is always to leeward of the mast when the others are to windward and vice versa.

'If one is making short boards, the mainyard is only lowered a little in going about; the tack is shifted to the other side, the sheet hauled over and the bowline hauled out again.'

Close-windedness was the primary quality of the luggers, and when the course was hard on the wind the three lower lugs had their yards hoisted inside the shrouds; the topsail yards passed between the lower and upper shrouds. The lug mainsail and main topsail had bowlines, led to the foremast and secured round it, while the foresail had not a bowline but a *foule*, which was a pole handled in the same way as the Viking *beitass* (*vide ante*). Thus the two simple pieces of gear that had given some degree of weatherliness to the Viking square sail continued in use unchanged to improve the windward trim of the more weatherly lug rig of the eighteenth, nineteenth and twentieth centuries.

The luggers' disadvantage was the number of men needed to handle them. With everything pinned in hard on the wind, straining bowlines holding the luffs of the sails up to weather, the *foule* compressed under the pressure from the foresail, they were the closest-winded craft yet to have appeared in the ages of sail, and not until the fore-and-aft rig was further improved by the use of cotton sails and wire rope rigging was their performance bettered. But either when going about from one tack to the other, or when changing course to bring the wind on to the quarter or further aft, a tumult of sail handling had to occur. Noguès mentions above that 'the mainsail is always to leeward of the mast when the others are to windward and vice versa'. This might have been so when making short tacks, but to have the best setting sails all of them had to be to leeward of their masts. Then when tacking the yards had to be lowered enough to dip the fore-end round the mast to the new leeward side. When passing from a beat to a broad reach or run, it was necessary to dip the yards wholly under the shrouds, since when squared off they could no longer be set aside inside this rigging. Thus the sails had to be lowered into a heap of canvas, and the

Two phases of
awkward
seamanship –
steam assisting sail
and opposite page
sail assisting steam

outer yard ends dipped under the shrouds, and the whole rehoisted. With the wind aft the luggers were trimmed wing-and-wing so that the sails did not blanket one another. Also, this trim gave the narrow and not very stable craft a better balance.

In the rivalry between smugglers and revenue men, the cutter and lugger rigs met in often violent competition. The cutters, for all their crush of sail and mechanically more sophisticated rig, had not the weatherliness of the luggers; but as elaborate sail carriers they were for their size unique. The reefing bowsprit might have been half the length of the hull. Both boom and topmast were long. The sail area carried in the mainsail, topsail, jib and forestaysail was thus large, and a ring-tail could be added to the mainsail. But these little ships, of about 60 feet in length, also carried an array of square sails, giving them the edge of speed over the luggers when the wind came abaft the beam. A large running square sail was set from a yard hoisted with the sail, while above it were double square topsails. In Europe and North America, cutters of this character became the immediate forerunners of the early racing yachts, in which the art of sailing to windward was yet further developed; though it was in craft that could have had few uses in the working world. The closer-winded lug rig, though very occasionally adopted in yachts during the earliest days of the nineteenth century, was quickly discarded owing to the difficulties of handling the rig over short racing courses. But it remained in use far into the twentieth century by fishermen, many of whom themselves spent their summers as paid hands aboard the yachts.

Sail-cloth had become a crucial element in world power, and the sources and quality of the pliable flax a constant preoccupation amongst maritime peoples. Of

all the materials from which sails had been made, flax had proved itself the most suitable, woven on foot-operated spinning-wheels in a widespread home industry scattered between countless isolated cottages, around which the sound of the looms continued all day. The character and treatment of the yarn was a matter of detailed specification when the best sails were involved, as too was the sailmakers' manner of making up the canvas produced by the weavers. Not surprisingly we find Samuel Pepys involving himself in the matter and writing of 'a high dispute' he had with Sir William Penn and Sir William Batten on the subject of how broad the canvas should be, how close together the seams in the sewn sail. The latter gentlemen insisted that the individual cloths should be narrow, this giving the sail many seams and making it less liable to stretch. Pepys opposed the view; and here he was wrong. The two Sir Williams were trying to minimize the fault in flax sails that to the end of their days was to detract from the performance of working craft.

Flax had strength and the great virtue of remaining soft and pliable when wet, the latter of great importance to the handling of sails under bad conditions. But as a corollary of this quality flax canvas stretched, sagged, and with use lost weight and became porous. The ability of the square-rigged ship to claw to windward was weakened by the character of her canvas; those 'white wings' beloved by generations of marine artists were wings that faltered. In this, as in so many respects, the limitations of seamanship were set by the materials available. It was the practice to wet down flax sails – sometimes known as 'skeating' – in order to shrink them and harden up the loose weave.

An American yachtsman of the present day has said that the British have tradi-

267

tionally misunderstood sails. It is undoubted that the American people in the last days of commercial and naval sail appreciated the subtleties of sail texture and cut better than those of Europe, and in the yacht-racing era that was to come it was to be one of their greatest assets. The sails of the Colonial Americans were of loosely woven flax inferior as a rule to the best European canvas. In the first decades of the nineteenth century they began to mix cotton with flax, and then to use all cotton. With the development of power looms, an altogether harder and more closely woven cloth was made, which was able to bring new power to sails. In the War of 1812, it was found that privateers and blockade runners using the new cotton duck were definitely closer winded than those with flax. A century and a half later the creamy cotton duck which had become the admired sail-cloth for yachts proved itself no less clearly inferior in weatherliness to cloth of the new man-made fibres, particularly the one now known as terylene, which was yet firmer and less porous than cotton.

Sails of terylene could have transformed the behaviour of square-rigged ships, but it came on the scene too late. Cotton duck, despite its merits in providing close-windedness lacked the strength of good flax; furthermore, when wet it became as hard and intractable as a board; and the greater sailing-ships ended their days handicapped by their flax sails.

Other materials were coming into use which would have been capable in time of transforming the behaviour of ocean-going sailing ships just as these ships were passing through their last phase. It was not until the mid-nineteenth century that wire rope was introduced for standing rigging. That in order to stay their masts ships of all sizes had had to depend upon ropes twisted from natural fibres, usually of the hemp plant, was a fundamental weakness of sail propulsion. Hemp rope stretches considerably and it was unable to hold the rig steady. The movement of the masts as shrouds stretched would cause the slackening of the stays carrying the fore-and-aft sails, which in turn could not then be trimmed for the most effective performance with the wind far ahead of the beam. The limitation on ships' performance in the ages of wooden structures and natural fibre rigging were due to the weakness of the materials quite as much as to any failure to grasp principles. Even had refinements of aerodynamic theory been understood, there were not the means available to give them practical expression. A Leonardo had been able to grasp the principles of flight, but their application had to be delayed until there were petrol engines able to provide power without excessive weight. As ships became larger, their inherent weaknesses increased while the stresses upon them increased at a faster rate than their size.

In naval dockyards riggers were being trained in wire splicing during the thirties of the nineteenth century, and ships began to appear with their lower shrouds of wire. By 1850 there were a few ships carrying wire rope shrouds for the lower, top and royal rigging; but it was not until the sixties that this became usual in the average vessel. It was this as much as any other feature of their construction and design that gave the tea clippers a higher sailing performance than any achieved before. Ships so equipped were able to make better days' runs than larger vessels despite the latter's potential advantage of size. And it was the use of steel instead of wood for masts that enabled a yet higher edge on performance to be achieved.

Opposite page
An extreme type of fore-and-aft rig induced by yacht racing and its rules of measurement, shown in a 30-square-metre class of yacht

The *lampschiff*

Shipping of the *Sir Thomas Lipton*

Wire rope was particularly valuable in adding to the efficiency of the square riggers' many fore-and-aft sails – the flying jibs, jibs and the staysails set forward and between the masts. Prior to the use of wire, these sails had to be set either on a hempen stay or simply on their own bolt-ropes (set flying) resulting in either case in the luff sagging and weatherliness being destroyed. It is significant that in the last and fastest clippers it became the practice, when sailing as hard as possible on the wind, to lower the staysails. Thus the very sails that in principle were the most effective for close-

272

winded sailing were unused owing to their potentialities being unrealizable. This would appear to have been due partly to their being set on hemp stays, and later when wire had replaced these, to the inherent bagginess of the flax canvas. It was the liability for staysails to be ineffective when hard on the wind that led to the retention of the square spritsail on the bowsprit long after the time when it might have seemed that the array of flying jibs, jibs and fore-staysails had rendered the spritsail otiose. Captain Cook's *Endeavour*, though the essence of simplicity in rig, carried two spritsails as well as a couple of jibs. These spritsails enabled the ship to be manœuvred with an assurance that would have been impossible had reliance been placed on the baggy flax jibs set flying on stretching bolt-ropes. But before 1850 the spritsail had disappeared, its yard alone remaining as a spreader for the shrouds of the bowsprit from which more efficient staysails and jibs were now set. Rigging screws (or turnbuckles) replaced deadeyes with lanyards for setting up the steel rigging, and geared winches for handling running gear and geared capstans for anchor work came into use as sailing-ships, in their decline, were mechanized and the new seamanship was making its appearance.

While the early steamships were floundering across oceans where sail was demonstrating its greatest competence it could have seemed that wind propulsion held great future promise. Only irresponsible fancy might see it succumbing to so awkward and alien an intruder.

The limitations of sail remained immense, with ships still restricted to the trade wind routes and able to achieve no better average speed, as we have seen, than about 6 knots; but this might be regarded as the eternal ordering of things. Whatever the weaknesses of sail, they were overshadowed by those, potentially so much more devastating, of early steam boilers. The steamer's independence of the wind was initially offset by ravenous coal consumption and consequent loss of time in making port for fuel; while the heavy, clumsy machinery and coal bunkers severely reduced carrying capacity. With steam power a new technique entered seamanship, that of fuel management. Having become independent of the wind, ships had forced on them a new dependence upon the land and chains of refuelling ports, and this among much else seemed to lay them open to competition from sail.

The use of steel tubes for masts and yards, as well as steel plating for hulls, enabled the last sailing-ships to be larger than any before and thus gain the economic advantage of size to sustain competition with steamships. Finally there was a reversion from the complexity of the big sailing-ship's rig, which thousands of years' development had brought to a climax of intricacy during the seventeenth and eighteenth centuries. The last and largest sailing-ships may have carried more masts and sails than any before them, but this was duplication rather than intricacy. The rigs showed the engineering attitude of the new day, with rigging as severe as a geometrician's diagram, compared with which that of the past generations of three-decked ships of the line was a network of tortured ingenuity – the 'magic intricacy' of the poets.

The climax of such development was seen in the seven-masted, 385-foot schooner *Thomas W. Lawson*, of more than 5,000 tons gross, built in Quincy, Massachusetts, and lost with all hands but one in 1907. Each of the seven masts was identical,

The signal station

consisting of a steel lower mast 135 feet in length and a 58-foot pine topmast. The sails on all but the foremost mast and the mizzen were also identical, consisting of a lower sail with gaff and boom and a topsail. All halyards, topping lifts and sheets were led to two large steam winches placed under the fo'c'sle and in the after deck-house, while there were four smaller winches amidships used for cargo handling and the lighter work of hoisting the topsails. The large ship, some twice the length of clipper ships such as the *Ariel*, was manned by only sixteen hands. She was a ship stranded between the mechanical age of seamanship and the much older one of sail, in which only, it continued to be assumed, a proper seaman could be bred.

Still, much older than sail, oarsmanship continued as the rugged working practice (emphatically no sport) of a few seamen. In 1812 it was written of the fishermen of Shetland that 'they are not probably surpassed in dexterity or long continuance in pulling. Frequently they pull the whole distance to and from the fishing-ground, which is universally allowed to be thirty-five miles at sea, and sometimes upwards of forty miles. . . . In these boats they frequently bring home a ton or ton and a half of fish, in the face of a gale.'

Material progress being so disparate throughout the world, with Stone Age ways

274

One of the most advanced fore-and-aft rigged craft in
the latter days of working sail – a New York pilot
schooner

of life persisting along with those of the Nuclear, it is not surprising that some of the
earliest forms of boats and rigs, and hence some of the first modes of seamanship, are
still in use today. Rather more surprising may be the fact that sailing seamanship is
still a preoccupation, if only for pleasure, amongst the most advanced peoples. And
the most advanced sailing yachts of today are able, by their still ineradicable
limitations, to throw into relief the achievements of past sailing ages.

The battle for weatherliness, which we have seen to have been a constant
preoccupation during the ages of sail for all those using coastal and narrow seas, has
not been won by the modern yachtsman, even in this, the eleventh hour of sailing
seamanship. It is a battle in which physical laws prohibit a victor. But at least the
modern yacht is able to put up a much superior fight against a head wind and sea
than even the most respected working craft of the past, such as the smart luggers of
the Brittany coast, the pilot cutters of the Bristol Channel, North Sea, or of the
Chesapeake, the best lateeners of the Mediterranean, or the fishing schooners of the
Grand Banks, some of which were built for racing and were essentially yachts.

With the racing yachts of the mid-nineteenth century the art of sailing to windward became an idealized pursuit with few extravagances barred. Racing was

organized to put a premium upon weatherliness. Yachting put no premium upon economy of means. Yet it should be recalled that it was the working seamen of the smaller craft, above all fishermen, who were called in to handle these thoroughbreds of sail. The profession of paid yacht hand was born and continued for a few generations, to be extinguished in our own egalitarian days. Briefly, there was a new kind of seaman out on the waters during the summer months, handling the most exquisite sailing machines yet devised by man, and doing so with a kind of skill rooted in all the best of traditional sailing skills, but refined, subtilized, perfected and lifted to a higher plane of pure sailing performance than ever achieved before. And with each winter the craft would rest their flanks in the softness of mud berths or lie hauled-out, pampered on shore, while their professional hands returned to simpler craft and rougher seas from which they would win fish instead of silver cups. The cream of the men who did this became the great skippers of racing yachts, a tiny select breed, with the small halo of fame that success in sport brings; often very temperamental people, for they were not just seamen, but artists of sail handling. As one of them once said, on the deck of the large racing cutter he commanded, to a group of his owner's yachting friends: 'If you gentlemen will come up to windward, you will be in the sunshine, altogether more comfortable *and out of the way of my main boom*.' This particular, and once much celebrated, racing skipper was noted for his unloving sarcasm. But it was such men who honed a new edge on to sailing seamanship, at the

The Brig *President*

time when sailing was becoming an anachronism except as a sport; but before there was today's legion of amateurs able to handle sail competently.

The efficiency of the best racing yachts, as they have evolved between about 1850 and today, is primarily due to the money available to spend on them. This has brought into being new trades, skills, techniques – or elaborations of old ones – that have had no need to justify their existence by making the craft more profitable or useful, only faster. To this extent the seamanship of yachting is too esoteric to be more than a footnote in the history of seamanship. But the best racing yachts as they have emerged from about one and a quarter centuries of development are able to illustrate the handicaps that former seamen under sail had to accept.

The seaman, like everyone else, has always been limited by the materials available for his use, 'availability' being largely a matter of price. The yachtsman today has sails of man-made fibres, a recent development from the beautifully cut cotton sails which were a feature of nineteenth-century yachts and a reason for their efficiency. These give a strength hitherto unattainable, a lack of porosity, and an ability to form themselves into aerodynamically appropriate curves without the bagginess and the irrelevant shapes into which the sails of working craft were liable to fall. The sails may be set from masts of light alloy tube having a stiffness and strength-to-weight ratio unknown in those of wood, supported by stainless steel

rigging with a strength and resistance to stretch beyond anything that could have been foreseen by the predecessors of the people who now take such materials for granted as they sail for fun. Man-made fibres provide them with ropes with which to sheet in sails with the ruthless power of low-geared winches.

A yacht can be worked to windward in the kind of offshore seaway that is kicked up by a wind of 25 knots – which is not far below gale force. Sails are strapped in with all the power modern mechanism can produce and the strength of rope or wire and spars withstand. And all these stresses are in turn transferred to the hull, upon which all the thrusts and tensions of the rig ultimately fall. And working into a head sea as she must, when going to windward, a yacht's hull and rig are all the time having to endure the inertial loadings which, as engineers are aware, are more destructive than loadings gradually applied. Even under these quite modest seagoing conditions modern yachts are liable to carry away gear.

278

The ultimate test of weatherliness – to sail round the world mainly against the prevailing winds and currents, from east to west, the contrary way to that of the trade routes under sail. This is the attempt being made by Chay Blyth in a modern steel yacht (*British Steel*) carrying an advanced rig

6

The Mechanical Revolution

The sailing-ship was a paradox all her days. The fettered limitations of her movements, the dawdling of even her best average speeds, gave man only a slight command of the seas.

The sailing-ship was a most imperfect device. Yet in it was an element of perfection, an ideal of motion, gracious beyond most words, never achieved by the mechanical ships of triumphant technology.

Two seamen observed their vessel under full sail one night from the detachment of the bowsprit end – the flying jib-boom – under trade wind conditions:

'. . . The sails were spread out, wide and high – the two lower studding-sails stretching out on each side far beyond the deck; the topmost studding-sails spreading fearlessly out above them; still higher, the two royal studding-sails, looking like two kites flying from the same string, and the highest of all, the little sky-sail, the apex of the pyramid, seeming actually to touch the stars and to be out of reach of human hand.'

One of the seamen wrote: 'I was so lost in the sight, that I forgot the presence of the man who came out with me until he said (for he, too, rough old man-of-war's man as he was, had been gazing at the show) half to himself, still looking at the marble sails – "How quietly they do their work."'

That was R. H. Dana in that classic of square-rigged seamanship *Three Years Before the Mast*. What a transformation of means lay between those aesthetically triumphant sails leaning on the night and the incomparably more effective steamer with her engines 'slam-banging home again. . . .'

> 'My engines, after ninety days o' race an' rack an' strain
> Through all the seas of all Thy world, slam-banging home again
> Slam-bang too much – they knock a wee – the crosshead gibs are loose,
> But thirty thousand miles o' sea has gi'ed them fair excuse. . . .'

But those engines of Rudyard Kipling's immortal marine engineer brought to ships a reliability of performance hitherto in the world of fantasy. Conrad described the sailing-ship *Narcissus* as she 'drifted slowly, swinging round and round the compass, through a few days of baffling light airs: 'Under the patter of short warm showers, grumbling men whirled the heavy yards from side to side; they caught hold of soaked ropes with groans and sighs, while their officers, sulky and dripping with rain-water, unceasingly ordered them about in wearied voices. During the short respite they looked with disgust into the smarting palms of their stiff hands, and asked one another bitterly: "Who would be a sailor if he could be a farmer?"'

Thus far had thousands of years of seamanship brought man under sail in one of the last and most highly developed sailing-ships. The philosophy of the simple engineer was as trite and sublime as any sailorman's before; but it reached into the future of seamanship:

'From coupler-flange to spindle-guide I see Thy Hand O God, – Predestination in the stride o' yon connectin'-rod.'

The sailing-ship may have banished the oared vessel from the oceans, but the idea of independent motion over the sea relieved from the tyranny of the wind was retained in some speculative minds, though not those of seamen, too preoccupied as they were with coaxing the winds to their purpose. Sporadic efforts had been made down the ages to regain the power of free movement. In the fifth century A.D. efforts had been made to drive a ship by paddle-wheels driven by oxen. Paddles driven by men had been tried, but it became evident that manpower was more effectively deployed on oars, which returned ideas to their starting-point. Neither animal- nor manpower could apparently master the oceans; so wind-power remained without competitor, until steam-power was harnessed.

With the development of machinery for the propulsion of ships, the sciences of thermodynamics and metallurgy entered the world of seamanship, forerunners of the other sciences on the doorstep, of which the latest has been electronics. In April 1838, and within twenty-four hours of each other, the *Sirius* and the *Great Western* completed the first two crossings of the Atlantic under steam. The former vessel had maintained a full head of steam throughout the passage, but had little coal left on arrival; the latter greatly impressed by not only steaming the whole way but having 200 tons of fuel left on board on arrival at New York.

The steam propulsion that ousted sail initially helped it in one important respect. This was in the steam tug. Hitherto the only means of towing a ship in or out of port was rowing-boats, which could not provide enough power in a wind or tideway. Smaller vessels might be shifted by using long sweeps run out through the gun ports. Otherwise resort had to be made to kedging and warping, which could involve some of the neater operations of seamanship. An anchor would be laid out by a boat in the desired direction and the ship then heaved up to it, the evolution having perhaps to be repeated many times. A pretty manœuvre sometimes adopted when shifting a vessel in a tideway was that of dredging, sometimes also known as clubbing. An anchor was lowered just to touch the bottom without being given enough cable to bite. By thus restraining the ship's rate of drift she retained some steerage way in the tide, and by a suitable use of helm she might then be worked across a tideway while losing some ground with the stream. The need to manœuvre in harbour and narrow channels, or to gain an offing before setting sail, was a restriction on ships' size and elaboration of rig from which the paddle-wheel steam tug released them.

The handling of the sailing-ship had depended basically upon ropes, and rope-work in its broadest sense was the heart of seamanship, nearly every operation depending upon it. The good seaman handled rope, whether making knots and hitches, splicing, belaying, reeving or hauling on tackles, as though the stuff had a personality which he knew how to bend to his will. Canvas work, too, though the

View through the lens of a lighthouse

special province of the sailmaker, was an essential part of the able-seaman's trade, and he handled the palm and needle with perfect confidence.

When sail had largely been driven from the oceans, there still had to be practised more of the traditional seamanship than might seem likely. The processes of navigation were yet untouched; merely simplified in practice because of the greater certainty about courses and speeds. The many changes to be wrought by radio were still some years ahead. Weather was still lore rather than meteorology. The many cargo-handling derricks and boat falls meant that the handling of ropes was still an important part of the seaman's trade, and the boats themselves were unchanged, moved only by oar and sail. It used to be said that you could judge a ship by the standard of her boats and boat handling. A ship was still always under the control of a helmsman steering manually by compass. Manual steering engines had made the work easier, and to control a steamship in a heavy sea was less exacting than struggling to hold the straining, tearing sailing-ship from the dreaded broach. But every engineer who had known the responsibility of holding a head of steam and engine revolutions to maintain a certain speed became aware of the difference between the good and indifferent helmsman; and how, when the latter had his trick at the wheel the necessary revolutions had to be increased. A steamer, too, required coaxing and 'handling'. And still in every port that the steamer entered,

The new Lundy lighthouse seen from the old

the smaller craft worked under sail, and the age of the new steamship was in many respects subservient to the old sail. Still on board the steamers were many who had once enjoyed making the report that was to become classic: 'Sailing-ship coming up astern, Sir!'

The triumph of mechanical power led to a dichotomy in the control of a ship. Deck officers remained for a generation or more men whose first experiences or longer had been in sail. Even when this time had passed, and the experience of young officers in sail had been confined to their early training, and perhaps over-emphasized during the course of it, the deck officer had no more than a rudimentary knowledge of marine engines. In the British Royal Navy as late as 1906 Admiral Sir Reginald Custance was writing of the contemporary naval officer: 'if he controls and manages the motive mechanism, he will do no more than the seaman of the Elizabethan age'.

In 1873 the *Baltic*, one of the earliest ships of the White Star Line, crossed the Atlantic at the record speed of over 15 knots. But the vessel was also rigged as a four-masted barque, having a course and two topsails on the fore-, main- and mizzen-masts, a jigger and a triangular headsail. The last two sails were not the only fore-and-aft elements in the rig, for unlike the traditional square-rigged ship and barque there was also on each of the square-rigged masts a fore-and-aft gaffsail, the primary function of which was steadying rather than driving.

283

In ships built for profit there was an inevitable pressure driving sail from the seas which was absent in the navies of the world, where tradition was a stronger force. The last days of naval sail produced many ships that represented a retrogression in seaworthiness. The English writer Sir Edward Sullivan, wrote at the end of the last century: 'Our ironclads are very disappointing. If they go slow they won't steer. If they go fast they won't stop. If they collide in a quite friendly way, they go down. . . . They have neither stability nor buoyancy. But this does not apply to British iron-clads alone. French, German, Italian, American, are all the same.' A revolutionary age had produced an uneasy period in ship design. And in some respects uneasy seamen, too.

Centuries of one kind of seagoing were transformed within a generation into something so different that neither those who handled the ships nor those who built them were certain of what they were doing. Especially in the navies, sails and their handling were still regarded as the root of seamanship. People's admiration was still aroused by such events as handling of a frigate by her captain, Sir Baldwin Walker, R.N. The ship was entering the Bosphorus under all plain sail and studding sails. The salute, lasting two and a half minutes, was duly fired. As the last gun went off all sail had been furled and the crew, figures in immaculate white, was manning the yards. Years spent working ships over the dangerous oceans and gaining faith in what experience had proved adequate, was not a background likely to give confidence in ships dependent upon graceless engines alone. And naval leaders not only knew nothing about machinery; it was also socially repugnant to them. An interest in engines was not even an amiable eccentricity, but a lapse of taste. This attitude was less strong in the merchant fleets, but it existed.

In the British Navy, then the largest and in some respects the most advanced, there had appeared as early as 1867 the first battleship setting no sail at all. She had just one short, naked mast. But many more canvas-loaded ships were yet to appear; the last British battleship of this kind did not come out until 1886.

The final days of naval sail were the first of sail training for its own sake, which today has again become so fashionable in a quirk of quaint and largely illogical maritime taste. Voices were beginning to be raised against canvas. It was becoming evident that not the least objection to sails and rigging was the fact that with all canvas spread to a joyful wind, the ships sailed so appallingly badly. It was long argued, in both the navies and the merchant fleets, that sail saved coal on long voyages. This was the hangover of the older, once sound contention that the un-reliability of engines and their greed for fuel made a ship without sail unfit for ocean voyaging. That time had passed. Now it was clearly demonstrable that the coal saved while plodding with ungainly gait under canvas was more than offset by the coal expended in carrying the weight and windage of masts, yards and their gear around the oceans at all other times. In the navies it became no longer reasonable to pretend that sails were other than a peace-time dressing to enable ships' crews to take part in the evolutions aloft with the fleet in formation – evolutions still congenial to proper sailors.

The lure of speed, which we have seen to have gripped those who handled some of the latter-day sailing-ships, became equally influential in some classes of steamship,

Outmoded in the West since the 15th century this type of compass is still used in China today

exaggerated now by the new pride and profit in steamers being able to maintain a regular, published schedule. On its maintenance depended, in the case of passenger ships, the good opinion of a line's clients, and when mails were carried the patronage of governments.

By the opening of the twentieth century the epitome of speed and reliability had been attained in the North Atlantic passenger service. The seamen of the Western Ocean mail ships had reached the height of their profession, running immense ships that appeared to be the ultimate products of triumphant technology; so when in 1912 the peerless and newest of its creations was sunk in the course of a few hours, the values of a whole civilization appeared to have been called into question and seamanship received a rebuff that shook its confidence, which subsequent disasters in the ensuing sixty years have not helped to restore.

From the point of view of seamanship, the central fact of the occurrence lies in the fact that when the *Titanic*, the largest liner (and ship) of her day, struck the fatal iceberg she was moving at the highest speed she had yet made on the voyage, nearly her full speed, despite the fact that she was in an area of ice about which several warnings had been received. A collateral point of significance is that no extra lookouts had been posted beyond the two who were always on duty in the crows-nest high on the foremast.

At the Courts of Inquiry that followed this disaster of hitherto unimagined magnitude, master after master of unimpeachable experience maintained in evidence that they would have done as had Captain Smith of the *Titanic*. In the Western Ocean a mail ship's speed was not reduced because of ice unless there was also fog. Reliance was placed on the ability of lookouts to spot or smell ice in time for avoiding action to be taken. If there was low visibility, extra lookouts would be

placed in the eyes of the ship. The necessary degree of fog to enforce a reduction of speed appeared undefinable.

The night on which the *Titanic* was rushing towards the gay welcome that such ships received on their first arrival in New York was an extraordinary one – no moon, no wind, no swell, an absolute calm of a most unusual kind. Whether there was a light mist such as often accompanies ice is uncertain. Evidence varies, but the doubt does indicate that any mist must have been slight. Nevertheless the curious conditions did make the sighting of an iceberg peculiarly difficult. The absence of waves or the least swell meant that there could be no ring of surf round the waterline of the iceberg, and there was no moon to reflect it. There was the further danger that an iceberg newly capsized and exposing its hitherto submerged surface to the air lacks for the time the crystalline quality that gives it some visibility. Added to these natural handicaps were a few due to organization. There is the amazing fact that the lookouts' binoculars had been mislaid at Southampton and nobody had provided them with any others. And the most urgent of the many ice warnings received had failed to reach the bridge.

Aperiodic magnetic compass

There was one ship's master at the British Court of Inquiry who did not go along with his colleagues in supporting Captain Smith's maintenance of nearly full speed. Called as an expert witness, he considered that in the face of the ice warnings that had been received speed should have been reduced. Also, the celebrated Antarctic explorer, Sir Ernest Shackleton, when questioned about maintaining a speed of $21\frac{3}{4}$–22 knots in an area of ice replied: 'You have no right to go at that speed in an ice zone.'

This question of speed under dangerous conditions reaches beyond the *Titanic* affair and becomes one of the most subtle aspects of latter-day seamanship. With mechanical power seamen had not only gained control of a ship's speed, but they had at their command greater speeds than at any period formerly. The handling of ships under some conditions was transformed. Fog usually being attended by windlessness, the master under sail had Nature's restraint on running into dangerous situations. Nor could the master of a sailing-ship be given tight schedules on the maintenance of which his reputation for competence would depend. No master giving evidence at the *Titanic* Courts of Inquiry mentioned what was so often discussed amongst ships' officers in private. They knew that the maintenance of high speeds in fog frequently led to the running down of fishing craft on the Grand Banks and in the English Channel. Rudyard Kipling when he wrote of 'The ram you, damn you liner' was not letting poetical imagery run away with him; as so often he gave precise technical observation a poetic and memorable form. There were well-qualified officers who refused to serve in the Western Ocean mail ships in the conditions under which they had to be handled. And at the time Joseph Conrad wrote bitterly: 'We shall have presently, in deference to commercial and industrial interests, a new kind of seamanship. . . .'

Such matters, though lying at the heart of steam seamanship never received guidance of any unimpeachable doctrine. Perhaps they never can, beyond the rule in the International Regulations now reading: 'Every vessel, or seaplane when taxi-ing on the water shall, in fog, mist, falling snow, heavy rainstorms or any other conditions similarly restricting visibility, go at a moderate speed, having careful regard for the existing circumstances and conditions.' Inevitably, ships' masters in many trades continued and continue to take what may or may not be well-calculated risks rather than lose reputation and possibly employment through what easily may become regarded as timid and inefficient seamanship. Forty-four years after the *Titanic* a barely lesser tragedy occurred, again to a liner of the most splendid type on the North Atlantic route. This is considered below.

Most intimately involved on the night of the *Titanic* were a very few of a new kind of seafarer with hardly a decade of tradition. During the crucial hours, over an area of the Atlantic whose radius was a few hundred miles and whose focus was the drifting ice, the morse flickered the tense messages that only the novices of this new power could call to hand. Yet they had the power to save, which at this moment had become beyond the abilities of the most experienced seamen. They were young men, not particularly well paid, and in the liners where they were usually found, often overworked. But they were dedicated to work capable of making the imagination glow; though it could not glow brightly enough to reveal the world of seafaring that was about to emerge as a result of the electromagnetic waves among which they were yet like children at play – often such gallant children.

The existence of electromagnetic radiation had been determined before any device was invented able to emit or absorb it. Guglielmo Marconi took out his first patent for wireless telegraphy in 1896. Within a decade a power of communication hardly less than miraculous to the lay mind of the early twentieth century was beginning to be put in the hands of seamen.

It is significant that the now all-pervading means of mass communication provided by wireless and its offshoot television should have found its more important original application at sea. On land there were already well-developed telephonic communications along wires; but still the ship, once she became the centre of her own horizon's encircling rim, for ever moving with her, was absolutely alone and divorced from the rest of mankind in the old immense solitude of the sea. It was for this reason an obvious place for the development of wireless telegraphy; and there was the further important consideration that at first communication by this means was easier across water than overland. But only half a century ago the most visionary could not have foreseen the numerous ways in which electromagnetic radiation was going to transform the major operations of seamanship.

It was the use of wireless as a means to make an end of a ship's helpless sunderance from the rest of the world when on voyage that was its initial importance. She ceased to be, as hitherto she always had been – in Joseph Conrad's words 'a fragment detached from the earth'. The first ship to be fitted with W.T. was the East Goodwin lightvessel in the mouth of the Thames, and this enabled her in 1898 to be in contact with the South Foreland lighthouse, over a distance of some 12 miles. When in the following year the lightvessel was rammed by a steamer and sunk, a wireless report to the shore station enabled the crew to be saved. It was a short distance and a small beginning compared with the tremendous ramifications of wireless at sea soon to be evolved.

While many larger ships were fitted with wireless by 1914, it was not considered at this date to be essential for ordinary vessels. But already the power that W.T. had to transform traditional seafaring was becoming evident. From urgent distress signals its use was extended to the broadcasting of weather warnings, ice warnings and time signals for chronometers. No longer did a seamen have to feel that the Greenwich time which he carried in his chronometer was a fragile and precious freight whose slight disordering would place his ship in danger. As the range of W.T. extended, the systems of warnings were expanded to include navigational dangers such as the failure or removal of navigational lights or marks, and even Press messages. Within the short space of a few decades the seaman was drawn into the organization of the land, and his millennia of separation from all that was connected with the shore came to a sudden end. One aspect of this still seemed strange when the First World War was fought and the navies in which W.T. was more highly developed than elsewhere found themselves being controlled strategically and even tactically by distant Admiralties.

During these years, and even before, it had been appreciated that the direction of the source of radio waves might be detected by a suitable receiver. This had an immediate tactical effect on the handling of fleets, but it led more importantly, though not immediately, to the technique of radio direction-finding, a totally new navigational aid which was to lead to those much more sophisticated of today; so that now in a fully equipped ship the seaman's ancient problem of finding his position is a problem only in a dire emergency.

The technique of W.T./R.D.F. (wireless telegraphy/radio direction-finding) was the initial step in the navigational revolution. To operate this a ship had to be able both to transmit and receive. A number of R.D.F. stations were established on the coastlines of various countries, equipped with the means to determine the bearing of radio signals from ships. The ship first called the station. The latter then asked the ship to transmit her code sign continuously for a brief interval. Then the bearing of the ship would be transmitted by the R.D.F. station to the ship. With such bearings from two or three stations within range, the ship was able to plot her position by the old, familiar system of cross-bearings, as taken formerly upon objects within sight and using the compass. There was a difference, however, that the radio bearings were true, not magnetic directions, while if taken at a considerable distance a further correction would have to be made, when plotting them on the conventional Mercator chart, since radio waves travel along great circles. This was an operation easily performed from tables.

Man so quickly takes for granted the marvels of yesterday, that we might with advantage record a scene in the wireless cabin (known to Americans as the 'radio shack') of a British battle-cruiser at her war station in 1914. Even sophisticated people could then still wonder at the sounds and voices drawn out of the air by the slim aerials at the top of masts which yesterday would have spread topsails: 'It was indeed "a wonderful night for wireless," almost unique in the experience of those to whom I was speaking. We heard all kinds of things on that night which are seldom heard together and under the same conditions. We heard the Russian Commander-in-Chief in the Baltic; we heard Madrid; we heard the German Commander-in-Chief, from his fastness across the North Sea. . . . We heard the British Commander-in-Chief in the Mediterranean. . . . As I was turning away a bitter cry came from the sea somewhere between Iceland and Ireland: "*Daffodil* to *Ranunculus*: 2,000 lb of marrowfat peas intended for me addressed to you at Happyhaven. Request you will, etc."'

It has been said that the lead and line was the first instrument used by seamen of which there is any record. Average seamen were not interested in the abysmal depths that plunged beneath their keels in mid-ocean; the few who were had to use the deep-sea leadline, with the result that as late as 1914 only some 6,000 deep-ocean soundings had been made.

The use of sound for the measurement of great depths was suggested by a French physicist during the first decade of the nineteenth century. In other nations, particularly Germany and the United States, people were experimenting on these lines in the early years of the twentieth. It was not until the 1920s that echo-sounding was first used at sea by the Centre d'Études of Toulon and by 1923 the U.S. survey ship *Guide* was fitted with an echo-sounder. Only by means of such an instrument could an oceanographic survey of the depths be conducted; but simultaneously the new technique was to provide one more instrument for ordinary navigational purposes, and the first in the family of electronic devices which have transformed navigation during late years. The uses of echo-sounding and radio direction-finding evolved together to change the average seaman's world, and before half the century had passed radar was to be added.

The problem of echo-sounding lay not in the principle but in its practical application. Sound travels through water at a speed that may be approximated for the moment as 1,500 metres per second. Thus, in depths of interest to the practical seaman the time interval between the emission of a pulse of sound and its echo returning from the bottom, is tiny. Sound will travel the depth of a fathom and return in rather less than one-four-hundredth part of a second. The time interval for a depth of 60 fathoms is 0·15 second.

Transmitter and receiver are in the bottom of the hull, and are connected

electrically to the recording unit on the bridge in which the interval is automatically converted into fathoms and recorded on a dial. A development made during the Second World War was the continuously recording echo-sounder by which is recorded a profile of the bottom as the ship moves. When sounding great depths allowances have to be made for the fact that the speed of sound in waters varies with temperature, pressure and salinity, and increases with them, within a range of about one half of one per cent. Such corrections are of particular interest to the oceanographer.

Until 1939 the only radio aid to navigation in general use – unless we include the echo-sounder – was the medium frequency direction-finding of the types discussed above. All radio navigational systems must use either bearings or distances from fixed reference points for the determination of position. The above used bearings. The navigational systems about to appear under such names as Loran (LOng RAnge Navigation), an American system, Decca, a similar British system, and Consol, make use not of bearings but of distances.

We have seen above that the major technological problem of the echo-sounder lay in the measurement of small time intervals. For the measurement of distance by radio waves instead of sound in water the time intervals involved, despite the greater distances, are minute. A radio pulse travels at about 162,000 miles per second. In a period of a 600-millionth part of a second the pulse travels about 100 nautical miles. To gain an accuracy of 6 nautical miles, therefore, the time must be accurate to a millionth of a second, known as a 'microsecond'. Once the problem of measuring time with this accuracy has been solved, at least the principle of how radio-measured distances may be used for obtaining a ship's position is not difficult to understand. The timing may be achieved by a cathode ray oscilloscope, which may be regarded as an electronic clock.

If two stations transmit radio pulses simultaneously, they will reach a receiver at different moments unless the latter is equidistant from the two. The receiver's position is then at any point lying nearer to one station than the other by the distance represented by the microscopic time difference. Such points lie on hyperbolic curves of which the stations are the focal points. A special chart designed for use with the particular stations involved has a series of such hyperbolae overprinted. A fix is obtained when time differences from two pairs of stations have been obtained, when the receiver's position will be at the intersection of two hyperbolae.

Using Loran, the navigator has on board his vessel the appropriate latticed chart with its hyperbolic grid. A pair of stations transmit synchronized pulses (it was said above that stations transmit simultaneously; for reasons that need not concern us while grasping principles, there is a certain time interval between the two) and the shipborne receiver measures the time difference between the reception of the two pulses. The hyperbolic lines on the chart join all points with the same time difference, and the appropriate one is selected. The same procedure with a further pair of stations will show another line, and where the two cut will be the ship's position, within an accuracy of about 5 miles. Thirty-seven transmitting stations operate the system, which at present covers part of the North Atlantic, the coasts of the U.S.A. and areas of the North Pacific. The range is some 650 miles per day and 1,400 miles at night. Loran does not yet extend to any useful extent to the southern hemisphere.

Decca is similar in principle but of shorter range, and here it is the phase difference, not the time difference between signals, that is measured. As hitherto, lines of constant phase difference between two stations are hyperbolae. Where these lines intersect is the ship's position. In this system a master station and three associated 'slave' stations are used for obtaining a fix.

A further system being developed by the U.S. Navy, at present known as Omega, operates on very low frequencies in order to provide the longest possible range. In time such a network could cover the world, and be accurate at distances of thousands of miles.

The hyperbolic methods of navigation are engineering systems dependent upon massive and costly arrays of equipment, all of it at present undergoing constant development and ranging from the special charts, through the shipborne receiving sets and calculating devices, to the widespread transmitting stations on shore; the whole depending on an elaborate organization for production and operation. Nothing could more vividly display the totally modern integration of seamanship with the land.

Wide areas of ocean are not yet covered by the system, though global coverage is clearly a future step that only an abrupt interruption in material progress could delay. Developed particularly for naval use and for aircraft, the expense of the

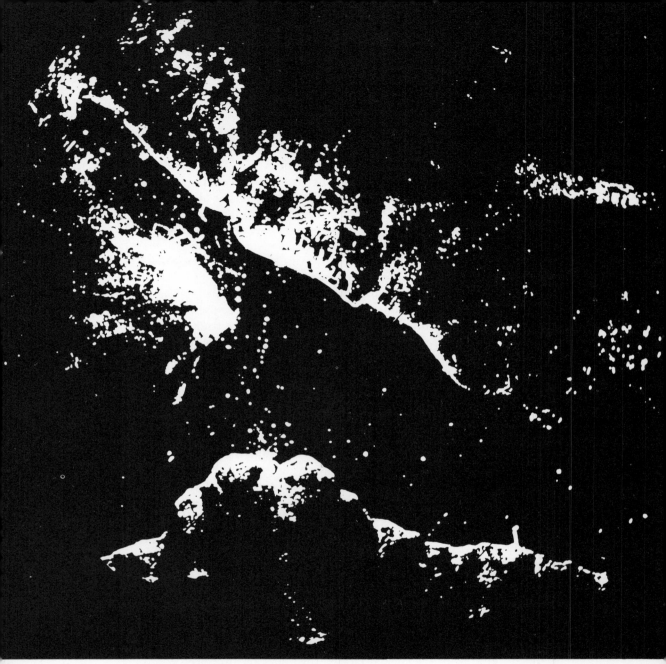

Approaches to Southampton on a radar screen

equipment is yet far beyond the economically acceptable for many merchant ships and equally in advance of their practical requirements, extreme accuracy in position-finding when in mid-ocean not being one of their needs. This applies with yet more force to satellite navigation systems. And it has always to be remembered, too, that no systems are yet immune from unpredictable time or frequency eccentricities.

Like the magnetic compass, the sextant is likely to remain in use long after more sophisticated devices and methods have been evolved.

Position-finding by the intersection of hyperbolae derived from the time taken for radio pulses to travel from transmitting stations on earth, have their counterpart in signals passed from man-made satellites.

The system was originated by the U.S. Navy. In use since 1964, some four years later it was released for use in merchant ships, including those of other nations. A number of man-made satellites are in polar orbits round the earth continually transmitting. Ground stations are at any moment able to establish the position of the satellites from the Doppler effect, or change in frequency, of the signal, as a satellite approaches or recedes. The positions of the satellites may thus be derived. By various computer operations, performed at the speed of light (i.e. of an electric current) the position of a satellite at short time intervals ahead are obtained and retransmitted to the memory storage of the satellite. The ship using the system receives these signals, together with the Doppler shift of the satellite in relation to the ship, and the information, together with the ship's motion, are fed into the computer on board, which returns the answer in terms of latitude and longitude. In the ship there has to be a special receiver, the device for measuring change in frequency of the satellite signal and a computer. As with Loran, Decca and Omega, satellite systems of navigation are undergoing subtle modifications in technique, and it seems probable that before they become the usual systems on board ship they will have become highly developed and common in aircraft, and inherited by the average oceangoing ship for which such sophistications are not essential for normal operation.

Inertial systems of dead reckoning at present fall into the same category.

A few years before the Second World War when all civilization was facing the prospect of bombing from the air, there was emerging a new form of radio direction-finding, which in its infancy was still called R.D.F. but later became known as Radar (RAdio Direction And Range). Devised for purposes of defence against aircraft, its marine uses soon became evident. Winston Churchill was to write a little irritably to the British Minister of Defence a few months before the war: 'The progress of R.D.F. especially applied to range-finding must surely be of high consequence to the Navy. . . . I cannot conceive why the Admiralty are not hot upon this trail.'

By the end of the war radar had been used widely in navies and in a few merchant vessels, which had had naval sets fitted, and then, for the first time, its peacetime applications were considered. Today the large, cage-like, continuously rotating radar aerials of ships large and small is almost as common a feature of the shipping scene as once were topsails. It has become a marine application of electromagnetic radiation second in importance only to the original use of radio at sea.

Radar should be compared not with the former methods of radio direction-finding but rather with the echo-sounder, the principles of which it reproduces, though in an infinitely more sophisticated manner. The echo principle of radar is easily comprehensible, but to apply it to a mechanism demanded the most advanced physics of the day. The seaman, who a few hundred years earlier could use scientific instruments and methods only when they had been simplified enough to accord with his crude modes of usage, and who with difficulty had been driven through the

The tanker *Texaco Caribbean* going down, one of the
numerous victims of the crowded conditions in the
English Channel today. It was a double disaster, the
German freighter *Brandenburg* later striking the sunken
bow section of the *Texaco Caribbean* and in turn also
sinking

Opposite page
The giant tanker. The two limiting classes of seamanship
in the world today are illustrated here and on page 307

The Meon Mark 3
anchor. This and
the pictures on the
three following
pages show the
changing shapes of
anchors in stone,
iron and stainless
steel

centuries to become the 'geometrical seaman', was becoming the fully fledged
'scientific seaman' of the second half of the twentieth century.

Short pulses of radio energy may be emitted and their echo from solid matter,
through which they cannot pass, be picked up on return by a receiver, the time

interval being proportional, as in the echo-sounder, to the distance. The major problem involved in the technique lies in the speed at which the pulses of radio energy travel, which is of course that of light and other electromagnetic radiation – 300,000 kilometres per second compared with the speed of sound in water, which is 1·5 kilometres per second. A second problem was that of emitting a pulse of radio energy capable of producing a sufficient echo over a distance. The first problem was solved by the cathode ray tube; the second by the magnetron.

Radar, devised in the first instance for the detection of enemy bombers developed into a powerful new tool to put into the hands of mariners, able to detect unseen obstacles in fog or darkness, and also within its range, providing a means of position-fixing. Its powers seemed almost spellbinding, with its ever-seeing eyes able to penetrate the fog and darkness which had led to the destruction of so many ships as they approached each other or the shore. Landfalls and crowded fairways would appear to have been divested of their ancient anxieties. On the bridge of the ship would be the radar screen – a picture adjustable for a range of say 10 to 50 miles showing perhaps the shore on one hand, the ships and buoys in the vicinity and a moving line indicating the course of the ship herself, and showing this though black darkness of dense fog covered the fairway ahead.

Yet with all its wonderful powers radar has not yet fulfilled the expectations that

Ancient stone anchor depicted on a Cypriot vase, 8th century B.C.

Stainless steel
'Digger' anchor

300

it not unreasonably raised. Partly this is due to the much greater number of ships that come together in the converging areas at the ends of the ocean routes – 300,000 ships per annum through the Straits of Dover. Here forty vessels may appear simultaneously upon a radar screen. Even when two ships alone are at risk of collision, radar is not necessarily the passport to safety. Experience during recent years has shown that it is when two ships are approaching end on, or nearly end on, that the greatest danger of collision exists. In earlier days, when all depended on the lookout's eyesight, this situation was safely handled by the 'Steering and Sailing Rules' of the *International Regulations for Preventing Collisions at Sea*. In daylight, or in darkness, when from each ship would be seen ahead both port and starboard lights of the other,

Tangara with its sophisticated anchor

Hydrofoil and planing craft, the fastest types of marine
craft in which seamanship touches the verge of
aeronautics. Vosper's fast patrol boat *Ferocity*

each ship was directed by the rules to alter her course to starboard so as to leave the other vessel on her port side. In fog, whether by day or night, no rule might save the ships becoming too close before sighting one another to avoid collision.

Using radar the ships will be aware of one another's presence, but without being able to see one another or their lights, a slight misinterpretation of the echo on the screen may lead to confusion about the other ship's course, and produce that common phenomenon a 'radar-induced collision'. The techniques for using the information that appears on the radar screen are now subject to acute controversy that may lead to a revolution in the form of the rules for preventing collision at sea.

A tragic example of a radar-induced collision occurred off Nantucket Shoals in 1956, when the Italian liner *Andrea Doria* was in collision with the Swedish liner *Stockholm*, the former approaching New York, the latter outward bound. Initially for the *Andrea Doria* there was thick fog, with visibility down to half a mile. On her bridge the radar screen eventually showed what was recognized to be the Nantucket lightship ahead, where it was expected, and course was changed. A little later the screen showed an echo ahead very fine to starboard. This was the yet unrecognized *Stockholm*. On *her* bridge the radar screen showed an echo which appeared fine on the port bow. It would appear, therefore, that the two screens were showing the same situation correctly. But the ships' masters interpreted the picture differently. The Swedish master accepted it as a case of two ships approaching end on or nearly end on, when the *International Regulations for Preventing Collisions at Sea* prescribe that each

302

ship shall alter course to starboard so as to pass on the port side of the other. The Italian captain interpreted it as safe passing of two ships on parallel courses – in this example, starboard to starboard. But unfortunately he decided it was not quite safe enough, and he therefore altered course to port in order to increase the passing distance between the two vessels. When, at much the same time, the *Stockholm* altered course to starboard, in accordance with the rule for an end-on meeting, the two ships became on crossing courses. The fog was lifting; but it was too late. In the Swedish ship it had appeared there should have been a safe port-to-port passing, each ship having altered course to starboard; in the Italian that it would be a safe starboard-to-starboard passing, the change of course to port having made it merely safer.

The *Andrea Doria* was struck on the starboard side somewhat ahead of amidships in the early hours of darkness and capsized in the middle of the following day. If, when the *Titanic* had sunk, the universal wonder had been that so large, efficiently handled and – as claimed – safest of all ships could go to the bottom in a few hours, now some two generations later the amazement was that another such ship could have a fatal collision when radar had been added to the means of handling ships without danger, together with a mass of other equipment and international rules and conventions. If amazement was common to both disasters, so was one of the causes – high speed. The *Andrea Doria* had been proceeding in fog at a fractional reduction of her full cruising speed – at 1·2 knots less than 23 knots, which was rightly described as a merely nominal reduction and in no way in accordance with the *Regulations for Preventing Collisions at Sea*. But this was the normal practice; and it

Hydrofoil

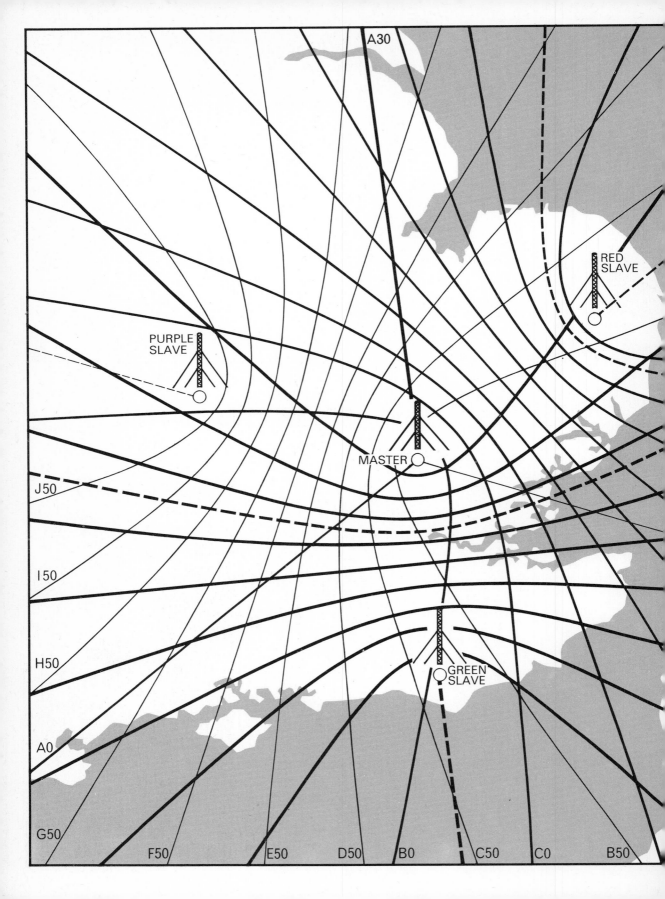

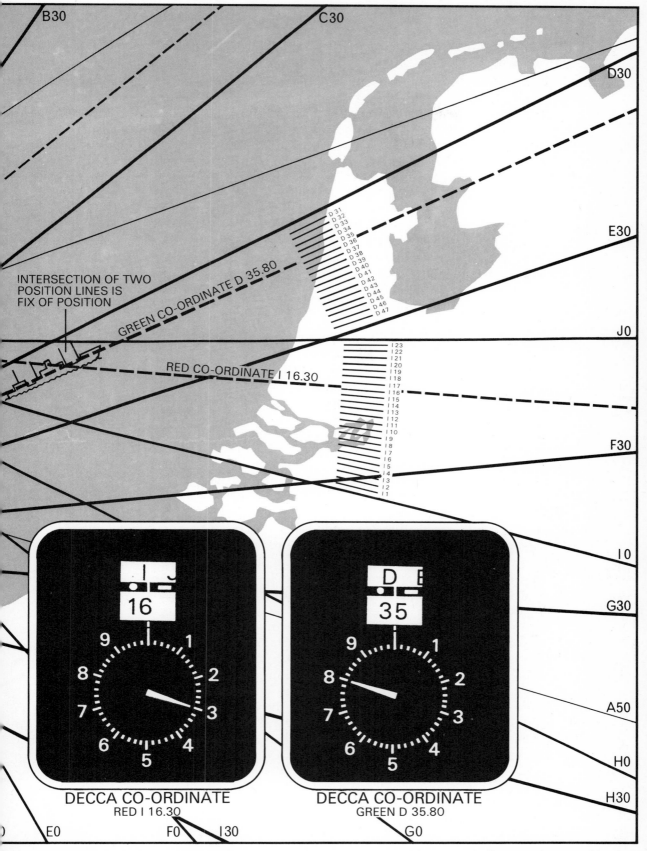

Decca navigator and its chart

was undoubtedly true, as pointed out at the time, that in the vicinity of the Nantucket Shoals that evening, in the same fog, plenty of other ships were proceeding at a speed less than the *Andrea Doria*'s only because their best speeds were lower. One of these was the *Stockholm*, except that she was in no more than a slight haze, and in darkness the onset of fog may initially be imperceptible. But at the subsequent Inquiry, when the questions of fog and speed occupied so much attention, the uncomfortable fact was revealed that though the *Stockholm*'s log-book recorded sixty-four watches in which there had been fog, on no occasion was it stated that there had been a reduction in speed. In this crucial aspect of ship handling, it might have been 1912 again.

The invention of the submarine fulfilled one of man's ancient aspirations, but initially had no striking effect on seamanship. Until the nuclear powered submarine was produced, submarines were essentially only surface ships capable of submerging for brief periods. They operated mainly on the surface, and submerged had a very low maximum speed which could be maintained for short periods only owing to the heavy drain on the batteries. With the nuclear submarine came a quite new instrument of seamanship, whose natural habitat was under the sea, where in regions of perpetual calm the highest speeds might be reached (appreciably higher than on the surface), the most flexible manoeuvrability be practised, which have received the name of aquabatics, and the greatest comfort be achieved; and the return to the sea's uneasy surface is to re-enter an area of reduced performance. During all periods until this, seamanship has been practised on the restless sea-air interface, which has been the cause of its major problems. Beneath the surface, where the nuclear submarine may remain for periods limited in practice mainly by the necessity for periodical dockyard overhauls, the bulk of the former preoccupations and the techniques of seamanship have disappeared.

And where Captain Cook was turned back by the Arctic ice, in a ship lashed by gales, blinded by fog, and with sails, ropes and men frozen under lead-grey skies, the nuclear submarine *Nautilus* passed beneath the ice in 1957, containing within her steel hull such amenities of soft living as air-conditioned warmth, excellent food, and books and film shows for relaxation.

If the skills practised by Cook and his men were seamanship, those practised by the crew of the *Nautilus* when she voyaged under the North Pole require a different name. Yet some old problems of seamanship obtruded, amongst them the oldest of all – that of maintaining a sense of direction. In high latitudes the magnetic compass swings at random, and even the gyro compass may lose its stability. When under the ice, in about latitude 86 degrees, the *Nautilus*' gyro compass became unstable, and man's latest and most advanced marine craft, navigating under 25 feet thickness of ice, was forced to depend on a magnetic compass behaving as wildly as any needle that had been touched by a lodestone and crudely pivoted. The ship, like so many before her, began blindly circling. After a transpolar voyage of 1830 miles there were again fears that the sense of direction might have been lost, and the submarine was brought to the surface through a hole in the ice so that the navigators, like true descendants of Cook, might take astronomical observations. The submerged dead reckoning on this occasion seems to have been much superior to so many disastrous dead reckonings in the past.

The single-handed voyagers of today are practitioners
of traditional seamanship, though assisted by
sophisticated rigs and some mechanical devices, such
as the self-steering gear, which might be regarded as
the ultimate development of the ancient side rudder

The solution to one set of problems commonly leads to the appearance of another,
and so it has proved in the seamanship of today. Traditionally the seaman has
operated in a world where his fellow travellers were sparse, and in general did not
incommode him, unless with the malicious intent of the pirate, privateer or the warship's press gang, dragging the merchant seaman from his vessel at sea. His perpetual
dangers were due to nature: the weakness of his ships; the gross limitations of his
ability to find the way; the menace of the coasts he must approach.

Even the twentieth century has not produced the unsinkable ship, but naval
architecture has gone so far that any well-found ship is safe under almost all conditions of seaway. Navigation, transforming itself from an art into a science, has turned
the oceans into a signposted highway and the approaches to the land into a brilliantly
lit street where the shores have lost their menace.

But while the natural obstructions to seafaring have been marvellously reduced,
the seaman now finds his chief danger and ever-pressing anxiety in his fellow

seafarers. On the deeper ocean he may still be relatively safe from them, but in the sea areas the reaching of which is his only object in crossing oceans – the approaches to the land – his dangers have been vastly accentuated. The capital problem of seamanship has been changed from that of finding the way to that of avoiding other ships. In 1963 it was reported that 1,800 ships of more than 500 gross tons were involved in collision. The number had been increasing annually prior to this, and has continued to do so since.

Several factors have combined to produce the situation, which may be summarized thus: a great increase in the number and size of ships all converging upon coastal areas that have virtually contracted owing to the greater draught of the ships confining them to narrower channels. The power of modern navigational techniques has quaintly increased dangers by assuring that the greater number of ships converge with more deadly accuracy on the bottlenecks in the seaways. The fact that even the largest ships may now have their engines as well as their rudder controlled directly and immediately from the bridge provides a security partly offset by the relative unmanœuvrability of very large ships, while excellent buoyage systems further congest the ever increasing numbers of ships into ever narrower channels. There is irony in the fact that in the Straits of Dover, the most dangerous waters in the world, where some 270,000 ships per annum, or more than 700 per day, pass through the 5-mile-wide channel between the Varne Bank and the English coast, the dangers have been increased because the English side of the Channel being better lit than the French, more ships choose the former side. Thus has ship handling been transformed in the pilotage waters, where a few sailing-ships within sight of one another would have once seemed a crowd; and where the lonely smuggler from the French coast could cross without concern the thin traffic of the shipping lanes, where many of the vessels were without lights and no rule of the road was acknowledged but that of custom.

The size of the biggest ships has been growing throughout history. Until the last few generations the growth was slow, and had ships continued to be built of timber and driven by sail this might have been permanently arrested at the size of the last wooden sailing vessels, which had a displacement tonnage of 7,000 tons and a length of 350 feet.

At no period have the biggest ships of their day been the most seaworthy. They were operating near the limits of their creators' abilities to make structures strong enough. It is a nice question whether the ultimate limit in the size of wooden sailing-ships would have been determined by the rig or by the hull, but certainly in both respects the maximum point of size had almost been reached when iron and steel construction and steam propulsion opened the way to the advances in size which have produced the critical position today. The contemporary situation was heralded by the *Great Eastern* of 1857, a vessel of some twice the length and five times the weight of any built previously, her dimensions revealing the new powers that steel and mechanical propulsion has given to shipbuilders. She remained the world's biggest ship for half a century.

That there has been a continuous increase in the size of average ships, is shown by the fact that the dredged depths of some harbour channels have doubled during the

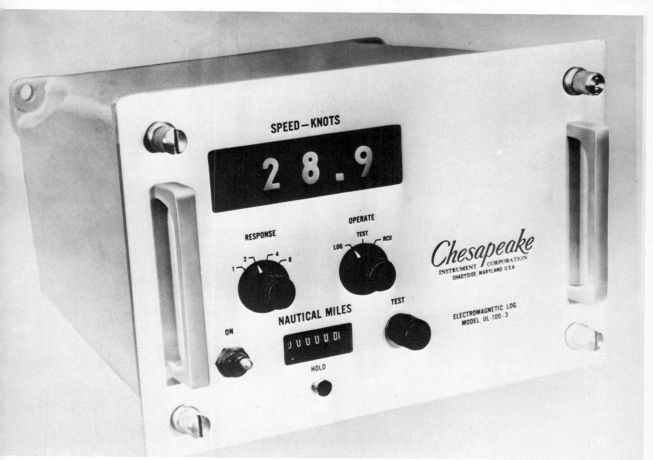

Electromagnetic ship's speed and
distance log-recording unit

century 1870–1970. This persistent growth in the size of most types of merchant
vessel has been accompanied by a sudden explosive growth in one particular class, the
influence of which is spreading to others. The cult of the gigantic in naval architecture is transforming the problems of seamanship. In former periods, while seamen
might be set grave practical difficulties in handling the biggest ships of their day and
be able to do so only by means of large crews, the size of the largest ships was still
limited by the constructors' abilities; whereas today there is the threat that ships are
growing beyond the size that can safely be handled by the resources of seamanship in
its present state. This is the problem on the threshold of the immediate future as
other types of ship, such as bulk container carriers, grow annually in size following
the wake of the supertankers.

A development having the effect of transferring part of the control of a ship from
the seamen on board to people on shore is the yet immature technique of 'weather
routing'.

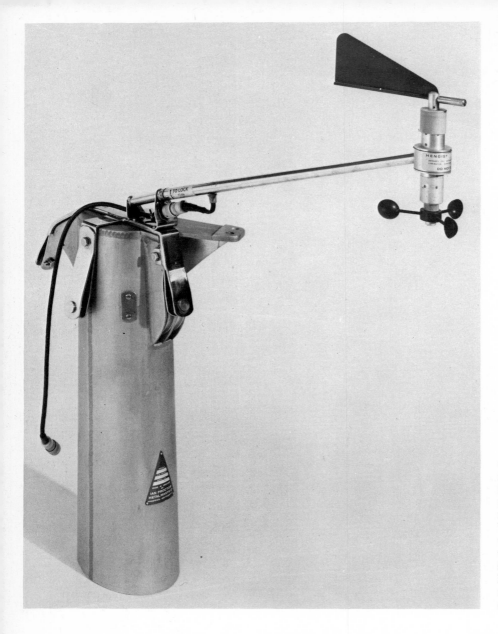

Gipsy Moth IV
navigational
instruments,
showing a distant
relative of the
Viking's wind
vane – a masthead
wind direction and
speed indicator
having dials
recording
electrically

It might be claimed that seamen practised this in a rudimentary form, with no aids from outside resources, when they followed the rules in the manuals for evading the track of cyclonic storms. Some will remember Captain MacWhirr's explosive opinion of such techniques in Conrad's *Typhoon*:

'Running to get behind the weather! Do you understand that, Mr Jukes? It's the maddest thing! . . . If the weather delays me – very well. There's your log-book to talk straight about the weather. But suppose I went swinging off my course and came in two days late, and they asked me. "Where have you been all that time, Captain?" What could I say to that? "Went round to dodge the bad weather," I would say. "It must have been dam' bad," they would say. "Don't know," I would have to say; "I've dodged clear of it." See that, Jukes? I've been thinking it all out this afternoon.'

Many people have thought about it since those days when wireless was in a very few ships only and on board the *Nan-Shan* MacWhirr was as isolated while at sea as seamen ever had been, though he did command a 'full-powered steamship'. Weather routing is the latest refinement in the techniques of directing a ship's movements

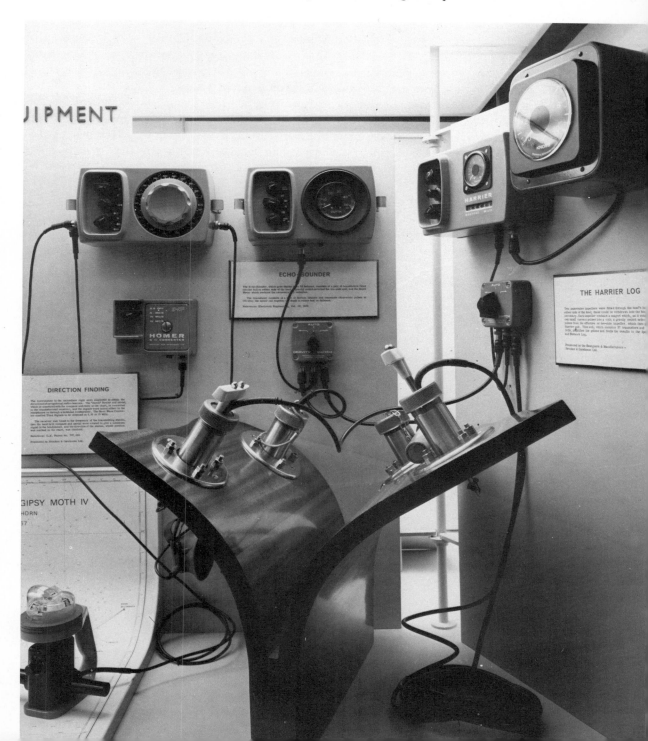

which were latent in the first use of wireless; but now it is radio in association with meteorology and oceanography.

The object of the operation is to guide a ship along the course where she will encounter the most favourable relationship between the seaway and the particular responses inherent in the ship, governed particularly by her length. On the one hand the naval architect has become increasingly capable of assuring certain characteristics of behaviour in the vessels he designs and of controlling their motions by the use of roll-damping fins, features of hull form, and of predetermined values of the pitching period. On the other hand, the increasing number of oceanographic records, providing the spectrum analysis of many seaways in different parts of the world, increasingly enables the character of seaways to be forecast in the light of meteorological tendencies. A ship may then be routed along a 'least-time-track', not necessarily the shortest, or great circle course, but the one on which she will be able to maintain the highest speed of which she is capable under the conditions.

All such judgements are beyond the Captain's control. There can be no question that in modern seamanship the seaman has become less, and his master equally so. The oceans are becoming controlled by those who are not seamen. The process has not gone very far yet; but it is advancing so quickly that we are within sight of the day when 'seamanship' in the old sense, will no longer be required.

GLOSSARY

Beating	To sail on a course dead to windward.
Binnacle	Non-magnetic housing for the compass, also containing the means of illumination and the compensating magnets correcting deviation.
Block	A pulley, but always called a block on board ship.
Bonnet	A strip of canvas laced to the foot of a sail to increase its area.
Boom	Spar extending the foot of a sail.
Brace	Ropes used to control the yards of square sails and made fast to the extremities of the yards.
Brail	Ropes used for shortening a vessel's canvas by gathering it into the mast or up to the yard.
Cable	The rope or chain carrying the anchor. Also a heavy rope or chain for towing and other purposes.
Carvel (planking)	The manner of building a vessel so that the side planks butt edge to edge, producing a smooth exterior.
Chain plates	Metal plates bolted to the hull near the gunwale to hold the deadeyes or rigging screws at the lower end of the shrouds.
Clinker (planking)	The manner of building a vessel so that the side planks overlap one another (see Carvel).
Close hauled	Sailing as close to the wind as possible without excessive leeway and whilst maintaining adequate speed.
Course	The lowest square sail on a mast.
Current	Horizontal movement of a body of water. Tides are one form of current.
Deadeye	Nearly circular block of hardwood bored with three sheavless holes, through which passes the lanyard to a lower deadeye, two deadeyes and the lanyard forming a purchase used to set up the shrouds or stays.
Deadwood	Area of flat surface in the hull, fore and aft, but mainly at the stern just above the keel.
Draught (draft)	The maximum depth of a vessel under the water, varying with the state of the loading.

Fetch	The distance over which the wind is blowing from the nearest shore up to weather.
Fluke (anchor)	The palms, or flattened ends, of the anchor arms at their extremities.
Foot	The lower edge of a sail.
Freeboard	The amount of the ship's hull lying between the waterline and the gunwale.
Gaff	The spar that extends the head of a fore-and-aft sail.
Gunwale	The upper edge of the hull's side.
Gybe	To steer so as to bring the wind round the stern from one quarter to the other.
Halyard	The rope by which a sail is hoisted.
Head	Upper edge of a sail.
Headsail	All fore-and-aft sails set ahead of the foremost mast.
Heave-to	To lay a vessel more or less up into the wind and with little or no way on her. To stop. To reduce speed to the minimum while riding out a severe seaway.
Jib	The foremost of the triangular headsails. There may be several jibs – inner, outer, flying – set ahead of the fore-staysail.
Keel	The lowest longitudinal centreline member of the hull structure to which the stem, sternpost, frames, and lowest strake of planking or plating are attached.
Leech	The vertical edges of a square sail. The after edge of a fore-and-aft sail.
Leeway	The angle between a vessel's fore-and-aft line and her course.
Line	The general term for all ropes on board a vessel.
Luff (of a sail)	The forward edge of a fore-and-aft sail.
Mizzen	The third mast from forward or the after mast of two-masted rigs when this mast is the shorter.
Port	The left-hand side of a vessel when facing forward (see Starboard).
Quarter	The part of a ship approximately midway between dead astern and on the beam.
Reaching	Sailing with the wind on, or just forward, of the beam (see Beating and Running).
Rhumb	A course making a straight line on a Mercator chart. A line following a constant course.
Running	To sail on a course with the wind right aft or almost right aft.

Running rigging   Lines used for trimming and controlling the sails as opposed to supporting the rig (see Standing rigging).

Set flying   A fore-and-aft sail set without having its luff hanked to a stay.

Sheave   The grooved wheel, or roller, in a block.

Sheet   Ropes controlling the clew(s) of a sail. For a fore-and-aft sail with a boom the sheet provides the chief, and sometimes the only, means of trimming the sail.

Shroud   Hemp or wire ropes, set up by tackles, deadeyes or rigging screws and providing the lateral, or athwartship, staying of a mast.

Sprit   The spar crossing a fore-and-aft sail diagonally and holding aloft the peak when there is no gaff.

Spritsail and Sprit-sail   In this work the fore-and-aft sail extended by a sprit is described as a 'spritsail'; the square sail set on a yard crossing the bowsprit a 'sprit-sail'.

Standing rigging   Hemp and wire ropes used to support the masts and bowsprit (see Running rigging).

Starboard   Right-hand side of a vessel when facing forward. Only applicable in this sense, and not to the right-hand side when facing otherwise.

Stay   Rope or wire used for the fore-and-aft support of mast or bowsprit.

Steeve   Angle made by a vessel's bowsprit with the horizontal.

Sternpost   The vertical timber or steel angle bar erected on the extreme after end of the keel. In wooden ships it usually carries the rudder.

Stock (anchor)   The cross-piece of an anchor, set in traditional anchors at right angles to the arms at the other extremity of the shank, to enable the anchor to bite.

Sweep   Long oar.

Tack (of a sail)   Angle between the foot and the luff.

Tacking   To work a vessel to windward by sailing alternately close hauled with the wind on the port and starboard sides.

Tackle   Any form of purchase, of which there are many, composed of a rope and blocks.

Thole   Pins fitting into holes in gunwale to serve as fulcrum for an oar.

Tide   The inflow and outflow of the sea under the influence of moon and sun. Compare with current.

Timbers   Applied generally to the various pieces of wood used in constructing a hull, and sometimes particularly to the transverse ribs or frames.

Warp   A rope, or hawser, used for moving a vessel under the power of her capstan; or for hauling her up to an anchor laid down ahead; or for securing her to a quay or mooring buoy.

Wear   When sailing to windward, to bring the wind from one side of the ship to the other by steering so that the stern passes through the eye of the wind (see Tacking).

Yard   A spar suspended from the mast and spreading the head of a sail.

INDEX